GENE KENTUCK OBERST OLYMPIAN ALL-AMERICAN & NOTRE DAME FOOTBALL CHAMPION

PARIS OLYMPICS CENTENNIAL EDITION

ROBERT D. OBERST

Version 3.0
July 2024
Paris Olympics—Centennial Edition

For information contact
Global Future Press
Solon, Ohio
RobOberst@sbcglobal.net

ISBN-13:
9780692754610
Paperback

Table of Contents

1: The Toss   6

2: Ancestry   15

3: Andrew Oberst   24

4: The Times   35

5: Oberst Home   42

6: High School   54

7: Notre Dame   69

8: Knute   74

9: Gene and The Gipper   88

10: Back on the Field   100

11: Back on Track   113

12: Blocking for the Four Horsemen   118

13: Exaltation and Deprivation   128

14: Records Shattered   139

15: The Olympic Trials   151

16: Olympic Voyage   155

17: Paris   169

18: Chariots of Fire Olympics   181

19: Joy of Victory   196

20: London   207

21: Victors Arrive Home   219

Afterword   225

About the author   228

Preface

It has been 100 years since young Eugene George Oberst won the first American Track & Field medal in the 1924 Paris Olympics, an amazing feat for someone who had been crippled since birth and had to wear painful braces, let alone someone who would be the first to watch the American flag fly over an Olympic stadium.[1]

The 1920s were the Golden Decade of Sports. Before then, participation in sports was reserved for the wealthy, for the average man or woman typically worked 60 to 70 hours a week and had little time for leisure activities.

One of Gene's best friends from the '24 Olympics, Jack Kelly, was the top rower in the world who had won over 200 consecutive races but was prevented from participating in the world's premier rowing event, the Henley Royal Regatta Cup in Great Britain, because he was a lowly bricklayer. Jack was emblematic of this golden age of democratic ideals, for despite this insult, he went on to win four Olympic medals, become a highly successful businessman, and run for mayor of Philadelphia. His daughter, Grace Kelly, would marry a prince, his son would become the president of the American Olympic Committee, and his ultra-athletic grandson, Prince Albert of Monaco, would compete in five Olympics.

After the war to end all wars, World War I, thanks to marvelous inventions such as the assembly line, washer machines, vacuums, and refrigerators, people had the time to participate in athletics. With the propagation of the radio, they could now follow their favorite team's heroes without attending the game or having to travel to another city.

In addition to his track and field competitions, Gene would become a star lineman for Knute Rockne's first football teams, blocking for the amazing, versatile Gipper and the astounding Four Horsemen when Notre Dame football became legendary.

1. Note: The U.S. Rugby team won gold medals on May 15, 1924, and the Shooting team won medals in late June, but because of their earlier scheduled events, they could not join the team on the voyage to France and Oberst's was the first U.S. medal awarded in the Columbes stadium and the first time the American flag was raised over any Olympic stadium.

The '20s would be the foundation of American sports when Gene would come to know many of the sports heroes and coaches of the 20th century—the legendary men who invented football, set Olympic records and were All-Americans, men who were the prime movers of track and field, surfing, rowing, hockey, swimming and the NFL, men who had films made about their lives. Gene's mentor, Knute Rockne, was the winningest college football coach in history (.941), for whom Gene would perform a remarkable service, as witnessed in 50 letters between the two. Rockne became the man who would guide his life.

————

Growing up in the idyllic 1950s, we did not have the opportunity to spend much time with our fathers. Many of my friend's dads had fought in World War II, and perhaps because of the horrors they endured, seemed distant, hardened, unapproachable. Although he directed a Navy officer training program, thankfully, due to his bad feet, my father did not fight in the war. Until the turbulent 60s and the women's liberation movement, there was a division of labor. Most of the moms in the neighborhood stayed at home and tended to the house and children, while the dads went out into the world to earn a living. Children went to school and, during summers and daylight-savings time, played until dusk when the streetlights came on. Our parents were not involved much in our activities and we roamed free. In a sense, our world had three interconnected dimensions—dads out in the world, moms at home, kids playing in the neighborhood, only stopping home to refuel. These three worlds rarely intersected except for evening dinners, holidays, and, for some of the luckier ones, an occasional family vacation.

I was the last of five children, considerably younger than my older siblings, but this was not unusual in our family. My father was 46 when I was born. His father, Andrew, was 47 and his grandfather Johann was 42 at Andrews's birth. Both my father and grandfather were the youngest in their families too. Reinforcing the tradition, Dad's uncle Johann, my great uncle, had five children in his 50s and 60s.

As a toddler, I remember Dad bringing home ten-cent Disney storybooks to read to me, such as Cinderella and Pinocchio, with gilded covers and stunningly-colored images resembling those from the movies. At four, while bouncing me on his knee, he urged me to box with him. I was reluctant to strike my father, but after repeated entreats, threw a punch with my tiny right fist that connected with his left eye. The eye rapidly swelled and soon became black and blue. He was embarrassed to tell his students or fellow faculty members that his 4-year-old gave him the shiner, for as an imposing figure at 6'5" and 320 lbs., it was difficult to admit such a thing. We did not seem quite as close after then, and like many children, I blamed myself for a while, but as I came to realize, he was enduring a major crisis and was in the process of changing careers that had nothing to do with me. Plus, since college professors at the time earned very little, he always had to work at least two jobs to provide for our family. My mother, two sisters and brother read me stories and taught me the typical things children learn along the way. We were not only born in four different states but in four different sections of the country – the South (VA), the Mid-Atlantic (PA), New England (upstate NY), and the Mid-West (OH).

Growing up, I loved baseball. All I had to do was throw my glove and bat over the fence in our backyard, cattycorner to Roxboro Elementary School's grounds, and hop over the fence. Home plate was in front of a huge poplar tree near that corner, whose heart-shaped leaves provided abundant shade for the team that was up to bat.   On many lazy, hot, endless summer days, we played doubleheaders, with a game in the afternoon and another after dinner. Since there was no air conditioning, the windows were open to let in any hint of a cooling breeze. Kids bounding down the street would call everyone out for the evening game, yelling, "Baseball!" when we would stream out of our houses and play until the streetlights came on. Starting at five, advancing through the various leagues, I would go on to play baseball or softball for the next 40 years.

When participation in sports followed the seasons, we did not have to concentrate on just one. As a relatively good athlete but not always the star, I was able to play on four teams in high school (football, basketball, track and baseball in the summers). I was also recruited for the cross-country and wrestling teams but could not participate in two sports simultaneously. I also threw the javelin in college, but not as far as my dad. Through junior high, high school and college, I enjoyed competing in many of the track and field events—the 50, 100, 220, 880, relays, high jump, broad jump, discus, shot put and javelin. Even though I had some of the fastest times, I did not like the intense tension at the line for the sprints, so I switched to the more relaxed field events. This provided an appreciation of the competitions at the Olympics and sports in general. After college, I continued to play seven or eight sports annually.

Our father was a wonderful dad, even-tempered and a fine example, who cooked delicious meat and potato meals, ready at precisely 5:00.

He celebrated all the holidays with fervor—New Year's Eve with plum pudding, Washington's Birthday with cherry pie, Valentine's Day with a pink, heart-shaped cake, St Patrick's Day with corned beef and cabbage for my Irish mum, Thanksgiving and especially Christmas. As a college professor, he had summers off, and although he sold real estate, we always took a vacation, usually to Stone Harbor, on the New Jersey shore. There we would body surf and play ball games in the sand, fish off the pier, play miniature golf, and go to Wildwood and Atlantic City with their enticing smells—salt water taffy, vinegared fries, cotton candy, and the rides and attractions on the broad boardwalks overlooking the scenic, mesmerizing ocean, the sound of waves continuously crashing onto the shore.

We knew that my dad had won an Olympic medal, and played football with the Gipper and Four Horsemen for Knute Rockne, but we did not pay much attention or really ask him about his experiences (what a shame). We knew that Knute Rockne had been a major influence on his life; after all, my brother Al's middle name was Knute, but we knew little about him or their relationship. Occasionally, a classmate would ask us about the Olympics or Notre Dame football, but we were too embarrassed to say much. The only time I remember paying attention to the notoriety was when the Olympics came around every four years, and I would shine up the tarnished medal with Brasso until it sparkled.

I came to know my father better when I went to college, and from then on, he was the major influence on my life. I would not have graduated from college without him. I suspect my brothers would say the same. Despite being average students, we all obtained master's or doctorate degrees, of which our dad was most proud. In addition to coaching, he taught political science and history at John Carroll University for 35 years—the family school, where all three boys, along with our sister Pat, went and Joan reigned as the Military Ball Queen.

With his appreciation of history, he accumulated hundreds of articles and significant memorabilia from his glory days at Notre Dame, the Olympics, and his coaching career, pasting these into a huge scrapbook. He had also written a diary, recalling his adventures at the Olympics in Paris in 1924, and saved boxes of other pictures, letters and memoirs back to the late 1800s, for he was the only one of his thirteen family members born in the 20th century. As I delved into his story, I became overwhelmed by the amount of material on him, on the Internet and in the Notre Dame archives, which, together with those boxes of correspondence and pictures, told a fascinating story, far more intriguing than I knew, remembered or imagined. The book kept growing and expanding, and I became absorbed in all the remarkable places he had been, the times he lived in, and all the amazing sports figures who were his friends.

Not that I was aware of this as a child, but as I learned from my research, he, struggling to provide for a family of seven, endured some extremely rough times, such as those during the Great Depression. Dad insulated us from these traumas, providing us with a normal and joyous childhood. I was particularly moved by the dozens of letters between him and Rockne; when starting out as a novice in his coaching career, much younger than me now, he was still surprisingly naïve. How could my father be young and naïve? It became apparent that after his father died at 20, Rockne, whose father had also died as a student at Notre Dame, became the father figure of his life—always there to help and guide him through the rough times and celebrate his successes. When I read his first-page headline, memorial article in the *Buffalo News* immediately after Rockne died, I understood what a wonderful man he had been and how much he influenced my Dad, and, by extension, his children—us. Without his beloved mentor to call on, he had to endure the depths of the Great Depression and unrelenting unemployment alone, constantly worried about how he would provide for his family.

But this book is not about the hardships. It is about the glory days when the Olympics and football were still young, naïve, and truly amateur. When Gene was born, men and women worked long hours, and at twelve, children went to work on the farm or factory, so there was little time to participate in or follow sports. Other than baseball, sports were primarily reserved for the leisure class, a strictly amateur pursuit. Gene's was the first generation to fully embrace athletics and develop a large fan base when interest in sports, accelerated by the new media, radio, exploded, during the "Golden Decade" of sports. This book is also about how Knute Rockne transformed Notre Dame, a tiny, insignificant Midwestern college, with no real entrance requirements, into a football powerhouse and highly respected university with an 11% acceptance rate, and how Gene played a key role in that transformation.

Gene and Catherine Harold Oberst have had five children, fourteen grandchildren, 28 great-grandchildren, and over a dozen great, great-grandchildren, for whom Gene's outstanding legacy continues.

1: The Toss

Befuddled, Kentuck was glad to hear the bell ring ending his second-year law class, wondering why he had chosen such a challenging major anyway. It was a warm, beautiful spring day under a bright blue sky, so he decided to walk on the newly green campus to clear his mind of all those obscure legal terms rattling around his brain, not aware of the event that would soon forever shape his life. Along his aimless stroll, he wandered by Notre Dame's Carter Field, where he heard the vibrant sounds of young men practicing their various events, sounds of spikes clicking on the cinder track, and the grunts from men hurling cannon-like balls, sounds somehow more intense and alive in the warm spring air, enticing him towards the field where he saw a myriad of athletes in shorts and t-shirts running, jumping, throwing and cascading over hurdles. He once dreamed of competing in the Olympics, but due to his deformed feet, he could barely run, so this was merely one of those childhood fantasies that had long since vanished.

As Carter Field drew Kentuck closer, he smelled the aroma of baking, volcanic cinders on the track, and fresh sawdust flying out of the jumping pits. Then he heard a "slish, thrump and boinggg" and suddenly turned to see a spear-like object rising eight feet out of the sod not far from where he stood. With its pointed tip, the weapon might have impaled him if it had flown just a few feet farther. As his anger rose, he heard a condescending voice urging him to throw the strange object back; it was Johnny Flynn thinking Kentuck might save him some of the tiring steps required to retrieve his errant javelin. Still angry, Kentuck yanked the wooden object out of the ground and then hurled the projectile into the pristine air, sending it soaring far above the approaching Flynn's head.   After turning to follow its breathtaking flight, gasping in disbelief, Johnny ran and told the track coach, Knute Rockne, of the incredible feat.

The next day, Kentuck consumed lunch with his best friend, Fernando Aviles, in the dining hall of Notre Dame's main building. As a tall, skinny, still-growing sophomore, the term might not apply because although the meat and potato portions were large and provided abundant nourishment, Kentuck always seemed hungry. He was startled when Rockne walked up behind him, tapped him on the shoulder, and said, "Hey, Kentuck! I hear you threw the javelin out of the park yesterday. How about going out for the track team?"

As an avid student of history, Gene read about the Greeks and the first Olympic festivals. Earlier, as a youth, while lying on his back on the green grass, he watched fluffy, white clouds roll by imagining waves carrying sailing ship-shaped cloud to the Olympics in some distant European port. Kentuck had heard fabulous stories of the Olympics from his football teammate and Olympian, Gus Desch, but because of his mishappened feet, he had not thought it possible to compete in track and field events. Looking straight into Coach Rockne's blue eyes, he enthusiastically accepted the invitation.

That afternoon, Kentuck walked to the field house adjacent to Carter Field, where he had played on the Notre Dame football team earlier that school year. Since it was late in the season, there were no more uniforms, so Rockne outfitted him with football spikes, baseball pants, and Rockne's sweatshirt that looked way too small on the tall Kentuckian. Rockne then instructed him on the basics of tossing the javelin. At first, Kentuck just stood there, wound up like he was pitching a baseball, and threw the spear in a sidearm motion. Showing him how to do so, Rockne told him to run up to the line before throwing, which felt awkward to the novice.

From football, Rockne knew that Kentuck could not run well, likely confirmed by his first attempts. Knute tried to teach Kentuck to throw overhand, but he just seemed to do better with his awkward sidearm motion. Kentuck's form came from pitching at home in Owensboro, Kentucky, where he was an outstanding pitcher. Rockne was a remarkable motivator and strategist, but he was also a great one-on-one coach who spent time with individual players and helped them learn their task, never belittling a beginner. Kentuck struggled with the set-up and was very slow in his approach. Knute was frustrated with Kentuck's progress but stuck with him. Given how much Kentuck struggled with this first stage during the run-up, Rockne found it difficult to understand how he attained such remarkable distances. He likely told him to try to run faster on the approach, keep practicing his lean, and that he would be throwing the javelin at Indiana University in a couple of days. Kentuck was pleased and excited with the coach's confidence in him.

Rockne wondered why Kentuck seemed to have such natural talent throwing an implement he had never touched. While growing up, one of Kentuck's favorite pastimes was to strip 5-foot horseweeds that grew wild near his home and see how far he could throw the shafts. The kids would play war using the weeds as spears in mock Roman or Grecian battles. Since they were soft, they didn't hurt much. Once hit, though, you were dead and could not participate in the ongoing battle. Sometimes from the top of the high cliffs overlooking the broad Ohio River, he would throw the horseweeds out to see how far across he could fly them, always aiming for the opposite shore, always falling short where they flopped into the current and were swept away.

Javelin

The javelin's roots trace back to the first spears, ½ million years ago and possibly as far back as 5 million years, when chimpanzees took broken branches, stripped 'em of their bark, sharpened 'em with their teeth, and used these rudimentary spears to hunt small animals. One can imagine a caveman, Ogg, walking along the African savanna, spying a massive saber-toothed tiger hiding in the tall grass ahead. Fear coursing through his veins, Ogg immediately takes flight, hoping to reach the jungle and scamper up a tree, but just as he leaps and grabs onto a limb, the big cat hammers him with a mighty blow, taking him soundly to the ground. Ogg looks into the 10-foot, 1,400-pound beast's steely, yellow eyes and foot-long incisors, prey to predator, about to give himself up, when he realizes that he still grasps the branch in his right hand. As the cat's massive saber teeth edge closer, smelling her rotten breath, he takes the broken branch and shoves it into her neck. The pointed tip slices through layers of skin and muscle into her jugular vein, after which the fearsome beast shakes fitfully then falls harmlessly to the side dead.

Such discoveries change the balance of power between man and beast and help in man's constant quest for food and protection. Thirteen thousand years ago, our American predecessors learned how to flake off Clovis points from shards of flint, attach these to their spears and while hunting in groups, take down the biggest of the prey—bison, multi-ton elephants and woolly mammoths, on which their tribes feasted for days.

Through his fascination with Greek history, Gene knew the story of the three hundred Spartans well, who deployed their spears and shields 2,500 years ago at the Thermopylae Pass to hold off 150,000 Persian invaders. Their victory helped the Greeks win the war, and led to the classic Hellenic age and Alexandrian Empire that stretched from Egypt to India. Later, warriors would carry various types of spears (pikes, lances and halberds) into thousands of battles throughout history to stab or throw at their foes. Most forms of the spear vanished with the advent of modern warfare, but during World War I, millions of soldiers attached bayonets to the tip of their guns, converting their riffles essentially into spears, before valiantly charging out of the trenches towards their enemy.

Perhaps more than anyone, adding motivation to his javelin endeavors, Gene appreciated the history of the event he now hoped to excel. At 8'6" and 28 ounces, the Javelin itself traces back to the first Olympic Games in Greece in 766 B.C., over 2800 years ago, when there were just a few events, all based on war skills, including the javelin, shot put, boxing, wrestling running, jumping, and equestrian events. These Olympics were a religious festival in honor of Zeus when wars between the city-states were suspended, and Greeks could travel freely to the base of Mount Olympus (Zeus's home), serving as a period of peace and unity, a release valve for their aggression and rivalries. Then, men could claim glory for their accomplishments other than just those in war. In the first games, athletes competed naked to see who could throw the javelin the furthest. In a separate event, they also vied to see who was the most accurate, for as a formidable weapon, this was the most important aspect in war. The modern Olympics did not continue the accuracy form of the event, though. In 1912 at the Stockholm Olympics, the two-handed javelin throw was contested, which consisted of consecutive throws with each arm, but this event was also discontinued.

To propel a javelin, you start by running; then as you approach the line, you turn sidewise to set up, lean back, and throw over your head. The goal is to use your legs, back, and all the muscles in your shoulders and arm, up to your fingertips to launch the projectile—nearly every muscle in your body. Throwing a javelin is a little like launching a three-stage rocket. The first stage is the run to gain momentum, the second stage is to lean back, like cocking a gun, and the third stage is a continuous firing of the shoulder through the finger muscles. As with a football, it is important to rotate the javelin as you release it by flicking your fingers to spin it through the air, thereby reducing air resistance, so it will travel further. It must land with the point sticking into the ground; otherwise, the throw is disqualified.

———

The meet was one of the last of the season, held on May 7, 1921, in Bloomington, Indiana. It is not clear exactly how the meet transpired for the 19-year-old sophomore, but this was the first track meet he had ever competed in, so he was likely nervous. He had no idea how far the others might throw or if his distance would be respectable.

The Indiana athletes no doubt saw the tall, gangly, poorly outfitted competitor as no threat whatsoever, and he felt a little embarrassed, especially when he saw how fast they ran and how fluid their motion was. With his slow approach and awkward setup, their judgment was soon confirmed. His first toss went far to the left further adding to their low estimation of his skill. Because he threw sidearm, his throws went way to the left, for which he was penalized, since measurements were made on the diagonal rather than on an arc as they are today.

To understand the difference between measuring on the diagonal or the arc, think of a quarterback throwing the football from the 20-yard line to a receiver at the goal line for a touchdown. If he throws the ball straight up the middle, he will toss it 20 yards. However, if he throws it to the receiver near the sideline, on the same goal line, the ball must travel nearly 32 yards—an extra 12 yards or 60% more. Kentuck would have to throw the javelin substantially further to register the same results as his straight-throwing competitors.

His second toss was little better again, falling far to the left, after which he heard a laugh, but when he turned around, ready to confront the perpetrator, he could not discern who it was as most of them turned their heads while smirking. Their condescending attitude stimulated his competitive urges. With fiery determination, he strode into the javelin area. Instead of starting at the back and running many steps until reaching full speed, he started a few steps from the line, ambled up to it, leaned back, and, with a mighty effort, released the shaft. He could feel that this was a good effort, fluid and somehow effortless, as the projectile kept rising until it reached its zenith then descended, finally sticking firmly in the turf. The other competitors were likely flabbergasted, unable to believe what they just witnessed. Johnny was proud of Kentuck, for, after all, he was the one who discovered him. Even though it was still far to the left, Kentuck could see that this throw was the furthest, which it was, winning the contest and setting the Indiana University record of 181 feet, 4 inches—not bad for his first competition. The next week he broke the Michigan State record with a toss of 165'1".

Notre Dame hosted the Indiana State Meet the following week. The attending eight Indiana teams consisted of Butler, DePauw, Earlham, Indiana, Purdue, Wabash, Rose Poly, and Notre Dame. For the meet, Kentuck wore the same baseball pants and pair of football shoes, but Rockne procured a Notre Dame jersey for him to wear. Rockne's sweatshirt had only gone down to his navel, so Kentuck felt he was a member of the team now.

Kentuck broke the Indiana Meet record with a toss of 171'11". Later, Knee of Wabash registered a distance of 175' 3". On his last throw, Kentuck dug deep and tried mightily, but his toss soared far to the left and fell far short of his previous mark. Knee finished first with a new meet record, and Kentuck finished second, having held the record for a few minutes, a remarkable accomplishment for an athlete who just picked up the implement two weeks earlier. His points helped Notre Dame win the Indiana Intercollegiate Track Meet with a score of 66 to Purdue's 38 ¾, who finished second. Rockne congratulated Kentuck on his performance. Later he listed Kentuck as one of the Notre Dame athletes who would compete at the first National Championships.

———

The 15-year-old National Collegiate Athletic Association (NCAA) decided to hold its first National Championship for any sport in the spring of 1921. (In 2024, it would host 91 such championships, including the lucrative Final Four Basketball Tournament and National Football Championship.) The guiding force behind the event was Alonzo Stagg, the famous football and track coach of Chicago University, whom Rockne, a Chicago resident, had hoped to play for. Stagg would be chairman of the NCAA Track and Field championships for its first twelve years.

Growing up dirt poor while studying to be a Presbyterian minister, Alonzo had struggled to earn his way through Yale. With little money for food, he succumbed to malnutrition, fainted, and had to be taken to the hospital. While there, a kindly professor rescued him, providing him with nourishing meals and a room in exchange for help around their house. This kind act not only saved Alonzo and his college career but turned out to be immensely fortunate for Yale.

Stagg was one of the two primary founders of football. He played for the "Father of Football," Walter Camp, at Yale, who, along with Stagg, established many of the young sport's rules. In 1889 starring as an end during his senior year, Yale won 15 out of its 16 games, when he became one of the first eleven All-Americans. The Ivy League, and especially Yale, dominated the sport for its first half-century, with Yale winning 17 national championships, the most of any college. It was not until the 1900s that Rockne, Stagg and Yost showed the nation that the Western teams could compete with the Eastern teams.

Alonzo established many of football's famous innovations, including the direct snap from center, T-formation, backfield shift, man-in-motion, draw play, hidden ball trick, Statue of Liberty play, place kick, and the fake kick. Amazingly, many of these plays still thrill College and NFL fans today. In 1889, he invented the forerunner of today's football blocking and tackling dummy by rolling and tying a mattress and then hanging it from the ceiling. It is difficult to fathom how one man could contribute so much to the game and what football might be without him.

Stagg unimaginably coached for over 70 years, passing away in 1965 at the age of 102. He and his mentor, Walter Camp, spanned the evolution of football in its first 100 years, from its birthing out of rugby in the 1860s to modern football in 1965, less than two years prior to the first Super Bowl. Alonzo would play a pivotal role in Kentuck's life, and later they would form a close relationship. Gene would even call him his second father.

Stagg's first track and field championships were held in Chicago on June 17 and 18. As a member of the U.S. Olympic Committee in 1920, Stagg thought this event would provide a vehicle to recruit, test, and inspire American athletes for the upcoming 1924 Olympics. One of the goals of the national competition was to stimulate interest and support for track and field and the future American Olympic team. Unfortunately, it rained most of the weekend, so the hoped-for turnout did not materialize.

Notre Dame's two Olympians would be at the event. John Murphy the national high jump champion in 1919 and 1920, and Gus Desch, the world record 440-yard hurdler, who took the bronze medal in the 1920 Olympics. Rockne's 1921 track team would be Notre Dame's most successful, so even though not all its members would attend the meet, they would be well represented.

On the relatively short train ride from South Bend to Chicago, Kentuck might have noticed the difference between the track team and his football team. Unlike football, track is primarily an individual sport. His football teammates knew each other well and struggled on the field shoulder-to-shoulder to win games, whereas other than the few relays, track success depended upon how an individual performed on any given day. There was no scoreboard, and it would be difficult for a participant or even coach Rockne himself to discern how his team progressed. Kentuck thought he might like track better, for it allowed him to show his mettle and stand out.

Due to his previous performance at the Indiana championships, and that the season was over for most of the team, Rockne awarded Kentuck a full uniform. When he walked onto Stagg field, Kentuck saw contestants from colleges throughout the nation, including those from the South, East and West. Kentuck rewarded Rockne's confidence in him with a high placement (Notre Dame recorded this as a 1st place and other accounts listed it as a 2nd, 4th or 5th. It is unclear why there is a discrepancy other than this was the first NCAA championship and student reporting of such events was not always accurate.) Flint Hanner of Stanford won the event with a toss of 191' 2". Notre Dame finished second with 16 ¾ to Illinois' 21 ¼ points.

The most inspiring story of this first NCAA championship was that of Leonard Palau of tiny Grinnell College in nearby Iowa in the premier track event, determining who would be the fastest U.S. college athlete—the 100-yard dash. In 1915 due to academic and financial challenges, Palau dropped out of Grinnell early in his freshman year. In 1918, he enlisted in the Army to fight in World War I, where, during the brutal trench warfare, exploding shrapnel injured him in four places. One fragment entered just in front of the right ear and came out through his right eye. Palau lost his right eye and ear. In addition, his right leg's stride was four inches shorter than his left. Due to his injuries, he ran with his head cocked to one side.

With the support of an early form of the GI Bill, he reenrolled in Grinnell. His best time until then was a 10.4. During the meet, he captured first with a blistering 10.0, barely beating Notre Dame's speedster Billy Hayes. Palau would later qualify for the 1924 Paris Olympics, but his wife would have their daughter around that time and he dropped out. His best time of 9.7 would have qualified for a medal in the *Chariots of Fire Olympics*. The previously poor student excelled in chemistry, physics, and math, becoming a teacher and a coach.

Living up to expectations, Notre Dame's Olympians Gus Desch won the low hurdles with a time of 24.8 and Johnny Murphy jumped 6'3" for a first in the high jump.

Although Kentuck never knew he received the distinction, the first five athletes were later awarded All-American honors. Including the four previously mentioned, Notre Dame had seven All-Americans at the meet with Eddie Hogan in the pole vault, Lawrence Shaw in the shot put and Chet Wynne in the high hurdles. Chet played fullback on the 1920 Irish National Championship team along with Kentuck and later coached Auburn to an SEC championship. In his three short years of coaching, Rockne had captured an NCAA Championship in football and a 2nd in track and field—not bad for the young, ambitious coach.

On the ride back to Notre Dame, the team rejoiced in their success. Kentuck played football with Desch whom he sat with on the victorious ride back. Johnny Murphy joined them and Johnny and Gus, an outstanding writer for the *Notre Dame Daily,* regaled him with stories of their fabulous trip to the 1920 Olympics in Antwerp. Gus was the first Notre Dame student to win a medal. Gene hoped he might be next. The following year Gus, a handsome 5'6" young athlete with wavy hair, would set the world record in the 440-yard hurdles at the prestigious Penn relays.

The term had ended, so when the train arrived at South Bend, Kentuck went to his dorm room and hastily packed his trunk. He returned to the station where he boarded a train heading for his hometown of Owensboro, Kentucky. He had not been home for nine months and he desperately missed his parents and 10 older siblings and could not wait to tell them of his fabulous year. As the train chugged out of the station, Kentuck reminisced about his sophomore year. He had played on an undefeated NCAA National Championship football team and a 2nd place national track team. His family and especially his alumni brother Albert would be proud. He felt he was finally living up to the expectations he formulated long ago.

He hoped to become a lawyer and join Albert's law practice but was no longer sure he wanted to major in law. He had done well in all his other subjects but struggled in law, the other subjects seeming so much easier and enjoyable. With the College of Commerce established that year, he thought he might change his major to commercial science, an up-and-coming field. Although there were opportunities for lawyers, commerce would surely grow rapidly in the

1920s and likely be very lucrative.

As the train rambled on, Kentuck dreamed of the 1924 Olympics in Paris, France. The Olympics were still three years away, and despite his early success, the route to Paris would not be an easy journey. How did this young man arrive at this pivotal point in his life, and how, with no formal training or technique, did he possess such amazing talent?

2: Ancestry

Fleeing starvation and seeking a better life in the mid-nineteenth century, Gene's immigrant father and pioneer grandparents emigrated from Germany to the New World. In a time before roads, they settled near the Ohio River, along the prime artery to the West. Like Abraham Lincoln, his mother was born in a log cabin less than 100 miles away from Abe's cabin in Kentucky. Their character, determination, and path in the new world would shape Gene's character and his opportunities in the United States.

Pioneer mother

Gene's great-grandfather, Johan Tennes, and his family were the first to immigrate to the United States in the 19th century. Born in 1802 in Wittersheim, Pfalz, Bavaria, the region had been part of the French Republic and would remain so until after Napolean's defeat in 1815. The rich alluvial farmlands along the Blies and Saar Rivers, which form the border between France and Germany had been settled by the Celts and later ruled by the Franks and Romans. As a result, the area had a rich blend of French and German culture. Paul Thennes (Gene's grandfather) was born on December 13, 1830, in what is now Germany to Johan and Katharina Fries. Paul was the fifth in the line of known Tenneses from that area extending back to the mid-17th century.

Although their names sounded the same, Paul's various ancestors' surnames were spelled differently—Thennes, Tennis, or Tennes, something not unusual for the time, for spelling was notoriously inconsistent with writers spelling words differently in separate documents or even from page to page. After all, Webster did not complete his first dictionary until two years before Paul's birth in 1828, thereby establishing a common resource for English spelling standardization. There was little standardization of German spelling either until later in the century, with their first dictionary in the mid-1800s.

In the late 1820s, shortly after Paul was born, harvests in Bavaria failed, and Paul's family immigrated to America for its abundant farmlands. Eventually, thousands would head for, the land of unlimited opportunities, "Land Der Unbegrenzten Moeglichkeiten." Likely living in Cincinnati for a few years, the family heard, through Father Joseph Kondek, of a new German settlement and available land in Jasper, Indiana.

Following the Indian Wars of the early 1800s, the government encouraged settlements in Indiana and neighboring states, selling land at low rates, with a standard price of $150 for 120 acres or $1.25/acre. The early pioneers had been predominantly British Protestants, but by the mid-1830s, that had changed.

Prior to Fr. Joseph Kundek's arrival in 1837, there were only 60 souls in Jasper. Since he spoke German, the bishop sent this Croatian missionary to Jasper to administer the sacraments to the five poor German Catholic families there. Until then, they could only attend mass once a month when a visiting priest stopped by. With few roads, early transportation to and within Indiana was primarily along the river systems. Therefore, the first settlements were concentrated in southern Indiana along the Ohio and Wabash Rivers and their tributaries, which, in turn, led to the Mississippi, forming a vital trade route for commerce to southern Indiana. Supplies and immigrants flowed from New Orleans up the Mississippi to Southern Indiana, where farmers sent their harvests downriver. The White and Potaku Rivers near Jasper led to the Wabash River, which fed into the Ohio River, where Father Kundek originated his journey in Vincennes.

The Buffalo Trace provided the other possible transportation route to Jasper, a 20-30 wide hoof-path formed by buffalo traveling from Illinois to the Kentucky salt licks every year for hundreds of years. With a small initial congregation, possessing indomitable energy, a missionary's zeal, and a unique vision, Father Kundig endeavored to persuade German Catholics from other areas in the U.S., such as Cincinnati, to move to Jasper.

Drawn by the fertile farmland, the Tenneses were one of the first families to respond to the invitation when they moved to Jasper in 1839, quickly cutting down trees and building a log cabin before the winter settled in. Testifying to Father Kundek's success, by 1840, there were 100 families in Jasper. They arrived in Indiana following a series of Indian wars, led by the legendary Shawnee chief Tecumseh, who cobbled together a large confederation of tribes and won several stunning victories. After a series of treaties, the government removed most of the tribes westward, including the Delaware, Piankashaw, Kickapoo, Wea, Shawnee and Potawatomi. The Miami tribe would not leave until 1846 after the Tenesses had settled in. From the Indian's perspective, this was a tragic invasion of their homeland. Somewhat insensitively, from the German settler's perspective, who had not fought in the Indian wars or experienced its trauma, thousands of square miles of flat, fertile farmland were now available for settlement.

The Tenneses lived through the Napoleonic Wars, and their ancestors endured frequent devastating wars in which their lands were fought over and passed from one lord or king to the next, so from their perspective, fighting for land was, sadly, nothing unusual.

Near the Ohio River, with relatively flat, abundant fertile land and a similar climate, Indiana resembled their homeland in the Saar River Valley. There was much less crowding and the land was inexpensive, but unlike German towns that had been established for centuries, they had to clear the forests, remove the rocks, furrow the fields for the first time, and build their own homes, town buildings and churches from scratch. They used the logs and rocks from their fields to construct their log cabins and split the logs to heat their homes.

With few of the support systems of their homeland, life on the frontier, with its innumerable challenges would be physically and mentally exhausting. Their families, community, traditions, common language, and religion offered solace during the difficult transition. The lifestyle these early German settlers led far up the rivers' artery system that connected the remote Indiana wilderness to the rest of the world, would more resemble their lives in Germany than life in coastal America—similar to that of the modern-devise eschewing Amish who still speak German today and live a mid-19th century lifestyle.

The following year they helped build a brick church to replace the earlier log one. The church was constructed entirely with the labor and materials donated by the small community. The Tenneses were likely involved in digging the clay, forming and firing the bricks used in construction, which the parishioners completed in December of 1841, just in time for Christmas services. This early experience with clay would later lead to their livelihood.

———

In 1832, in Baden along the fertile southwestern corner of what would later become Germany, near the Rhine, the French border and the Black Forest or Swartz Wald, the Kiefers welcomed a beautiful, blond daughter named Josephina into the small German farming village of Pfaffenweiler. At the beginning of the 19th century following the Napoleonic wars, when Baden was in the hands of the French, the area suffered much devastation. Depending on who won the war, this area, adjacent to Alsace-Lorraine, was sometimes part of France and sometimes part of Germany, resulting in a fascinating blend of German and French culture. Only 40 miles away, Strasbourg is the seat of the European Union Parliament.   This was a rare peaceful period when farmers could tend their crops and families without fear. With its mild, oceanic climate, Baden proved to be an ideal region for growing crops, especially grapes for fine wines such as Riesling, Sylvamer, Pinot Gris, and the spicy Gewürztraminer.

During the peace, likely a joyful time for Josephina and her family, Baden experienced rapid population growth, increasing by a third in a mere 30 years. Rather than passing land to the eldest son through primogeniture, common in many European nations, fathers divided their holdings among their sons. This practice led to smaller and smaller parcels, barely enough to support the large, primarily Catholic families.

When Josephina turned 17, the peaceful period dramatically ended. Influenced by the French Revolution and seeking democracy, thirty-nine German States revolted against their aristocratic leaders. The Baden people overthrew Grand Duke Leopold in 1848 and established an assembly. Shortly afterward, the Prussian army from the north stamped out that revolution, reinstalling the duke. Then, in the early 1850s, there was a terrible famine throughout the region. Due to the same potato blight that infected Ireland, over half of Baden's potato crop rotted in the fields. Moreover, a poor grape harvest led to poor wines—their cash crop. Because of the famine and large population, many families, such as the Kiefers, struggled to provide for their children.

Desperate for food, reeling from the revolution and crackdown, with few funds to draw upon, the townspeople searched for solutions. Back in Indiana, energetic Father Kundig, still endeavoring to build his small congregation, aware of the drastic conditions in Pfaffenweiler, sent a letter to the town's leaders inviting them to join his new parish. But traveling to Indiana would be an epic journey of unimaginable expense for the poor, distraught villagers to afford or endure.

The village decided to sacrifice their only remaining resource to pay for the costly and lengthy trip so their young people could have a better life. They clear-cut their portion of the Black Forest selling the timber on the condition that their youth signed a paper stating they would never return. One can imagine the traumatic scene at the dock along the Rhine of families splitting at the seams, children and young adults queuing up for the boats leaving for an uncertain fate in an unfamiliar land, parents staying behind, growing older, never to see their children again or their, yet to be born, grandchildren.

The first group to make the epic voyage consisted of several of Josephina's close relatives (cousins, aunts, and uncles) among the 85 Pfaffenweiler men, women, and children. Few of these pioneers had traveled far from Baden or seen the ocean. During their trip, a fierce storm welled up off the petulant Atlantic Ocean. Facing mountainous seas and fierce winds, thinking the ship would capsize, sentencing them all to a horrific, watery grave, fearing for their lives, they prayed to God for deliverance. Finally, when the tumultuous storm abated, the skies cleared and the ocean lay calm. After they survived, they vowed to erect a monument upon their safe arrival in Jasper. Following their 52-day trip to New Orleans, they likely kissed the ground before completing the remainder of their arduous trip to Indiana. Not long after they arrived, they erected the promised sculpture to express their thanks to God—a cross that still stands today.

Josepha's father, Josef, died when she was nine. Induced by glowing reports from their Kiefer relatives of fertile, Indiana farmlands, fetching Josephina, her mother Therisa, handsome brother Anton, his wife Caroline and their three young children, Gustavus (9), Joseph (8) and Emilie (3) decided to leave Pfaffenweiler. Josephina and her family traveled down the familiar Rhine on a steam-powered paddleboat, viewing picturesque vineyards, towns, cathedrals, and castles along the way as the river grew gradually wider. They boarded a larger ship for Le Havre, France at the mouth of the Rhine River in Rotterdam, Holland. Next, they sailed across the broad, open, often treacherous Atlantic on the Valcluse, likely enduring cramped, foul-smelling quarters and poor rations. Never having seen the Ocean before, with the memory of their relative's terrifying voyage in mind, they had to endure the 7½-week crossing to reach the new world. Such a trip, leaving all they knew for an unfamiliar and possibly hostile land, took courage to undertake, but considering the devastating conditions of their homeland, they felt they had to risk it.

No doubt exhausted by the long, seasick-inducing voyage, they arrived in New Orleans on April 15, 1854. Whereas a trip from England to New York, where many immigrants would arrive, is about 3,500 miles, they had already traveled nearly 6,000 miles but their trip was not over. With another 2,000 miles to go, on the fourth leg of their arduous journey, they steamed up the Mississippi then up the Ohio River on a paddleboat to Troy, Indiana. On foot, with all their worldly possessions in tow, they walked the final 25 miles to Jasper and their relatives' open arms, arriving nearly three months after leaving home. Their families and former neighbors likely held a joyful feast with their favorite foods—schnitzel, bratwurst, spaetzle, and beer followed by kuchen, to celebrate their safe arrival.

Largely due to Father Kundig's German immigrants, the population of Jasper's Dubois County had roughly doubled from when Paul Tennes came until Josephina's arrival to over 6300. Shortly after Josephina arrived, after the second harvest, after they had adjusted somewhat to the new world, on November 27, 1855, with their jubilant families in attendance, Father Kundig wed Josephina Kiefer to Paul Tennes. They moved into a log cabin the families constructed, with a brick fireplace, on a hillside surrounded by pine trees, with a spectacular view of the surrounding countryside, overlooking a stream where they would gather their daily water.

In their cabin on August 6, 1857, Josephina had her first child, Mary Josephine (Gene's mother). Initially, Paul worked the farm, and Mary started out as a farm girl performing the typical required chores, helping with the harvest, tending the garden, caring for her younger sister, helping her mother in the kitchen, and canning. One day, on a visit to town, Mary spied the infamous outlaw, Jesse James. At first, startled and afraid she feared he might shoot her, but she soon realized he seemed like a fine, upstanding gentleman—not threatening at all. She rushed home and told her parents about the exciting man she saw.

Jasper had over 200 immigrants from Pfaffenweiler. Perhaps to heal the wounds of traumatic separation, today, the two towns are sister cities, whose citizens frequently travel to each other's towns and have an active student exchange program. To celebrate the connection, Jasper has an annual street festival, Strassenfest, with a beer garden, bratwurst, wiener schnitzel, streusel and numerous events presided over by the beautiful, young Miss Strassenfest. Germans regularly travel from Pfaffenweiler for the festival.

Picture of the Tennes Cabin where Mary was born
Painted by Gene Oberst in the 1930s

During the Civil War, from 1861-1865, the South blockaded the Mississippi River making it impossible to operate the long-established trade route between southern Indiana and New Orleans. Since there was no train route to Jasper, the farmers in Jasper, lost their primary route for their supplies and harvests. With access to the Mississippi trade route stunted, the emphasis on transportation and subsequent population growth shifted to northern Indiana along the Great Lakes and the new, expanding railroad lines.

Testifying to how short life could be, Paul lost his 23-year-old brother John in the Civil War, and his youngest brother John Adam would die in a gunfight in Missouri. Paul also lost his older brother Benedict who drowned as a student at Heidelberg in Germany.

While the nation engaged in the horrendous war, movement from the northern to southern states, which had been fluid, slowed to a trickle. Just thirty miles south of Jasper, across the Ohio River, lay Owensboro, Kentucky, a border state claimed by both the North and South. One of the stars on the Confederate flag represented Kentucky, but the South never controlled it, and many Kentuckian men fought on both sides, with one of the first Confederate Companies in Kentucky formed in Owensboro. Confederate troops occasionally raided Owensboro, disrupting the vital river traffic the area depended on and burning down the courthouse. After the war, when relocations were again possible, some of the numerous Germans, drawn by Father Kundek to settle in southern Indiana, moved across the river to the growing community of Owensboro, Kentucky.

Life in the new settlements like Jasper was tough with little healthcare and no doctor. Josephina tragically lost three of her young children, and in January of 1867, they lost their fourth. Paul Tennes had likely joined Josephina's brother, Anton Keifer, making bricks in Jasper. By 1867, perhaps because their clay had run out or due to the lack of development caused by the war the demand in Jasper had waned, so they moved on. Anton settled in nearby Washington, Indiana, where he again started producing bricks.

Tall, with a full, trimmed beard, a long attractive nose, deep-set eyes, a square face defined by a square, dimpled jaw and high cheekbones, with the large, barreled chest and the arms of a man used to toiling on the farm and hefting bricks, Paul Tennes cut an impressive figure.

Paul scouted the Owensboro area across the river, where he saw rich deposits of red clay where the roads had been cut out of the earth. The southern portion of Daviess County also included abundant coal deposits and coalmines, a necessary resource for making bricks. Paul reasoned he could use this coal in kilns to fire the red clay to make bricks. He also thought that the growing town could use his bricks, so he bought 14 acres on the edge of town where there were rich clay deposits and decided to construct a brickyard. Soon the family moved 30 miles due south, crossing the Ohio River on a ferry into Owensboro. Shortly afterwards, they rejoiced at the birth of their son, Joseph.

Owensboro lies on the southern portion of a large bend in the mighty Ohio River. Its first settlers floated down on flat boats around the beginning of the 19th century. The river's current forced the boats to the outside of the dramatic bend where Owensboro lay above striking yellow cliffs. In 1804, Lewis and Clark wintered there with their Corps of Discovery prior to their monumental trip of exploration and cataloging throughout the West, eventually making it all the way to the Pacific.

By 1870, in addition to the Tenneses, their household contained two servants and six German brickmakers. Sadly, Josephena died that year, leaving three children behind, with Mary, the oldest, who was barely 13. By now, Paul sadly had lost three brothers, four children and now his beloved wife. Adding to his grief, he would lose his dad, Johan, the next year. Paul needed a nanny to care for his young children. Through contacts in the German community, he heard of Christina Oberst and hired her while he tended to the brickyard.

———

Christina Oberst had immigrated to the U.S. when she was 22. She landed in New York on May 4, 1965 on the *Mercury* out of La Havre, France, just as the Civil War ended during the rambunctious celebrations. After two months living with her aunt Elizabeth in Poughkeepsie, Christina moved to Owensboro with an active German community. She worked for various families in the area as a nanny and housekeeper. Then she became the governess to Paul Tennes's three children, Mary, Albert, and Joseph.

In 1871, with her three charges in tow, Christina went down to the docks to meet her brother, Andrew, who was due to arrive from Germany via London and Poughkeepsie. Andrew had only 15 cents to his name when Owensboro appeared high on a yellow cliff around a bend in the river. As the boat docked, he saw his sister smiling along the side of the boat with a beautiful young girl standing next to her.

3: Andrew Oberst

Genealogical research, including church records and DNA testing, shows that the Oberst lineage traces back to Switzerland in the mid-16th century and possibly back to the 14th century. According to family lore, the name originated long ago in a Swiss village nestled into the Alps. One fine summer day, the villagers decided to hold a race up the mountain. The young men raced quickly up the first slope of the mountain, with one contestant lagging behind. Unlike the others, Johann realized it would be a long race and wisely paced himself. About halfway up, he began passing the others, who exhausted by their effort, fell abruptly to the ground. He too felt his heart pounding rapidly in his chest, but with a steady pace and steely determination, he progressed ever higher up the grueling mountain. Within sight of the peak, the last competitor fell, and Johann reached the summit far ahead of the rest to the cheers of the elated villagers. So impressed by his feat from that day on they called him Zobrist: first-up. Henceforth, he and his heirs were known as the Zobrists. Later, they dropped the Z resulting in Obrist.

The word Oberst traces back to feudal times in Germanic areas where an Obrist or Oberst was a senior knight. Oberst corresponds to the rank of Colonel in the Germanic countries. Initially, the name referred to the tribe that lives the highest on the mountain or the family that lives the highest in the village—giving credence to the family legend. According to the dictionary, all of which is a little much, "The usage derives from the superlative of ober(e), the upper or the uppermost. Used as an adjective, oberst means top, topmost, uppermost, highest, chief, head, first, principal, or supreme."

In 1517 when the early Obrists lived in northern Switzerland, Martin Luther, outraged by the sale of indulgences by the Catholic Church that, for a price, would forgive all sins, posted his 95 theses on the Wittenberg Cathedral in Germany. Cited as the start of the Protestant Reformation, the schism spread throughout Europe, causing periodic conflicts and wars. Lasting from 1616 to 1648, the Thirty Years' War erupted between Catholics and Protestants, in which 4.5 to 8 million soldiers and civilians died from the battles, famine and disease. Although the war included nearly all of Europe, most of the fighting occurred in Germany, which lost over a fifth of its population. They also lost much of their infrastructure, their homes, farms, shops, roads, mills, livestock, etc. Some German communities lost over half of their loved ones. To bring peace, the Holy Roman Emperor, Ferdinand III, signed the Treaty of Westphalia, stating that each ruler could declare the kingdom's religion, to which its subjects would adhere. The provinces in northern Switzerland became Protestant, whereas most of what is now southern Germany became Catholic.

As Catholics fearing persecution, the Obrists left Basel, Switzerland, and eventually settled in Bingen, 250 miles down the Rhine River, about 40 miles southwest of Frankfort. There, the population had been devastated by the protracted Thirty Years' War, so available land and opportunities were plentiful for the Obrists. Later, the Obrists settled in nearby Mandel, in the picturesque Rhine region where fertile, green hills flowed into the expansive Rhine River. Like many southern climes, life was more relaxed than in the northern reaches of Germany. People in the South enjoyed their schnitzel, bratwurst, kuchen, beer, wine, and festivals.

Before Gutenberg invented the printing press in the fifteenth century, few people could afford books; therefore, few could read or write. Last names began to take hold in the 1300s, but the spelling often varied, so there were several variants of the same name: Obrist Oberist, Zobrist, and Zoberist. Even though the pronunciation and meaning were the same, the Germans spelled the Swiss Obrist as O-b-e-r-s-t. One of Andrew's ancestors who moved out of the Basel area after the war had half of his eleven children named Obrist, while the later half were named Oberst. In the United States, at Ellis Island, it was not unusual for new immigrants to Americanize their names when they arrived, or, since many could not write, those who processed their applications would often spell the name as it sounded, a spelling that would carry forward to subsequent generations, similar to what occurred to the Oberst's when they moved to Germany.

———

During the mid-19th century, Johann and Katrina Oberst lived in Mandel, Prussia near Bingen, a small village in the Rhine valley about 40 miles downriver from Frankfurt. Due to its moderate climate and proximity to the river, Johann's four-acre vineyard thrived in this ideal wine-growing region, growing Riesling, Silvaner or Mosel white grapes. After the grapes ripened in the fall, the family spent long hours harvesting and then mashing the grapes into juice and pouring the juice into barrels to ferment. After fermentation, when the alcohol content peaked and the taste was just right, they poured the delectable liquid into casks or bottles and sold it at the market. The nearby Rhine, the German superhighway of the 19th century, provided the avenue to thriving markets from Switzerland, Germany and France to the docks of Rotterdam in Holland. Keeping the tradition alive, today there are seven wineries in Mandel, which sponsors an annual wine festival.

Their youngest son, Andrew (Gene's father), was born three weeks before Christmas on December 5, 1853. Johann named his son after his older brother, who had fought with Napoleon's Grand Armée during the invasion of Russia, commemorated in Tchaikovsky's *1812 Overture* with its booming cannons. On the horrific march back from, of the 680,000 soldiers that set off for Moscow, nearly all were captured, killed, or died from starvation or exposure. Uncle Andrew was one of twenty-five thousand survivors who had made it out of Russia alive. He was very lucky because only 4% survived—what a disaster for France.

Before the 19th century, there was no German nation; rather, there was a collection of 300 kingdoms. One militaristic northern kingdom, Prussia, began conquering and consolidating the others into its realm, including Mandel. Prussia continuously added more territory, eventually establishing the German nation in 1871 following the Franco-Prussian War, with its capital in Berlin.

The Prussian regime expected its young men to serve in the military, a concern for the Obersts. Its Army was composed of conscripts rather than regulars, meaning that all military-aged males were required to serve. One of Andrew's older brothers, Johann, was drafted and would fight in the Franco-Prussian War in 1870. Like Gene, Andrew had deficient legs, which would make his service unusually difficult, and, therefore, he did not relish serving in the Prussian military. In addition, since it was a conquered area, those in Mandel's province did not feel especially loyal to the militaristic Prussians.

In the early 18th century, the Prussian kingdom was among the first enlightened realms to institute mandatory elementary education from age 5 to 14, teacher colleges, certification and mandatory testing. Beyond merely the three Rs, the curriculum included other subjects such as ethics. In 1868, at 14, after Andrew had completed 8th grade and his examinations, his parents discussed what Andrew should do next. He was a bright student, but secondary education was reserved for the wealthy; therefore, high school was not an option. Perhaps the Obersts sensed the Franco-Prussian war coming in a year or two and wanted to protect their youngest son, so they decided to send him to London to live with relatives from the Mandel area, Charles and Sophia Oberst, from whom he would learn the baking trade.

Bustling, vibrant, cacophonous mid-19th century, Dickensian

London, differed vastly from Andrew's pastoral Mandel. Andrew arrived in London during the peak of the Victorian era (1837 -1901), during its "Golden Years" (1850-1870), with London the center of the British Empire, an empire that spread throughout the world—in essence the focal point of the world's trade, economy and power. The driving source of its prominence came from its role in leading the Industrial Revolution and its naval dominance of the world's oceans and consequent trade routes. At the turn of the 19th century, the population of greater London stood at one million. By the time Andrew arrived during those "Golden Years," London had grown to four million people. To accommodate all the newcomers, housing prices had escalated, as did crowding, leading to the emergence of teeming slums.

Based on his family's experience in debtor's prison and being sent to work in a factory at age 12, Dickens wrote inspired books such as Oliver Twist and A Christmas Carol, which told the remarkable story of the wretched working and living conditions the poor endured. But industrialization also led to the emergence of a burgeoning middle class, who patronized Charles and Sophia Oberst's bakery.

Life for the Obersts and the middle class in general was much better, for they had an abundance of cultural and entertainment opportunities such as the circus and newly formed brass bands, who due to London's frequent rains, played in the newly constructed, covered bandstands, their music permeating the parks on a sunny, Summer, Sunday afternoon, something Andrew with his appreciation of music and participation in the church choir likely enjoyed.

The bourgeoisie adhered to the high moral standards that defined the Victorian era. There was a spirit of libertarianism, as people felt free since taxes were low and government restrictions minimal. Even though the middle class did well, they too had to deal with the crowding, unsanitary conditions and air fouled by hundreds of thousands of coal fires that frequently blocked out the sun and covered every exposed surface with black, sticky soot.

At first, the crowds, noise, foreign language and foul-smelling, coal-black-infused air would have assaulted Andrew's rural-tuned senses. Still, London was a fascinating city, the center of the largest empire in the world, at the height of its powers—quite an experience for someone so young, just starting out on his life's journey.

There, under master baker Charles' tutelage, young Andrew apprenticed in the baking trade. He probably started doing the heavy work such as carrying hefty flour bags and kneading the daily bread, baked while it was still dark when the air was cool and moist before noisy London awoke. The large kitchen would soon become hot, but the smell of baking bread was delightful. His duties also included making deliveries, notably pigeon pies to Cardinal Manning, who presided over the Catholics in London, something his parents back in Mandel would be proud to learn. Family legend also contends that during one of his deliveries, Andrew saw Queen Victoria in one of her gardens. She would have been about 50 at that time. Eventually, he would have begun to bake tastier treats like kuchen, cakes, pies, and cookies.

After a three-year apprenticeship, when he had learned passable English and his trade well, Charles suggested that Andrew migrate to the United States to live with his sister. In September of 1871, at 17, he left from the port at Liverpool, sailed across the Atlantic, and landed in New York, a city as crowded, noisy, and confusing as London. From there he traveled up the Hudson River to Poughkeepsie to stay with his aunt Elizabeth and her family. It is said that he only had 15 cents to his name, which he used to purchase a piece of pie. Elizabeth Oberst Ramsteder Schindler immigrated to the U.S. in 1954, leading the way for her niece Christina and nephews Andrew and later John to come, a practice called chain migration.

Picture of Andrew
In Poughkeepsie, NY
At 17 just after immigrating to the U.S.

Two months later, this thin, tall. attractive, young gentleman with pensive brown eyes and dark hair, set off for Owensboro, Kentucky where he would join his sister Christina and her employer Paul Tennes. Using his acquired skills as an apprentice, he hoped to establish a bakery there. Andrew likely traveled by train through Pennsylvania to Pittsburgh, where he boarded a paddleboat to transport him down the Ohio River to Owensboro. The scenery along the way was much more pleasant than crowded London or New York, reminiscent of his faraway home in Mandel along the Rhine. With fresh air filling his lungs, feeling renewed, Andrew would have looked forward to seeing his beloved sister, meeting Paul Tennes, and starting his new life in this New World ripe with opportunity.

As the boat docked, he saw his sister smiling along the side of the boat with a beautiful young girl standing next to her. For

Andrew, it was love at first sight: someday, he would marry this attractive tall girl with long legs, a slightly upturned, chiseled nose, and high cheekbones. He was very shy yet excited to embrace his sister and meet the beautiful Mary Tennes. Christina introduced Mary as one of the children for whom she was the nanny. Andrew would live with Christina, Paul Tennes, and his five children in their home along with a servant, farm hand and six brick makers, until, with their assistance, he opened his own bakery in town.

————

Andrew soon became acclimated to Owensboro, the county seat of Daviess County. Owensboro's livestock included both cattle and sheep, the sheep outnumbering the cattle two to one. As early as 1834, Owensboro churches started barbequing mutton and burgoo in a lengthy process that involved slathering the meat with a vinegar-based sauce. Burgoo is a stew with barbequed mutton, other meats, and vegetables. Christina likely introduced Andrew to the local delicacy at a church barbeque with Mary.

Mary became a tall woman of nearly six feet. Andrew was over six feet tall too. True to his first sighting, Andrew Oberst married Mary Tennes in 1876 at St. Joseph's Church, given away by her proud father Paul. Andrew was 22, and Mary was 18. Christina was delighted to see her handsome brother marry the lovely girl she cared so much for.

By then, Andrew operated a bakery on St. Ann's Street across from the rebuilt county courthouse destroyed by Confederates during the Civil War. The smell of fresh-baked bread, kuchen, pies, and other tasty treats permeated the air enticing those on the square and lawyers from the courthouse to the bakery.

In 1877, not long after the wedding, Paul died at 45, leaving the brickyard, house, extensive property in Owensboro, and 18 acres to his wife Christina. Paul's life was a testament to the land of opportunity the Germans and other immigrants dreamed of when they faced deprivation and starvation back home. When he was a baby, his family left all they knew, undertaking a journey of thousands of miles, landing in a new and unfamiliar land. The family was one of the first to settle in Jasper, Indiana, where they carved out a log cabin home, a church, and a community out of the wilderness. In the New World, the bricks he, his lineage, and their crew made helped build Owensboro. Many of those buildings are still standing nearly 150 years after his death. Paul is one of the founders of Daviess County, appearing in the first history of the county. A stained-glass window dedicated to Paul Tennes, originally at St. Joseph's, currently resides at the Owensboro Museum of Art.

Andrew took over the management of the brickyard for his sister

Christina after Paul's death and eventually became a partner. Three months after her father died, Mary gave birth to their first son, Andrew Jr., in 1877. The family lived at 1500 West Fifth Street in Owensboro, close to the brickyard. This 1100 square-foot brick house, likely built with Oberst bricks, stood there until 2020 and is now a field. The young family grew quickly with the addition of a child every two years or so:

Josephine in 1879 (named after her grandmother Josephina Tennes),
Paul in 1881 (named after his grandfather Paul Tennes),
Albert in 1883 (named after his Great uncle Anton Albert Kieffer), and
John in 1885 (named after his grandfather Johann Oberst).

Interesting how their names honored their grandparents and significant uncle.

When the house became too small for a family of seven, they bought a larger property adjoining the brickyard at 1409 West Fifth, just a few houses down the street. To carry the family, the Obersts also bought a Phaeton Surrey from the Owensboro Wagon Company, one of the largest in the U.S., which Andrew enjoyed driving around town with his large family.

Like the Tenneses, many German families moved from southern Indiana to burgeoning Owensboro. Within the community, they spoke German. At first, they attended St. Stephen's Catholic Church, but due to the differences in culture and prejudice against Germans, parishioners asked the Germans to sit in the last pews. Indeed, many of the first pews had doors with locks on them to keep the Germans out.

During the 19th century, there were few restrictions on immigration and no quotas, therefore Western Europeans suffering from war and famine, sailed across the broad Atlantic to the United States unimpeded. However, earlier settlers such as the English Protestants and Catholics in Owensboro looked upon these people with their different languages, customs and drinking habits as inferior beings. Two major groups immigrated to the U.S. during the mid-19th century—the Germans and the Irish. Concern regarding these interlopers, who might be taking their jobs or at least reducing their wages, led to the establishment of the Native American Party, commonly referred to as the Know Nothings, who soon took over the governments in locals such as Philadelphia, DC, Massachusetts, Maine, Pennsylvania San Francisco, California and Louisville.

In the 1850s, when Paul and Josephina lived in Jasper, to maintain their political power, the Know Nothings conspired to keep these foreigners from voting. Seventy miles upriver in Louisville, they set up thugs in front of voting places to stop Irish or Germans, those who did not have yellow tickets or buttons, from voting. If they insisted on their right to vote, the Know Nothings severely beat them or stabbed them. Then they ravaged their communities, burning down a German brewery, destroying shops, firing a cannon at a Catholic church, killing a priest, and burning houses and apartment buildings down to the ground.

Between 20 and 100 people were mercilessly slaughtered. The reason the precise number was unknown was that the evidence was covered up. Since the Know Nothings won the election by a landslide and controlled all the levers of government (the mayor, council, police department, fire department), nothing was done—justice was not served. A year later, several more voters were killed further upriver in Cincinnati, and in 1857, an additional seven were slain in Washington, DC. Gene Oberst's future wife, Catherine, had a great uncle Quinn who was a large property owner, who was killed in the Louisville massacre after his townhouses were set ablaze as the fire department watched the conflagration and did nothing. The Know Nothings shot his tenants as they fled. Then they stabbed, shot and threw Quinn back into the fire.

The Know Nothings were a protestant group of men, but xenophobia also extended to the Catholics, with the early Catholic settlers not tolerating the German Catholics and later extending the same prejudice to the Irish Catholics. The Irish Catholics, likely due to their common language assimilated more quickly, but they and the Germans did not get along either.

Because they felt unwelcome in St. Stephens, the Germans built a parochial school for the German children in 1868, which the young Tenneses and Obersts attended where classes were taught in German. Mary said that the teacher demanded strict discipline and when they misbehaved would pinch their skin until it bled. They built their first German Catholic church in 1871, which was destroyed by a lightning fire in 1878. The parishioners, including the Tenneses and Obersts, raised enough money to build a new church, opening St Joseph's in 1880, which still stands today. Continuing the tradition started in Jasper, donated Oberst bricks were likely used to construct the new church.

With an added influx of Irish after the potato famine, St. Stephen's again became too crowded. The affluent Irish, who operated most of the bourbon distilleries in town, were known as the "whiskey people." Due to the abundant corn harvest, there were 18 distilleries, which turned corn into mash, fermented it, distilled it, and then aged the 80-100 proof delectable liquid in charred oak barrels to produce fine Kentucky bourbon. At the time, Americans consumed immense amounts of whiskey on and off the job.

The affluent, Irish, whiskey people did not want to join St. Joseph's because they could not understand German, there were stark cultural differences and the Germans like the Protestants and those at St. Stephens rejected them. The mass at St. Joseph's was conducted in Latin, but the sermon, announcements, and readings were in German. The whiskey people built a third church, St. Paul's, dedicated in 1889. So, in Owensboro, there were the teetotaler's Catholic Church, the Irish, the whiskey people's Catholic Church, and the German, beer-drinker's, Catholic Church. This was not unusual in the late 19th and early 20th centuries, when immigrant communities banded together in their own churches, speaking their own language, and practicing their time-honored traditions. Today nationalistic tendencies have been resolved in Sts. Joseph and Paul Catholic Church.

———

In 1888, Herman became the first baby born in the new house, followed by Joe in 1890. By now, there were six boys and only one girl, so Mary was elated at the birth of her second daughter in 1893. They named the new baby Mary after her mother. Frank was born in 1895, followed by Louis in 1897.

Andrew's older brother, Johann, the one who had fought in the Prussian army during the Franco-Prussian War in the early 1870s, moved to Owensboro during the 1880s, to work in the brickyard too. While he was in his 50s and 60s, in the 1890s and 1900s, he had five children who would play with their Oberst cousins. The family lived a block away on Fifth Street. One of Gene's best friends was his cousin John Oberst who was in his class in grade school. Christina, her stepchildren, and the two children she had with Paul (Catherine and Francis) also lived nearby, establishing a rather large Oberst community who visited each other regularly and celebrated the holidays together.

The brickyard produced 20,000 bricks a day, enough to build two or three standard-sized homes. By 1900, the population of Owensboro quintupled from about 2,500 when Paul arrived to over 13,000. Oberst bricks helped provide housing, stores and businesses for the rising population.

Adjacent to the brickyard, with its abundant supply of bricks, the house expanded as the family grew until it became quite a complex with numerous outbuildings, gardens, and livestock that sustained the large family. True to his roots, Andrew maintained a grape arbor, which he harvested every year to make his wine and grape juice, something he and his family had done in Mandel.

Johann and Katrina Oberst circa 1860

Gene Oberst's Ancestry

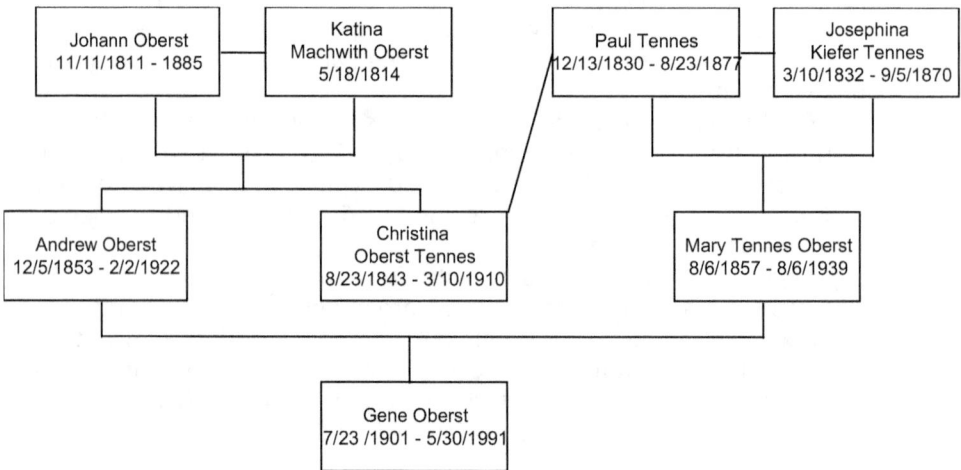

4: The Times

Eugene (Gene) William Oberst was born on July 23, 1901, in Owensboro, Kentucky, to Andrew and Mary Tennes Oberst. He was their 11th child born in this Ohio River town during a pivotal time in American history when opportunities seemed endless and the American Dream shown bright.

At the turn of the twentieth century, after defeating Spain, a vast European power, in the Spanish-American War, there was a sense that this would be the American Century. Innovation permeated the atmosphere with new inventions every week such as the automobile, telephone, light bulb, moving picture, airplane, and hundreds of mechanical marvels to improve the home, factory, and farm. Just that year in December, Marconi invented the radio. That 4th of July marked the 125th anniversary of the United States. Throughout the burgeoning nation, cities and towns alike held their biggest celebrations of the year with patriotic fervor at a fever pitch, stoked by a crescendo of booming, flashing fireworks lighting the night sky. Fulfilling its manifest destiny, the nation now stretched comfortably from the Atlantic to the Pacific.

After a 63-year reign, Queen Victoria died in January, capping the Victorian period in Britain and the Imperialistic Era for the world. The United Kingdom dominated the 19th century with possessions spanning the globe. Much of the British success had been due to its dominance in maritime trade and its preeminence in manufacturing, but by 1900, the United States began to assume that role, producing 24% of the world's goods versus 19% for the UK. GDP grew at its fastest pace, averaging 9.7% from 1870 through 1890. Part of the booming economy would be due to the immigrants such as Andrew for the U.S. population had grown by 63% over those 20 years.

———

This stunning transition was largely due to three men who monopolized the most important industries of the 19th Century: Carnegie in steel, Rockefeller in oil, and JP Morgan in banking, railroads, and electricity. Two would become the wealthiest men the world had ever known—Rockefeller and Carnegie, whose combined wealth would be approximately a trillion dollars in 2024. In 1901, JP Morgan bought out Carnegie to form U.S. Steel, controlling the market for this vital ingredient of the Industrial Revolution. These men amassed their huge fortunes by buying out competitors and consolidating vital industries into monopolies, which vastly increased America's industrial might, but severely reduced competition and led to controversy. Those who had been bought out or were forced to work in extremely dangerous conditions for wages barely enough to survive were not particularly fond of the prosperous industrialists.

In 1896 in nearby Ohio, a Cleveland iron, oil, and coal magnet, Mark Hanna, allegedly elected and controlled fellow Ohioan, President McKinley. By 1900, sentiment continuously grew against the "Robber Barons" because of some of their nastier tactics, such as undercutting competitor's prices to force them out of business. William Jennings Bryan spoke eloquently of the evils of capitalism and his plans to dismember the monopolies. Fearing this anti-monopoly presidential candidate, Carnegie, Rockefeller, and Morgan each donated $25 million (in today's dollars) to the McKinley campaign, an unprecedented sum at the time. Vice President, Garret A. Hobart died towards the end of the term leaving the ticket open. Republican leadership concerned about the progressive, up-and-coming, New York Governor Theodore "Teddy" Roosevelt, persuaded McKinley to select Roosevelt as his Vice President—a do-nothing position at the time, thereby sidelining him.

During the economic panic of 1993, as unemployment soared to 20%, during a labor dispute at a Carnegie Steel mill in Cleveland, Leon Czolgosz lost his job. While living on his father's farm near Cleveland, only able to find periodic work, he tried to understand the cause of the panic. He turned to a relatively new worldwide movement, **anarchism**, believing that the greedy capitalists and their corrupted politicians took advantage of the workers, making them little better than slaves in their moneymaking machines. On an extremely hot day, September 5th, 1901, President McKinley attended the Pan American Exposition in Buffalo. There Czolgosz, pretending to wipe his brow with a handkerchief to conceal his gun from the Secret Service, shot the president twice in the abdomen. President McKinley died sometime later in a tragedy that rocked the nation.

Teddy assumed office on September 14, 1901, proclaiming with his big stick policy and booming voice, that America was now a world power. Like Gene Oberst, Teddy had grown up handicapped and as a thick-glassed weakling, suffered from severe asthma attacks and cholera morbus, either of which could lay him up for days at a time. But Teddy was a force of nature, who valiantly worked through his pain and maladies, built up his body and became a relentless ornithologist, outdoorsman and hunter. A voracious reader, he excelled at Harvard, shortly thereafter marrying his delicate, beautiful, aristocratic wife Alice. Four years later, after giving birth to their daughter Alice died. His mother, Martha, who he was very close to, tragically died on the same day.

Teddy sought solace in the depths of the Dakota wilderness, where he founded cattle ranches and assumed the life of a rugged cowboy. There, after three robbers stole his newly constructed boat, after a relentless search down ice-filled waters, facing tortuous winter conditions, he captured them and brought them to justice. With his big toothsome grin, bushy mustache, and clear spectacles, Teddy became an intriguing mix of strong, burly, mountain man and erudite intellectual, who could be at ease tracking a buffalo for days through the deep snows of the Dakota wilderness with temperatures below zero, bounce between balls with the upper crust of New York society, or speak dynamically at a political party hall to a raucous proletarian group. He also excelled as a professional writer whose *The Naval War of 1812* and multivolume *The Winning of the West* garnered critical acclaim.

With mansions in New York City and the shore of Oyster Bay on Long Island, Roosevelt hailed from a 250-year-old, upper-class, Dutch American family but felt that the industrialists wielded too much power over the American political system. As the "Trust Buster," he moved to reduce the "Robber Barons" dominant influence, most notably by breaking up J. D. Rockefeller's Standard Oil monopoly that originated in Cleveland, until the 21st century, the largest company in the history of the world. Just two of its many pieces, Exxon and Chevron, are still two of the world's largest companies today. If whole, the estimated value of Standard Oil's pieces would be over a trillion dollars in 2024. Even though Rockefeller lost his monopoly, his stake in the thirty-split companies would be worth $600 billion in 2017, making him arguably the richest man of all time.

In the early 1900s, the "Muckrakers" called attention to the putrid conditions in the meat packing industry and the dangers in other industries such as Rockefeller's oil, Carnegie's steel and Morgan's railroads. Roosevelt established meat inspection and the FDA (Federal Drug Agency) to ensure drug quality. Teddy's progressives also organized to enforce child labor laws. At the time, the typical factory workweek was 12 hours a day, for which the worker made about $6 a week, or 10 cents an hour. Many children worked in these factories and although their time was not supposed to exceed 10 hours a day, it was rarely enforced. In addition, Teddy established the national park system, providing 17 million acres of public parks and forests for posterity.

———

In the late 19th and early 20th century, inventors such as Bell, Edison, Ford, and Goodyear, dramatically improved living through their innovations and businesses with Edison, Ford, and Goodyear taking annual "camping" vacations together. A couple of years after Gene was born, two nearby inventors in Dayton, Ohio, Orville and Wilber Wright, became the first men to fly. The West, as the U.S. called the Midwest was the center of innovation. The Wrights, Edison, Ford, and Goodyear happened to live nearby in Michigan and Ohio, encouraging Western young men to become inventors too. The inventors, along with the monopolists, were an example of how much one man could accomplish in a lifetime, an inspiration to young Gene.

Women's dresses at this time covered their ankles. Before modern appliances, they spent around 40 hours a week on meal preparation and cleanup, 7 hours on laundry, and another 7 hours on housecleaning for a total of 54 hours a week which does not include caring for their children. The average housewife baked half a ton of bread or about 1400 loaves a year. Gene's mother Mary's chores would have been overwhelming. With up to 13 mouths to feed and a large house to clean, the household duties would consume over 100 hours a week. Fortunately, her daughters, Josephine and Mary, helped with the load.

Few people had the conveniences long taken for granted in the 21st century. Only one in three American homes had running water so they had to fetch water from a well or pump it with a hand crank. Only one in six had toilets, so regardless of the weather they had to go out to the outhouse. Only one in thirty was lit by electricity, therefore light was supplied by candles, oil lamps or gas lamps all of which led to frequent fires. Owensboro opened its first electric plant just seven months before Gene's birth on New Year's Eve 1900, so electricity would soon be available to the Obersts—what a luxury. Only a few families could afford central heating, so most families gathered around the stove or fireplace during the cold winter months. In time, the Obersts' would acquire all of these 20th-century conveniences, but when Gene was born none existed in their home.

————

Gene's birthplace, Owensboro, Kentucky, typified America. It was a river port along a broad expanse of the Ohio River, the largest port between Louisville and St. Louis, the third-largest city in the state after Louisville and the capitol, Lexington. Steam-powered paddleboats docked there on a regular basis, delivering supplies and picking up tobacco, produce, manufactured goods, corn and bourbon whiskey, made from the corn in Owensboro's numerous distilleries. The burgeoning city had several factories with hundreds of farms surrounding it. Flanking the town square were dozens of Federalist-style buildings most built with bricks from the Oberst's brickyard.

Then three out of five people lived in towns in rural America with populations of fewer than 2,500. Owensboro with over 13,000 was larger than most. The country was in the process of transforming itself—leaving the first, agricultural wave and moving onward toward the second, industrial wave. This transformation caused tension between the rural and urban populace. Most of the early inhabitants had been conservative Protestants who settled in rural farms and towns. The later immigrants were largely Catholic who moved to large cities like New York or Philadelphia, taking industrial jobs. In tune with the culture of their homelands, they tended to drink whiskey, beer, or wine, whereas the more Puritanical, Protestant sects, seeing the evils of alcoholism, called for its prohibition.

At the turn of the century, there was a renewed interest in spirituality and religion of all kinds. As in Owensboro, the number of churches and attendance was expanding throughout the nation. As a boy, Gene snuck into a tent where an enthusiastic Holy Roller revival meeting was underway, fascinated to see people rolling on the floor. Religions encouraged values of virtue, industry, and thrift, with the expectation that one would be rewarded with material success.

The average life expectancy in 1900 was 48, with men outliving women, largely due to mothers dying in childbirth. The average married woman bore six children and spent much of her childbearing years pregnant. Twenty-five percent of children died before their 5th birthday. If they survived, fifty percent of children would lose at least one parent by the time they were 21. Sadly, Gene's mother Mary Tennes Oberst exemplified these statistics losing her mother as a child and her father before she was 19, when he was only 46. She saw four of her younger siblings perish but fortunately, the stout Mary had not lost any of her eleven babies: two girls—Josephine and Mary and nine boys—Andrew, Paul, Albert, John, Herman, Joe, Frank, Louis, and baby Eugene. Extended families banded together to take care of their orphaned children and aging parents in a time before Social Security, Medicare, Medicaid or welfare.

Family Picture before Gene was born
Circa 1899

———

Andrew, Gene's oldest brother, initially worked at the brickyard and attended Jasper College. He later worked as a millwright at the Owensboro Foundry where he was 2nd in charge, and his father was on the Board of Directors. Gene would later come to know his oldest brother better when he worked at the mill and walked with him to the mill. Andrew was a superb piano player.

When Gene was born, his second-oldest brother Paul studied at the Christian Brothers College in St. Louis and later studied to be a priest in the Passionist order at Mount Adams in Cincinnati. When ordained, Paul took the name of Bonaventure. Gene would not meet him until he was three years old when he, his mother, and brother Herman visited Bonaventure in Cincinnati. Gene was afraid of the tall figure dressed in black until while touring the Cincinnati Zoo, he looked over a wall into a snake pit and ran into his brother's arms, who quickly scooped him up and comforted him. Over the years, Gene would see Bonaventure more than he would see any of his other brothers.

Gene came to know his favorite brother Albert when Albert was severely sick at 17 and they would play together on his bed. By 1903, Albert enrolled at Notre Dame, where he would obtain a law degree in 1906 when it was possible to attain such a degree in three years versus seven. He was an altar boy at Albert's wedding and was thrilled to receive a dollar from him.

Josephine, a lovely woman and a nurse, who never married, dedicated her time caring for her large family. Some said she never found a man the equal of her brothers—at least her nine brothers said so.

After John graduated from college, he began working at the post office becoming an official, where he worked all his life. John visited a nearby glassworks, where he acquired a glass hammer that stood above the family fireplace, which Gene used to hammer nails and, of course, broke. Afraid, he hid in a closet in the kitchen and from then on felt intimidated by John. He would bring milk from their cows to John and his wife Emma, who, being quite an intellectual, saved foreign news briefs for Gene to read. In one column, the briefs summarized events around the world, which Gene found highly interesting, instilling in him an interest in world affairs.

Herman, Gene's second-favorite brother, whom Gene thought to be the most handsome, was a brilliant person. He loved adventure and sang in light operettas and with the church choir along with their father. He owned a saloon, a tobacco farm, and a general store near the family home. Since Herman was well-read, he had collected many books, which Gene spent months reading, including his favorite, Pushing to the Front. Herman also taught Gene how to hunt and fish.

All of the boys were over 6 feet tall. A picture in the Owensboro paper showed Andrew with his nine sons, enough for a baseball team. Before modern conveniences, it would have been difficult for Andrew and Mary to provide for the eleven children, but they found numerous ways to survive and thrive.

5: Oberst Home

With so many mouths to feed and a decent, but limited income, the Obersts had to become self-sufficient. Andrew's brickyard across the street supplied ample building materials to expand the family home and grounds over time. With nine tall, strong, industrious sons to provide the labor, expansion projects and chores were readily accomplished.

The initially small antebellum house on 1409 West 5th was expanded greatly by the addition of a second floor and additional rooms in the rear. The family home eventually included a parlor and sitting room two bedrooms, large dining room and kitchen on the first floor and five bedrooms and a bath on the second floor—seven bedrooms and a bath, which was a vast improvement over the outhouse. A porch enveloped the home on the south and west sides. The south-facing half of the porch was fitted with removable windows. In the winter and with the aid of a steam radiator this became the conservatory where there was an orange tree, a lemon tree, a night-blooming Cereus, various ferns, and other tropical plants, which were protected from the cold. With the sun shining through on a cold winter morn, the tropical room provided a welcoming environment for the Obersts to sip a cup of coffee and read the local paper before launching into their day.

As the youngest child, much of the additions to the home were completed by the time Gene was born with the last coming when he was six. Mary and her two hard-working daughters fed the family well and kept the house running smoothly. Below is Gene's recount of his childhood home, which highlights how independent and self-sufficient many families were in a time before supermarkets and modern appliances. The story provides perspective on the life of a child growing up in an early 20th-century, Ohio River town. It also gives insight into Gene's early environment, enterprising family and motivations.

Let me tell you about our home, which by no means was typical of others in our neighborhood. I never realized at that time that our house and yard, occupying almost an acre, was any different from the laborers small homes for almost a half mile on all sides.

Now to the outside of our home property. The front and side was surrounded by picket fences, large sycamore trees grew in the front, a few catalpa bordered our next door neighbor's alley way and also shaded the brick lined stable yard in the rear of our house. From outhouse to the side street there were gardens for flowers and vegetables and a few trees of each of the following fruits; apple, pear, quince, plum, peaches, cherry and most interestingly some ten paw paw trees and stunted fig trees. The paw paw trees produced a delicious tasting fruit in late August. Our next-door neighbor had an enormous persimmon tree and we relished eating this fruit in October and November...

Our major supply of walnuts for winter candy came from excursions into the woods several miles from home where we brought back bushels of nuts to be shelled of the outer covering, then dried and packed away.

Our grape arbor produced a variety of grapes which we cut for eating, bushels for canning (jam and jelly), and to make several big barrels of wine, which my father, expert in wine making learned in his youth along the Rhine. When the time was right the wine would be put into bottles for table use.

We picked gallons of red and purple raspberries from our bushes in May and early June (Oh ! how delicious with sugar and the thick cream supplied by our cow). The vegetable gardens supplied us with onions, radishes, lettuce, cabbage, tomatoes, okra, asparagus, beans, potatoes, corn, egg plant, celery, rhubarb, chives, mustard greens, kale and spinach. There was also a number of herbs some of which I remember as sage, horehound, mint, fennel, and rosemary. During the appropriate seasons, my two sisters and mother canned hundreds of jars of fruit and vegetables and stored these into the fruit and wine cellar. I seldom recall seeing a store canned item in our kitchen. We picked black berries from nearby hillsides and canned many gallons.

We had a number of chicken coops with laying pens in shelves in sheltered houses. The number of chickens varied between fifty to one hundred at a time, supplying us with eggs and eating chickens.

There was a two-story brick stable with two stalls for cows, one large stall for our buggy and riding horse. Attached to the stable was an enclosed buggy shed with surrey and phaeton. In the loft above the shed there was a special provision for pigeon nests where we could readily reach squab for table usage, which some on toast and gravy provided a delicacy, reserved usually for guests of whom there were many, particularly priests of the Passionist Order, friends of Bonaventure. Squab on toast, fresh creamed asparagus, corn on the cob, fresh green beans, new small buttered potatoes, wine, coffee, delicious home made bread, and peach ice cream. Yum! Not bad for middle class people with a rich heritage of education, culture and health, but not too much money in the bank.

There was a driveway from the side street to the stable yard. Back of the driveway and stable was about ¼ acre of garden land. One entered the driveway of about 75 feet through a swinging gate. One should note that practically all the homes in our area were surrounded by fences for protection of yards from stray animals and particularly from herds of cattle driven down our front road sometimes in droves of hundreds brought in from western ranches by train to be taken to feed pens for fattening at the distilleries below town, where the cattle were fed the remains of corn mash after the essentials for whiskey making were extracted from the corn.

Besides the aforesaid items, we had a summer kitchen attached by a large shed to the kitchen, which was largely used for washing clothes. A brick smoke house seasoned hams, bacon, sausage, made up by my father from several large dressed hogs bought in the fall. A milk house with deep cold well water pumped in by hand kept the crocks of milk and cream cool in the cemented brick trough. A cistern supplied rain water for clothes washing. With no sanitary sewer in our area, one more outhouse was about 75 feet from our back door—it had two- and one-half seats. I was pretty well grown before we had a full bath room in the house. The last mentioned outhouse was sheltered by grape vines, rambling clematis, and morning glories.

Our family had a huge iron kettle used for rendering lard from various parts of the hogs processed for the winter. A wood fire was started back of the porch shed. The kettle raised on bricks was filled with hog parts to produce lard and eventually the remaining parts were placed into a special rendering press where every remaining fat was pressured out and the substance which remained was known as cracklings-- not too bad to nibble on. The rendered lard was placed in large tins or crocks to be used for frying food on our large kitchen coal stove, which had attached a compartment for heating our hot water, stored nearby in a fifty-gallon galvanized iron tank. In the spring of the year all the fat *remnants, bacon rinds etc. were placed in the huge kettle outside with added lye and after a considerable period of boiling a precipitate of home-made soap became available for using to wash clothes.*

Probably the most interesting items that I recall are the paths around our yards, banked by an almost unbelievable variety of roses, daises, evergreens, sunflowers, hydrangeas, lily of the valley, petunias, salvias, snapdragons, hyacinths , dahlias, iris, carnations, hollyhocks, phlox, mums, flowering moss, daffodils, tulips, bushes of bleeding hearts, flowering almonds, bed of elephant ears, a bush of sweet smelling calathea snow ball plant, ferns, fences with morning glories, forsythia, Virginia creeper, honeysuckle, clematis, climbing wild roses, morning glories, passion flower vines, and lilacs.

My sister Josephine's pride and joy was her large several tiered flower bench about 15 feet long and quite wide on which she grew sensitive flowers; ferns, wax plants, night blooming cereus (bloomed with extremely large long stemmed sweet smelling flowers only one night a year), potted palms and perennial potted flowers, all of which was transferred in the winter months to our L shaped porch (along the entrance and east side of the house), where glass windows were installed and heated by radiators. Her flower display along with her dwarf orange and lemon producing trees were the talk of all visitors.

One can conclude that with all of this flora, fauna, animal life including cat and dog, this made the family almost self-sufficient for life's sustenance, independent of most outside sources. My mother baked great loaves of bread and kuchen. My sisters made delicious pies and cakes and were expert at making candies of a variety of names.

Gene describes his childhood home, which had grown over the years. Throughout his childhood, the Obersts would add modern conveniences such as electric lights, indoor plumbing, toilets, and central heating, but these did not exist when he was born.

The above outside picture of my home surroundings must be supplemented by the inside features of our home. Seven bedrooms, foyer, parlor, living room, large dining room, kitchen with coal burning stove and pantry, and off the hall; on second floor a huge attic to store ancient furniture and gadgets, where we put together shot gun shells and wash was hung to dry in the winter time. Electricity was installed in 1907 as was also hot water radiators replacing the usage of coal oil lamps and four fireplaces. Outdoor plumbing was supplemented by interior facilities and a fair size bath installed replacing a tin and wood tub in a hall on the first floor.

Our Parlor kept immaculately clean contained a piano and period red velvet covered walnut furniture, Fortunately, my sister Mary and brother Joe were excellent (piano) players and accompanied me in singing many old songs. Many times my brothers would gather around the piano and have a song fest. Albert's favorite was " Asleep in the Deep. Mine were Smarty, Daisies won't tell Dear and Silver Moon.

Each person in my family had work chores about the house until they were old enough to have outside work. My task at about age 6 was to close all the outside shutters on the house. Later, I assisted my brothers in yard sweeping, cleaning the chicken house, bringing in coal, chopping wood to start the morning fire in the kitchen stove, plucking feathers from chickens after their heads had been removed and the headless chicken dipped into scalding water to loosen their quills. At eleven my other brothers had been introduced to milking the cow (a chore I hoped not to assume). Fortunately, my father now no longer with the brickyard management took this onto himself as well as gardening.

Oberst home, Owensboro, KY – painted by Gene Oberst

Before Gene started school, a spider bit him, and much of his body became extremely swollen, restricting him to bed for weeks. As the swelling increased, his mother worried about her dear youngest child, concerned that he might die. The doctor said all they could do was keep him in bed and let time heal. As Gene became older, his parents noticed that he limped. Periodically, they took him to see their family physician, Doctor Todd, who had served in the Confederate Army operating on maimed soldiers. Gene enjoyed his stories immensely, thereby becoming sympathetic to their cause— *The South shall rise again*, a common sympathy in the South. Even though the war had ended 40 years earlier and Southerners loved America, there was still some lingering resentment expressed in this common phrase, which few took seriously. Gene had extremely swollen ankles and flat feet that looked like clubs attached to his legs. As a result, he could walk in pain but could not run well.

Likely due to his crippled feet, Gene became an avid reader, consuming the family's extensive collection of books. Being born with this disability, Gene or Hutsi, as his mother called him, did not know what it was like to walk without pain and run with abandonment like most toddlers. In some families, eight brothers would have tortured their younger brother for his deformity, but Andrew and Mary would not allow such behavior, and although there was likely some sibling rivalry, there is no evidence that the Oberst boys picked on each other or fought regularly.

Since his older brothers were much older than he and his closest brother, Lewis, was exactly four years older to the day, Gene depended on neighborhood boys for play, and there were plenty of boys to play with in this growing, Twain-like river town. Being crippled, it would not be unusual for the neighborhood boys to tease him, and for him to become embarrassed. Soon they relented and he joined in their games and adventures. The rambunctious boys grew up freely like Huck Finn and Tom Sawyer, seeing the paddleboats sloshing by, hearing their whistles at the dock, running barefoot during the summer. As a young boy in the expanding, 1900rds boy's-world, Gene had to establish himself. Being embarrassed about his handicap, he did not want to call attention to himself, complain about his condition, or pain, or ask for special consideration. Motivated by their games and adventures, he soon learned to bear the pain and keep up as best he could. Here is his recollection of those days and how boys in the river town grew up.

> As a youngster, I lived a veritable Tom-Sawyer-like existence; with huge space in the brick yard across from home, ravines, woods, farmland nearby, the Ohio river only five blocks away, open field areas all around for play. We

kids enjoyed every type of play known to youths of that day. Like Dan Boone; we hunted Indians, played Jesse James, beacon around the brickyard, hiding in the ravines, caught frogs and snakes, fished for crayfish, fished in the ponds and the Ohio river, rode horses, hunted squirrels and rabbits, parched corn for eating by using tin sheets over outdoor fires, baked potatoes in the kilns in the brick yard, walked the railroad tracks just two blocks away from home (some daring kids hopped the trains, but not me). We went barefoot everywhere after May 1, but wore shoes on Sunday much to our disgust.

Most of us were proficient in baseball, but basketball was only for the uptown kids at the YMCA. There was not much snow for winter snow games and ice skating. Almost every year gave us sufficient cold for snow and ice to get a touch of building snowmen, getting out homemade sleds, using these to hitch rides in back of delivery wagons, and to go skating on rather thin ice, which usually resulted in breaking through and then drying out by a fire built outdoors.

We had homemade bows and I used arrows made from iron weeds with a nail stuck in the pith for weight at the end. There were a number of throwing projectile gadgets. The one I liked best was made of a string attached to a three foot willow branch and then stuck into a notch of a foot-long dart made from roofing shingles. These might sail up to a hundred or so yards. All of us were skilled in mumbly peg (a knife game) and a jumping game using a paddle hitting a small cylindrical wood piece cut like a torpedo. Great fun in the spring was to make stilts and to walk with these through mud and jump into sand pits from banks of clay.

Did we smoke? Yes—such things as pieces of old cane buggy whips, mullein, rabbit seed, cuts of dried grape vines; and most of us had experience making cigarettes from tobacco and rice paper. I did not relish smoking tobacco, particularly with home made pressed burley soaked with sorghum molasses brought to school by farmer lads. I tried several times only to get green in the face and deadly sick for hours.

Our great summer vacation fun was to give a hand signal to boys in the neighborhood. If a boy nodded affirmatively after looking to see that his folks were not looking, he would then meet the gang at the big tree down the street. After assembling, the gang would go to a small lake on the outskirts of town, or as we got older we would go several miles below the city on the Ohio river and enjoy a couple of *hours of swimming and play both in the morning and afternoon. We did not know that swimming suits had been invented, consequently, when we got home for noon meal or evening supper, there was no wet clothing to give us away.*

Summer days in Owensboro sizzled, with most days in the 90s accompanied by uncomfortably high humidity. The family ate their main meal in the early afternoon when the heat intensified with a smaller supper in the evening. Working at the brick kilns would be oppressive during the hottest time of day so a midday respite provided welcome relief. When Gene was a little older, his father and mother decided to open an ice cream parlor downtown. With no air conditioning, ice cream was a delightful treat on those scorching summer days in the first decades of the 20th century. Ice cream cones became a favorite at the St. Louis Fair in 1904, and by 1910, sodas, sundaes, and banana splits were concocted. Gene visited the parlor as often as his parents would allow, often accompanied by a band of his smiling pals parched after a hot game of baseball.

Picture of Mary with her eight younger children
At Jasper IN homestead (circa 1901)

From right: Josephine, Louis, Mary holding Eugene, Frank,
Albert, Joe, Herman, John

The Younger Sons

Andrew sent Gene's three older brothers out of town to college-
Andrew Jr. to nearby Jasper College in Indiana, Paul (Bonaventure) to
Christian Brother's College downriver in St. Louis, and Albert up north
to Notre Dame College in South Bend, Indiana. These were relatively
expensive, and by the time his younger sons were ready to attend
college, due to declining clay deposits, the brickyard was less
profitable.

Andrew, the father, received a good grade school education in
Prussia but was unable to progress further because his family was not
wealthy.   He had accumulated an extensive family library and
regularly attended the Chautauqua lectures, both of which he used to
educate himself further, but he and Mary wanted their sons to have a
college education if at all possible. Fewer than 3% obtained a degree
then, and Andrew and Mary thought a college education would vastly
enhance their sons' prospects and lives. He thought a local college
would provide the education he wanted his younger sons to acquire,
so he helped to establish Columbia College in Owensboro in a wealthy
former resident's mansion, where the boys could stay at home, work,
and attend school.

It seems intriguing that a mother who grew up in a log cabin and
a father who only had a grade school education would care so much
about their children's education. After all, not even one out of thirty
young men and hardly any women attended college. But like
immigrants in the 21st century, they saw America as the land of
opportunity, in which your children could advance themselves through
hard work, disciplined study and obtaining a professional degree.

Andrew's fifth son, Joe, whom Gene thought to be the most
intelligent and second most handsome, spoke eloquently and could
walk on his hands for 75 feet. Joe graduated from Columbia around
1913, married, and moved to Atlanta where he became an insurance
agency manager.

Mary, a tall, attractive woman, attended a finishing school and
taught her younger brothers' etiquette and how to play the piano.
Gene taught her how to drive, which she learned in the first lesson.
She started working for the sheriff's department and eventually
became a highly respected deputy sheriff. The next in line, Frank,
also attended Columbia and lent Gene his physical education books,
which Gene put to good use.

Louis had been born four years and one day before Gene and was
the most daring of all the brothers, testing the ice on the frozen lake
even though he sometimes fell in. During frequent hot summer days,

the boys would go to the Ohio to swim, where there were shallows, sand bars, and, when the river was low, an island with a long beach. They did not bother to wear swimsuits but rather swam naked. During one excursion to the river, a boy named Badger grabbed six-year-old Gene, took him into the river, and told him to swim back to shore or drown. Afraid Gene struggled to swim back but made it. Louis, defending his younger brother, argued vehemently with the older Badger, who chased Louis along the beach, intending to beat him up. They ran for about a block, where a group of girls was sitting on a yellow bank high above the river, who, upon seeing the two naked lads below, started giggling. Embarrassed by their lack of clothing, Badger immediately reversed direction, followed by Louis. To the boys assembled on the beach, it looked like Louis now chased the much-bigger Badger and they wondered what he had done to strike such fear into the bully. Gene thought of his older brother as his hero.

The family looked forward to Christmas, which, at the time, was not celebrated throughout America to the extent it would be later in the century. For Germans, though, it was the major holiday of the year, whose Christmas tree and Santa Claus would soon sway the nation. Gene felt thankful to receive a book and apple as presents rather than the threatened alternative—a lump of coal.

On Christmas Eve in 1909, after the family prepared for the festivities, they heard screams outside. Louis, now 13, had been run over by a team of horses pulling a road leveler, his ear hanging by a thread. The family quickly raced him to Dr. Todd, who, being well-practiced as a Civil War surgeon, restored the ear. The horses' hooves injured Louis's head, though, and at times, as Gene said, "His sanity would leave him." Unfortunately, due to the injuries, Louis met a premature death in his mid-thirties.

Picture of Andrew and Nine Sons
Gene 1st on left

Like his older siblings, Gene enrolled at St. Joseph's German Catholic School where he learned German in addition to English. When he was 14, he traveled to his brother Bonaventure's Passionist monastery in St. Louis in hopes of healing his deformed feet. There, he stayed with his brother from August until December while doctors operated on his feet and fitted him with braces. The clunky metal braces eased the pain, enabling him to walk further and run slowly. This provided Gene with an opportunity to get to know his brother better too. As the General Consulter of the Passionists (Vice President), Bonaventure would later travel the world to faraway places such as Italy, England, Ireland, Austria and Poland, establishing and supervising monasteries. Much later, Bonaventure would be in charge of St. Martha's in Bethany, Palestine in the turbulent times of the founding of Israel in 1948. The church had protected 60 Jewish, Polish refugees from the Nazis during World War II.

After Saint Louis, after they operated on his feet after he received his braces, he could run a little, and although there was less pain, running was still painful with the metal braces digging into his flesh. He had learned not to let the pain restrict his activity—he never made excuses, and he never willingly let anyone know of his deformity. All he wanted was to be treated and be accepted as a normal boy.

Childhood passed quickly, and, before he knew it, he graduated from St. Joseph's grade school and headed to Owensboro High. Many of his grade school pals would not attend high school; instead, they would work at their parents' farm or shop, or seek a job in town. Gene looked forward to High School where he would meet those from other nationalities and religions.

6: High School

As a child, Gene devoured a surprisingly extensive family library, especially for a middle-class family that greatly influenced his life as he sought wisdom, knowledge, and an understanding of history and the world.   In the living room, there were several bookshelves containing books such as:

- Stoddard's Lectures,
- Real American Romance,
- 20 Volumes of the Civil War in photographs,
- American series by Prescott and Parkman and Robinson,
- Four leather-bound *History of the World* by Ridpath.

Also included were Classics by Tennyson, and Longfellow, books by Marion Crawford, Irving Cobb, Jack London, Horatio Alger, and some forty books by G. A. Henry dealing in historical fiction and highlighting important phases of World History. The Bible, much of Shakespeare's work, Defoe's *Robinson Crusoe, Treasure Island, Putman Hall Cadets, Rover Boys, Motor Boys, and Tom Brown at Oxford, adorned the shelves, as well as* a series of books by Father Finn such as *Harry Dee and Ted Playfair, Ben Hur, Fabiola, Mysterious Island* and *20,000 Leagues Under The Sea* and others by Jules Verne. He read every one of these books and hundreds more from the Carnegie Library.

His particular favorite *Pushing to the Front, Success Under Difficulties* by Orison Swett Marden, a volume of inspirational essays showed how to overcome obstacles and become successful. Marden's parents died before he was seven, leading to an extremely arduous and transient childhood.   Samuel Smiles from Scotland, a similar motivational writer, inspired him towards greatness, after which, as a polymath, he worked his way through college, earning degrees in law, medicine, and science, along with several in the arts. He published the book in 1894 with 50 editions to follow during the ascendance of the "American dream."   Remarkably, much of it still applies today. Similar to the self-help books that would follow, *Pushing to the Front* instructs young men on how to construct their lives and pursue values in the pursuit of lofty goals.

The book has over 60 themes represented in distinct chapters, each focusing on a particular personal attribute such as drive, determination, discipline, courage, perseverance, character, thrift, beauty, college, etc. The author brings in hundreds of examples from famous artists, philosophers, writers, inventors, and American presidents to illustrate his points:

- Philosophers such as Aristotle, Socrates, Plato, Descartes, Rousseau, Adam Smith and Hobbes
- Presidents and national leaders such as Garfield, Grant, Jefferson, Washington, Wilson, William Jennings Bryant, Henry Clay, Nelson, Napoleon, Sir Walter Raleigh, William Penn, Disraeli, Thomas Mooreland and Teddy Roosevelt
- Writers and artists such as Shelly, Tennyson, Byron, Keats, and Daniel Webster, Shakespeare, Milton, Lamb, Michael Angelo, Beethoven and Gibbon
- Inventors such as Watt, Bell, Morse, Ford, Edison, Goodyear and the Wright brothers
- Entrepreneurs and explorers such as Rockefeller, Carnegie, Chase, Vanderbilt and Columbus

One common theme is how many of the great men were born into poverty, often growing up in a hovel or log cabin, and how, through the characteristics Marden highlights, they overcame immense difficulties, acquired a formal or informal education, and eventually became stunning successes. The book includes hundreds of examples, antidotes, stories, and quotes from the great men who started at the lowest rungs of society and changed the world. During their ascendance, they became leaders, helped their fellow man, acquired fame and usually became wealthy. In a sense, Marden endeavored to accumulate and present the combined wisdom of the ages for an ambitious young man to potentially benefit from. What more would an idealistic young man like Gene want at the turn of the century when, from his perspective and his immigrant family's example, America offered infinite possibilities?

Some of his advice like his guidance upon cleanliness and the importance of bathing once a week and washing your hair once a month—twice if you have oily hair is outdated. Much of it is in sync with today's thinking though—quoting anti-smoking literature, or support for women making the most of themselves, aligning with women's rights, and their obtaining the vote.

Gene read the book multiple times and adopted it as the map for his life. He would follow its precepts, expecting that through perseverance, hard work, discipline, clean living, and thrift he would be successful.   In a sense, it became his bible containing the accumulated wisdom of the ages that would guide him.

Below are 20 key quotes, which helped to inspire Gene's personal philosophy:

Inspirational Quotes from *Pushing to the Front*

How to Succeed
"Great men never wait for opportunities; they make them. Nor do they wait for facilities or favoring circumstances; they seize upon whatever is at hand, work out their problem, and master the situation."

"This striving for excellence will make you grow. The constant stretching of the mind over problems which interest you, which are to mean everything to you in the future, will help you expand into a broader, larger, more effective man."

"We constantly see men of mediocre ability but with fine personal presence, superb manner, and magnetic qualities, being rapidly advanced over the heads of those who are infinitely their superiors in mental endowments."

"The weakest living creature, by concentrating his powers upon one thing, can accomplish something; the strongest, by dispersing his over many, may fail to accomplish anything."

"The trouble with a great many people is that they are not willing to make present sacrifices for future gain. They prefer to have a good time as they go along, rather than spend time in self-improvement. They have a sort of vague wish to do something great, but few have the intensity of longing, which impels them to make the sacrifice of the present for the future."

Interaction with others
"A large part of the value of a college education comes from the social intercourse of the students."

"The man who mixes with his fellows is ever on a voyage of discovery, finding new islands of power in himself, which would have remained forever hidden but for association with others.

"Timid, shy people are morbidly self-conscious; they think too much about themselves. Their thoughts are always turned inward; they are always analyzing, and dissecting themselves, wondering how they appear and what people think of them. If these people could only forget themselves and think of others, they would be surprised to see what freedom, ease and grace they would gain; what success in life they would achieve."

Positive outlook

"The human mechanism is so constituted that whatever goes wrong in one part affects the whole structure. There is a very intimate relation between the quality of the work and the quality of the character. Did you ever notice the rapid decline in a young man's character when he began to slight his work, to shirk, to slip in rotten hour, rotten service?"

"The 'blues' are often caused by exhausted nerve cells, due to overstraining work, long-continued excitement, or from dissipation. This condition is caused by the clamoring of exhausted nerve cells for nourishment, rest or recreation."

"We were made for happiness, and gladness, to be prosperous. The trouble with us is that we do not trust the law of infinite supply, but close our natures so that abundance cannot flow to us."

Beauty

"We admire the beautiful face, the beautiful form, but we love the face illumined by a beautiful soul."

"All great works of art have been produced when the artist was intoxicated with the passion for beauty and form which would not let him rest until his thought was expressed in marble or on canvas."

Learning

"A home without books and Periodicals and newspapers is like a house without windows."

"If a man empties his purse into his head," says Franklin, "no man can take it from him. An investment in knowledge also pays the best interest."

"There are so many good correspondence schools today, and institutions like Chautauqua, so many evening schools, lectures, books, libraries and periodicals, that men and women who are determined to improve themselves have abundant opportunities to do so."

Women

"Multitudes of women in this country today are vegetating in luxurious homes, listless, ambitionless, living narrow, superficial, rutty lives, because the spur of necessity has been taken away from them; because their husbands, who do not want them to work, have taken them out of an ambition-arousing environment."

True riches

"People who keep their minds bent in one direction too long at a time soon lose their elasticity, their mental vigor, freshness, spontaneity."

"Some men are rich in health, in constant cheerfulness, in a mercurial temperament which floats them over troubles and trials enough to sink a shipload of ordinary men.   Others are rich in disposition, family, and friends. "

"What power can poverty have over a home where loving hearts are beating with a consciousness of untold riches of the head and heart?"

Despite social media and all our technology, surprisingly, much of Marden's advice still applies in the 21st century. Interestingly, 60 years ahead of its time, he supported women's liberation.

Guided by Marden, Gene eventually developed a winning personality and learned how to interact with people well while maintaining a positive outlook on life.   He would cultivate an appreciation of music, literature and art, eventually producing numerous paintings, writing short stories, teaching himself how to play the piano, read and compose music. He, too, would become a polymath or Renaissance man.   Gene would maintain a life-long appreciation of learning, continuously expanding his knowledge until his last days.   At times, like most people, Gene would be highly paid and at other times, he would struggle to get by, but he realized the importance of the true riches in life, such as family, friends, character, education, travel and teaching the young.

———

Periodically, the Chautauqua Institute visited Owensboro, providing stimulating lectures, music, art, and intellectual pursuits, which Gene greatly looked forward to. The institute was, and still is, located in Western New York, adjacent to Pennsylvania's panhandle, near Lake Erie, less than 50 miles from Ohio. It is a non-denominational, spiritually based institution offering a broad variety of cultural pursuits, including philosophy, art, dance, theatre, politics, literary arts, economics, and science. Its music program attracts talented young musicians from throughout the world and boasts concerts and symphonies by talented musicians along with popular national groups. Many world-renowned speakers lecture on various topics, such as the Middle East, global issues and world economics. Wandering around the expansive institute in a beautiful natural setting with other similarly-minded individuals seeking knowledge induces peace, serenity, and intellectual curiosity.

There are a variety of recreational and boating activities along picturesque Lake Chautauqua that adjoin the institute to balance the mental stimulation. One caution though, in accordance with its roots—no alcohol is provided, although personal, moderate consumption is allowed. Other facilities around the lake provide contrast, particularly at Bemis Point with its lakeside restaurants and stately, 1880, Victorian Lenhart Hotel, reminiscent of Cape May, NJ, where one can sit in a rocking chair sipping a snifter of Grand Mariner while looking out over the broad, beautiful lake and possibly hear a jazz concert on the lake.

In the late 1800s, the Chautauqua movement began as a way to disseminate culture and learning throughout the country by transporting their programs to larger towns throughout the nation like Owensboro. Part of its purpose was to encourage people to improve their minds and seek culture, rather than sitting idle or hanging out in taverns drinking alcohol. When most people lived in rural towns and small cities, before many of the cultural and art facilities had been founded, people outside of the eastern metropolises had little opportunity to enrich their lives. For the culturally starved, the Chautauqua movement provided intellectual stimulation. Gene's brother, Albert, would become a long-time member of the movement in Owensboro, serving on its board.

Jobs

Gene performed odd jobs at the brickyard, such as turning and stacking the bricks. His first outside work came when he was 10, cleaning the law offices of his brother Albert. This took about three hours on Saturday, for which he received 25 cents. The money plus savings from the brickyard jobs allowed him to accumulate about $3.00, with which he bought a complete baseball uniform. As he relates, "I remember appearing with the gang at a game, the only one so dressed and proceeded to play the worst game of the day. That was the only time I wore the suit." No doubt his friends did not appreciate the uniform.

Occasionally he went across the railroad tracks with a bunch of kids to pick water buckets full of beans from nearby farms to be processed and canned by the Ritter Canning Co. After being weighed, they received 5c per bucket. Some of the pickers tried putting clods of dirt in the bottom of the buckets to increase the weight, which upon being discovered, they were quickly fired.

Nearly 6-foot tall at 13, he obtained a temporary job at the Canning Co. during the tomato season, where he stacked boxes filled with ketchup in the warehouse. He loved drinking the thinner-than-Heinz ketchup straight out of the bottle.

At 14, after he got his leg braces, he started his first real summer job at the Owensboro Forging Co. where his father was on the board. His task was to pack buggy tubes into the wooden boxes he constructed for shipment to buggy companies in various cities. He worked 56 hours a week, receiving 15c per hour, which he dutifully turned over to his father. Toward the end of summer, he ruined a few of the tubes by driving nails into the packing boxes penetrating the tubes, making them worthless. The foreman talked to his father and had him switch to shoving wheelbarrows filled with scrap metal up a long, arduous incline into a rail gondola. Realizing the strenuousness of this job for one so young and crippled, his father looked at his spent young son and decided it was time for him to quit, to which he gratefully acquiesced.

Blacks

In stark contrast to the burgeoning opportunities for whites, unfortunately, good opportunities for African Americans were few and far between. In 1896, in Plessy versus Ferguson, the Supreme Court sided with Southern states that wanted "separate but equal" facilities and institutions. This case reinforced the segregation and discriminatory voter laws of the South. President Teddy Roosevelt spoke out publicly against the law citing racism and discrimination, appointing many blacks to lower-level Federal offices.

The brickyard employed numerous blacks to dig the clay, form the mud into bricks, dry the bricks in the kilns, stack the red bricks, and then transport the bricks to the thriving construction industry throughout Owensboro, nearby cities and states. It was an oddity of the South that, although they lacked many rights and it was a deeply segregated community with very set, unjust rules, the relationship between individual whites and individual blacks was sometimes congenial. Andrew and Mary, neither of whom grew up in the South, owned about ten shacks near their brickyard, charging $1.25 to $1.50 a week for rent, which Gene sometimes collected. These blacks were an extension of the family with respect flowing both ways. Gene knew dozens of them by name, liking many of them. Indeed, there were some he counted among his best friends, former slaves who told him fascinating stories of the cotton fields down South, their oppressive treatment, and their heroic escapes.

When he went downtown, he could just as easily walk a couple blocks north toward the river and transverse a white neighborhood, but he preferred to travel through the seven-block black neighborhood, where he would likely see many of his friends and joke around with these fun-loving folk. They seemed to know something about life and relationships that perhaps his industrious, hard-working, somewhat staid German family might not.

On one occasion, as he walked through the black area, he heard angry cries coming from a porch: "What are you doing in our neighborhood, white boy?" They left the house and started to follow him, continuing their nasty taunts. He had never seen these fellows before. Fear and alarm suddenly coursed through his body. Should he face them or run? Because of his braces, he knew he could not run fast and they would easily overtake him. So, he continued down the street, walking tall, trying to ignore them and appear unaffected. As they closed in on him, he thought he would soon have to face this potentially ugly situation, but before he got far, several people interceded, standing in front of Gene, saying something like, "This is Eugene Oberst, one of the Oberst boys who lives down the street with his eight **bigger** brothers. Don you ever talk to him that way or we will run ya'll out of town on a rail." His friends apologized to Gene, saying that these fellows were new to town but that they would "learn 'em good." Those who yelled at him apologized and walked away sheepishly. After this event, Gene continued to walk down this street to downtown, passing time with his friends.

Later as a coach, Gene learned that it was not the color of a young man's skin or their nationality, but their ability as an athlete and their character that would define them. He never discriminated against anyone and, despite intense resistance, supported his trend-setting African American athletes, some of whom were the first to be accepted on the school's team.

———

Gene soon attended Owensboro High. He had always been the tallest in his class, but because of his clubfeet, he did not think he would be able to keep up in the football practices, let alone be as effective a player during the games. When he was a junior, needing more men for the line, some of his friends convinced him to join the team. That year, Owensboro turned out to be a steamroller. Lauded as the state football champions, the Red Devils outscored their opponents by a total of 405 points to 2 points that year. Indeed, the only ones to cross their goal were themselves when they gave up a touchback for two points. During their last game against Henderson, they scored a record 20 touchdowns, registering a devastating 124 points to zero. Henderson took some solace in the fact that they only gave up four extra points. Over 100 years later they still held the record for the most TDs scored in any Kentucky high school game. Throughout the year, there was a spirit of excitement resonating throughout the halls.

Gene enjoyed pitching baseball in the spring and summer, winning nearly every game. With his large frame and well-developed upper body from his jobs, he hurled a blazing fastball. Basketball was relatively new and football, which had been played for only a few decades, was still developing. The best teams resided along the East Coast, where football originated, but Western teams like Notre Dame were starting to gain recognition. There were some semi-pro teams, none of which amounted to much, and one could not make a living playing either football or basketball.

As the national pastime, baseball was an entirely different matter. Baseball players earned a decent living, working six months out of the year, and occupied a unique position in the national psyche, which appealed to young Gene. With his success in high school, he dreamed of being a professional pitcher. Not far up the Ohio River, the Cincinnati Reds played ball, and a little down the Ohio River, Saint Louis had two teams—the Cardinals in the National League and the Browns in the American League. It was not unusual for the president to throw out the first pitch of the year as Woodrow Wilson had done in 1916. That year, Tris Speaker of the Cleveland Indians led the league with a .386 batting average.

The 1917 season started with Babe Ruth of the Boston Red Sox pitching a three-hit shutout against the New York Yankees at the Polo Grounds. He led Major League Baseball the previous year with a 1.75 ERA when he won 23 games. In 1917, he added a game to this record, winning 24 out of 38, completing 35 games with an ERA of 2.01. Gene longed to be like the Babe. That year, Ty Cobb accumulated a 35-game hitting streak and led the majors with a .383 average. The White Sox beat the New York Giants 4 games to 2 in the World Series. In 1917, Babe Ruth made $5,000, Tris Speaker $15,000, and Ty Cobb $20,000—unbelievable sums for playing a game. Gene dreamed of such a baseball career.

———

On April 6, 2017, Gene's carefree world abruptly changed when the United States declared war on Germany, and the nation mobilized. Before this time, the Obersts had been proud Germans and might have even rooted for the Germans in 1914 when the war started. Peace-loving Andrew had lived under Prussian rule and moved from his home to avoid mandatory service in their Army and had left before the German nation formed, possibly because he or his parents could see what was coming. They and the rest of the German community supported the U.S. fully since this was their country now. Occasionally, they sensed resentment in the community, and Gene was careful not to refer to Germany or speak the German he knew well.

The school system encouraged students and their families to grow gardens and sell war bonds. In the summer of 1918, with a labor shortage due to World War I, Gene at 16, and his best friend, Herman Pfeiffer, began working at the Owensboro Flour Mill where he became a truck driver picking up wheat from farmers and delivering flour to stores. The Milling Co. had an agency for the sale of chicken and cattle feed in 100 lb. bags. He and his companion won praise from their employer for the speed they achieved loading and unloading freight cars. The pay was 30c per hour for 60 hours of work per week. He felt rich when he got the $18.00 paycheck, with no tax deductions, since it was before income taxes were levied.

His older brother Frank signed up for the Army and would eventually become a captain. Following the war, Frank served in Panama when the canal was opened to civilian traffic in 1920. Possessing a string of ponies, Frank enjoyed playing polo there, something the Obersts in Owensboro could not have imagined.

Reading the papers daily. Gene followed baseball religiously, continuing to dream about becoming the next Babe Ruth. In 1918, the baseball season was shortened due to the war. Babe Ruth's Boston Red Sox team won the World Series, 4 games to 2 against the Chicago Cubs. That year the Babe won 13 out of 19 games, posting an ERA of 2.22. There were no designated hitters, so the Babe also led Major League Baseball in home runs. Two years later, Babe was traded to the Yankees, initiating the "Curse of the Bambino," after which the Red Sox would not win another title for a devastating 86 years.

While Gene was in high school, Columbia College failed. As an investor, his father received some of the college's assets, including boxes of textbooks, some of which Gene read, and physical education equipment, including dumbbells and numerous Indian clubs. That summer before his senior year, he used the sporting equipment to work out before he joined the Owensboro football team. He could not run much, but he could run some with his braces. In the Red Devil's games, he was usually the biggest player. Gene easily blocked opponents on the line, opening wide holes for the Owensboro backs to run through. His father did not profess to be a fan of or understand American football, but Gene was proud to see his father in his phaeton watching a game. Owensboro hoped to repeat as the Kentucky champions, but an insidious force would prevent them from doing so.

Spanish Flu

During the war, the Spanish Flu, a pandemic, spread throughout the world, infecting 500 million people (one-third of the world's population), killing 50-100 million—far more than the war. In the midst of Gene's senior football season, the dark, dreaded flu descended upon Owensboro. There were not much more than a dozen members on the football team, so when many team members came down with the "Flu," the games had to be canceled for several weeks. Owensboro's theaters, churches, and public gathering places also closed. To avoid gathering at churches, burials were only performed at graveside ceremonies. People who had to venture out did so with muslin masks over their mouths and noses.

The flu struck seven out of eight Obersts still at home, including Gene. The only one who did not catch the deadly disease was his father, Andrew, who had been active outside performing stable chores and gardening. Andrew also took a periodic swallow of bourbon from a bottle in his closet—medicine, as he called it, which he claimed saved him from the flu. For several days, Gene had a high fever, chills, and horrible dreams while sleeping. After a week, though still weak, his appetite returned; although for some time, coffee had a most disgusting taste. After several months, the flu thankfully abated.

That spring, the Owensboro paper featured an article about Andrew and his nine tall, strapping sons – enough to field a baseball team. All were over six feet tall, a half-foot or more above the average male's height of 5'6". By then, Gene had become the tallest.

Picture of Andrew and his nine Sons
From left to right – Andrew Sr., Andrew Jr., Bonaventure, Albert,
John, Herman, Joe, Louis and Eugene

Owensboro's principal asked Gene, an outstanding student, to be the commencement speaker at his high school graduation for the class of 1919. Below is an excerpt from his speech on "The Future of Air," delivered on May 30, 1919, at the Grand Theatre.

Eleven years earlier in 2008, up the Ohio River and connecting the Miami River in nearby Dayton Ohio, the Wright Brothers demonstrated their "aeroplane." Even though they had first flown in 1903 at Kitty Hawk, with remarkable unschooled engineering skills, ingenious, life-threatening experimentation, grit, and determination, it took five years to perfect their flying machine. Sadly, those throughout the U.S. and even in Dayton did not pay much attention to the first flight because it was not sustained with the prerequisite turns. Like the race to outer space in the '60s, in a multi-national race to be the first to fly, it was not until 1908 that their immensely successful demonstration of distance and control in Lemans, France caught the imagination of the world.

By 17, Gene had already seen miraculous new inventions such as the radio and airplane begin to dramatically alter how people communicated with each other and traveled around the country. Shortly after surviving the deadly pandemic and winning "the war to end all wars," in the flowery style of the time, his speech gives insight into his thinking and idealistic nature at a time of hope and infinite possibility for him and his optimistic classmates. It is interesting to note that over 100 years ago, Gene focused on how transportation and wireless technology would revolutionize the world, which is something a modern valedictorian might speak of today.

> *Tho I am neither a prophet, nor the son of one, nor do I aspire to be a prophet, my words this evening will border upon the prophetic.*
>
> *We have gradually gone out of an age that was as slow in its methods of life, as the snail in its mode of traveling; ... From its beginning, this new era demanded inventions that would husband time and labor. To meet this need, ingenious minds have invented various machines, that were thought to perform apparent miracles. A few of these contrivances are the distance abridgers; such as, the steam boats, railways, telephones and telegraphs;...*
>
> *As the world progressed farther in this mechanical era, more skillful inventions for bridging space were demanded: and as a result, wireless telegraphy was made possible. And all of you know the good results of this invention, ... how distress calls from ships were quickly received and answered thus saving hundreds of lives... Who can predict the future of wireless telegraphy?*

....*American ingenuity, however saved the day for air service, when on the 17th of Dec. 1903 the Wright brothers made man's first successful sustained and steered flight, in a heavier that air machine, driven by a gas engine, over the sand dunes of Kitty Hawk, N. Carolina.*

....*The most beautiful, inspirational, and serviceable of man's inventions, was rapidly improved, and will shortly be wholly at his service; carrying mail, freight, and passengers for long distances,... doing a score of things that no vehicle hitherto at our disposal has been able to effect. In fact, the aeroplane will soon reach that state of perfection, that all of our home and international trade and traveling, will be carried on by it, in preference to the slow moving steam ship, and the expensive railways.*

......*An aeroplane with a velocity several times greater than that of the fastest bird, will also soon be flying, with a capacity of several hundreds of passengers, from one city to another. This passenger express will be equipped with every convenience known to modern life and in extreme cold weather, the passengers will wear electrically heated clothing, to keep them warm.*

You may go to Switzerland on a vacation, since it will only take a day to travel there from this country then instead of wearying yourself by climbing the almost precipitous mountains to catch a glimpse of famous scenes, you may fly above and about the snow covered Alps seeing the undisturbed mountains, -that have stood as mute sentinels, gazing upon the events that have occurred in the dim ages gone by, -rise high above the surrounding country, impressing you with their grandeur and sublimity, and fully testing that there is no limit to the beauty of the workmanship of the Divine Creator.

...*Their great French scientific prophesier, Jules Verne, was once called "an insane dreamer because of his predictions regarding submarines, balloons, and electricity; yet everything that he foretold has already come true.*

The future of the air is unlimited. And the people living in 2019, will look back into the history of this period, and scorn the inventions which now excites our wonder, because they will no doubt possess contrivances, which the imaginative brains of Jules Verne and Thomas Edison could not fancy.

*The future of the air, a future presaged by the motive power and achievement already demonstrated, **will have an inevitable effect upon industry and society in general, for it will revolutionalize the world,** and take us* *farther toward the goal of Utopian perfection, which shall be the outcome of a superexcellent civilization*

Much of what Gene predicted regarding the future of flight came true. Soon planes were carrying dozens and then hundreds of passengers at ever-faster speeds. Less than ten years later, Charles Lindbergh crossed the Atlantic, ushering in the era of transoceanic flight, eventually making it possible to be in Switzerland flying over the mountains in less than a day as he had predicted.

Gene and his classmates would live through the most productive period in America's history, from the 1920s until 1970. Those in his generation, the first of the "Greatest Generation" born from 1901 to 1925, would help invent amazing devices, including world-changing innovations such as the polio vaccine, penicillin, atomic energy, television, radio, jet planes, satellites, space travel, the moon landing, modern management techniques, transistors, microchips, mainframe computers, microcomputers, and even the Internet.

The family was proud of this honor. Now that Columbia had closed, Andrew and Mary discussed college for young Gene, who wanted to follow Albert to Notre Dame. Currently 65, Andrew had retired from the brickyard several years earlier. Gene was an excellent student with bright prospects, but money was short, and Andrew did not think they could afford it. Later in the century with his grades, size, athletic ability, and membership on a former state championship football team, Gene would have been a shoo-in for an athletic scholarship, but few were offered at the time.

After Mary's stepmother, Christina Oberst Tennes, died in 1910, Mary inherited some of her property that was split among the five siblings. Mary decided that she would use some of this money to help Gene attend Notre Dame College, but there would only be enough for his first semester. He would have to earn the rest himself and could not afford to come home for Christmas, Thanksgiving, or Easter holidays. Since *Pushing to the Front* detailed, how many great men had worked their way through college, Gene thought this was certainly possible and even looked forward to the challenge. He was ecstatic about the proposal and applied to the university, which at the time accepted nearly all applicants, believing that anyone who wanted to attend Notre Dame should be able to do so. Since Frank decided to stay in the Army after the war and would no longer need most of his civilian clothes, he gave these to Gene to wear at Notre Dame. Gene could not wait to start the next phase of his life and live up to his exalted expectations. Because he had only played a limited amount of time on the football team at Owensboro High, he hoped to prove himself on Notre Dame's football squad and excel on the Norte Dame baseball team before his ascendance to the major leagues. Little did he know that his plans would not pan out.

7: Notre Dame

During the fall of 1919, Gene Oberst arrived at the Owensboro train station ready to embark on a new and exciting chapter of his young life. Imagine this first solo trip, like that of any freshman starting out into the world on his or her own, leaving his close-knit southern roots and heading up into unfamiliar Yankee territory. His mother, father, and older sister, Mary, accompanied him in the Phaeton carriage pulled by their old horse, Moxie. As the coal-fired, steam locomotive pulled into the station puffing and wheezing, they said their final goodbyes. An effusive, fetching, tall, thin southern belle, Mary gave him a big hug and kiss. Gene was surprised to see his father Andrew, normally an unemotional German, choked up telling him in his German accent to study hart. Andrew shook his son's hand vigorously then abruptly had to turn away. With tears welling in her eyes, his mother had a gaunt look, a look Gene had not seen before. He was the last of her eleven children, her baby, and he too was leaving the nest. Now a mature college man, Gene had to wrestle with his emotions, holding back tears, while looking into her tear-soaked eyes to say, "Goodbye mama." "Goodbye Hootsi," she replied.

He settled into a seat as the train chugged and hissed, slowly pulling away from the station, the engine belching black smoke with each stroke, the smell of burning, black coal heavy in the air, the rhythmic chucking sound increasing its cadence till it blended into the background and the steam whistle blew—chuck,,,,chuck,,,,chuck,,,chuck, chuck,chuck,chuck,choooooo, woo-woo. He waved a long goodbye. Still a little choked up, the cord attached to them stretching, he sat back, feeling a mixture of elation to be on his way and regret for he knew he would not see them again until the following June. As the countryside sped by, he spied the familiar red Kentucky clay on the train bed's banks his father employed to form the bricks at the family brickyard; in a sense that clay would pay for his first semester.

After a transfer in Louisville, they crossed the bridge over the Ohio River and into Indiana. Some of the people on the train were already speaking in the unfamiliar Yankee accent heading to their homes up north. He had never ventured far from the mighty river, and it did not take long before he was the furthest north he had ever been.

Not far from where the train wound its way north, in Dayton, Ohio, two brothers, Orville and Wilber Wright, invented the flying machine he referred to in his speech.

Lulled by the train's persistent clack, clack, clack, Gene slowly drifted into sleep. The locomotive eventually pulled into South Bend station. The extremely tall, thin Kentuck was a handsome lad with a broad smile, introspective brown eyes, and thick, curly brown hair. Eugene William Oberst had arrived in South Bend, anxious to begin his studies at Notre Dame College, ready to change the world.

He had only turned 18 a little over a month ago. The small college contained fewer than a dozen buildings and a few hundred students.   Unbeknownst to Gene, Notre Dame was about to dramatically explode onto the national scene due to a powerful catalytic force working magic on the football field that fall. And Gene would perform a vital, although yet unknown, role in the school's pivotal transformation, as that force would also forever transform his life.

Even though he was one of the youngest freshmen, the six-foot-four Oberst towered above his fellow collegians at a time when few stood above six-foot. With difficulty, a porter pulled the black steamer trunk from the baggage compartment and offered to wheel it to the departure area, but Gene declined the offer, largely because he was on a tight budget and wanted to avoid tipping. Instead, he hefted the large black trunk he acquired from his mother containing all he owned onto his broad shoulders. It weighed a mere 120 pounds; about the weight of the grain bags he toted that summer working for the Owensboro Flour Mill. He might have thought about carrying the trunk to Notre Dame but saw a bunch of students boarding a noisy bus with Notre Dame lettering on the side, so he tossed the trunk effortlessly on top with others and climbed onboard.

Unlike students today who might visit several prospective colleges, Gene had never seen Notre Dame, but as it rose above the trees, he would have spied its glistening, heralded golden dome far in the distance. Below the dome stood the school's main building, housing most of the classrooms, two cafeterias, and the administrative offices. The vehicle weaved through the lovely gothic campus along a dusty dirt road, which had a few dorms, a chapel, several outbuildings, and two picturesque lakes adjacent to his approaching dorm. When he climbed out of the bus, he remembered what his brother Albert said: "During the initial confusion, the upperclassmen robbed valuables from the new freshmen, so keep a close eye on your trunk." He considered stealing a despicable thing for supposedly upstanding, young Catholic men to do, but carefully guarded his possessions from the unscrupulous upperclassmen.

Before coming to Notre Dame, he had leafed through his brother's

Dome yearbook so he knew a little about the college, campus, and its activities. Plus, he heard many stories about Notre Dame from his brother so he already had a picture of it painted in his mind, but it looked even bigger than what his brother had recounted. Once he settled in, one of the first things he did was to walk to the main building and look up at the inside of the inspirational golden dome painted with a religious scene with what looked like a few students throughout the ages studying under the inspiration of angles and the Holy Ghost, what he thought the Sistine Chapel in Rome must look like.

Following Albert's example, who had graduated in 1906, Gene decided to major in law. Being a tall Kentucky lawyer, like Lincoln and his successful brother would be a glorious profession. Besides, he loved reading, and Albert always seemed to have his nose nestled into one of his law books. Gene especially looked forward to joining the Notre Dame Football team, coached by Knute Rockne, who had just barely started coaching last season when the season was cut short because of the war and Spanish Flu epidemic.

If he wanted to stay in school, Gene would have to earn his way through college with summer jobs and working at the Notre Dame law library, the priests' dining room and the Greek restaurant in town. Funds were tight, so there would not be enough money to purchase a train ticket to come home for breaks, and no funds for socializing. Gene desperately wanted to see his large family, but accepted his fate, looking forward to letters from home to stay in contact.

————

After being a starter on the dominant State Championship Owensboro team, Gene found it tough to be a scrub on the Notre Dame football squad that fall. Being a key member of the Owensboro team did not prepare him for the complexities of Rockne's system. Rockne's early teams only had about 22 -27 athletes. Since the starters went both ways (offense, defense, plus special teams), they did not need more. But, if a player left the game, they could not return. Rockne's philosophy was that freshmen would not play until their sophomore year, but they could serve as scrubs for the upperclassmen to practice against, like red-shirted freshmen today. The freshmen would learn the opposing team's offense and defense and then simulate it for the varsity. Gene's ego took a blow since he did not enjoy being a practice dummy for the upperclassmen to push around.

Most of the guys on the team had nicknames. Due to his Southern accent and manner, they christened him "Kentuck," which he enjoyed because he was proud of his Kentucky roots.

One advantage Kentuck had was a front-row seat on the bench to watch George, *the Gipper*, Gipp perform. He had never seen an athlete dominate a sport so thoroughly in the air, on the ground, on defense, and kicking too. The Gipper was an indomitable force even against perennial powerhouses like Army, Nebraska and Michigan State. That year, largely due to this phenom, Notre Dame had an unblemished record of 9 and 0 and was the NCAA national champion. After the season ended, Gene decided to concentrate on his law studies and his passion, baseball.

Gene also played on the Brownson Hall dorm football team along with his best friend, Fernando Aviles, the first Hispanic he knew, who also played on the freshman team. The intramural dorm teams were a key source of recruits for the varsity   Nine years earlier Rockne played on the Bronson team as did Gipp three years earlier.

Like many freshmen, Gene had a difficult transition to college life. Even though it was only 250 miles by train, the trip was the furthest of his life and home seemed far away. Adding to his loneliness, northerners, with their unfamiliar accents, did not seem as warm or friendly as those in Kentucky. Most students came from well-to-do families in the Midwest who picked up the tab, with few having to work their way through college, which Gene looked forward to doing. His favorite book *Pushing to the Front* provided guidance and examples of those who done so, such as James Garfield who grew up dirt poor in Ohio and worked as a janitor at Hiram College, eventually becoming its president and then the U.S. President.

That first Northern winter was a long and bitterly cold one. Unfathomably for a Kentuckian, there were a couple of days below zero. It rarely snowed in Owensboro, but it snowed a lot in South Bend. Since it was on the southeast side of Lake Michigan, the dominant northwest winds picked up warmer lake moisture and dumped snow onto South Bend. Spring did not arrive until April, a dreary month after Kentucky.

Since nearly all of his hard-earned money would fund his books, tuition, room and board, he had little left for socializing or spending other than perhaps a candy bar or an Eskimo Pie once a week, so he became lonely. He especially missed his family during Christmas when all the other boys left campus and boarded trains for warm Christmases with their close-knit families. Instead, he dined with the brothers, priests and foreign students whom he got to know better. Fernando, who was from Cuba, also stayed on campus during the holidays, which made the lonely time easier. He looked forward to the spring when he would try out for the Notre Dame baseball team.

———

Throughout the cold winter, he waited tables and concentrated on his studies. Finally, as spring approached, dreaming of being a starting pitcher that season, he went to the field house to work on his arm and ready himself for the upcoming tryouts. Up until that time, Notre Dame was more noted for baseball than football. They had outstanding teams, with many of their stars making it into the pros.

When Kentuck went to the gym to work out, he saw a shot put on a mat and thought that if he threw the heavy object, like a medicine ball, it would help strengthen his arm that much faster. To toss a shot put, you place what is essentially a 16-pound cannon ball in your hand, grasping it below your chin and facing the back of a circle. First, you jump back a step and rotate your body, using the larger muscles in your legs and back to gain momentum. Then you fiercely launch the projectile forward with your arm. Unfortunately, Gene did not know this, so he picked the shot put up, brought it behind his head as he lifted his leg, and threw the cannonball like a baseball. He heard a snap in his arm and instantly felt a sharp pain. He had sprained his arm, and the long-honed dream of becoming a famous major leaguer instantly vanished.

That summer, he finally went home to see his family. He missed his mother most. Since Hootsi, as she called him, was her last child, the baby of the family, she tended to spoil him a bit. She and his two sisters made his favorite meals. He also missed his father, Andrew, and his brothers, sisters and the growing flock of nieces and nephews. Since his oldest brothers were in their 20s when he was born, like many families of the time, he had nephews and nieces close to his age. He loved playing with them as they roamed the rooms of the seven-bedroom house. He was especially close to Albert's children, who lived nearby.

Gene went back to work at the Owensboro Flour Mill again as a truck driver picking up wheat from the farmers and delivering 100-lb bags of flour to stores. Late in the summer, he injured his back after he started carrying the heavier 180-pound oat bags, so he left the flour mill's employ.

Gene felt badly that he would not be on the baseball team, but perhaps a glorious baseball career was not to be his destiny. After all, few star high school athletes made it to the major leagues. He would, therefore, concentrate on his law studies and his new job at Notre Dame, overseeing and coaching the younger Minims, the grade school on campus. Since he was now a sophomore and could actually play on the varsity, he looked forward to joining the football team, expecting to command the line as he had done in high school. Knute Rockne, who had only become the head coach two years earlier and had only graduated from Notre Dame six years ago, was already acquiring a reputation as an outstanding coach. He also looked forward to playing with the legendary George Gipp, college football's most versatile athlete. He would enjoy opening up holes for Gipp to run through and getting to know the star better.

8: Knute

Northwest of Oslo, between snow-capped mountains and expansive fiords, lays Voss, Norway, a town of approximately 5,000 interdependent souls. There, rugged, granite mountains fold into verdant valleys, surrounding winding rivers that cascade into waterfalls and deep-blue cold lakes. In many ways, this picturesque landscape resembles the spectacular snow-capped Cascades in the Northwest. Not far from the Arctic Circle, one might expect this to be a frigid, deserted expanse, but warmed by the Gulf Stream, the average high reaches a more moderate 49 degrees, a few degrees below that of northern Great Lakes cities. During the desolate winter, with as few as seven hours of dim light, darkness permeates Voss, but by the summer solstice, the sun shines on Voss for 20 hours a day.

It is easy to imagine Viking warriors casting off from such stunning shores in their longboats to conquer the British Isles, Iceland and North America. At the close of the 19th century, on March 4, 1888, Martha and Lars Rockne welcomed their son, Knute, to Voss. As they viewed their firstborn, they, like any parents, hoped he would succeed but could not imagine how this tiny blue-eyed, blond fellow with a chubby, round face could play such a pivotal role in a strange, far-away land. Could this helpless baby possibly live up to the legends of those epic Norse explorers, such as Erik the Red, who discovered Greenland, and his son Lief Ericson, who discovered America over 400 years before Columbus in the 11th century?

Martha Rockne had descended from doctors, educators, and scientists, imparting an appreciation of culture and learning to her children. Under her caring tutelage in their hearth-warmed Nordic cottage, Knute acquired his aptitude for science and education. Knute did not, however, acquire his father's mechanical talents.

Possessing deft skills as a blacksmith and mechanic, Lars Rockne crafted fine carriages. His Kerisol became the first to support the seat with springs leading to a more comfortable and secure ride. Kaiser Wilhelm II of Prussia, one of Queen Victoria's grandchildren, while vacationing near Voss tried Lars' carriage and found the ride so comfortable that he ordered one for himself, extolling its virtues to others.

Encouraged by his growing reputation, Lars exhibited his innovation at the Liverpool Fair where he won a distinguished prize.

Emboldened by this success, he decided to exhibit at the 1893 Columbia Exposition and Worlds Fair in Chicago, setting off for the Brave New World in 1891. Eighteen months later, his family joined him.

By then, Chicago, with a population of over 1,000,000, had become a bustling, gritty metropolis, second only to New York in size. America represented a huge adjustment for the young family from tiny Voss. Fortunately, a large Norwegian contingent had settled in the city, easing the family into the new world.

The Columbia Exposition celebrated the 400th anniversary of Columbus's discovery of the New World, presenting an amazing amalgamation of the arts, innovation, and commerce along with entertainment from the likes of the Buffalo Bill Wild West Show to the exotic, sensual Ziegfield Follies. At a time when the U.S. population stood at 63 million, over 27 million attended the fair, with over half traveling from foreign lands. The magnificent White City occupied the fair's center—lit by thousands of electric lights, miraculously transforming night into day. Coming from rural Norway, this might have been the first time young Knute saw an electric light, let alone such a wondrous display.

Lars won the 2nd Grand Prize in the International Fine Arts and Applied Arts Division for—"Supreme excellence in design and craftsmanship." He soon found a position as the engineer for the Norwegian paper in Chicago, where he would use his superior mechanical talents to keep the presses running.

———

By the late 1800s, football, still in its formative stages, resembled the sport it sprang from—rugby. Knute Rockne played on pick-up teams as a youth, but his high school did not field a team until his junior year in 1904. Underscoring the transitory nature of the game, they were only able to play a few games before the league disbanded.

Young Rockne, his parents, and his four younger sisters hoped Knute would attend the University of Chicago. J.D. Rockefeller had established the university the previous decade, where Alonzo Stagg, one of the two major innovators of football, coached. Alonzo led Chicago to become one of the dominant teams in the West. Stagg learned football at Yale in the 1880s from football's legendary founding father, Walter Camp, where he became one of the first eleven All-Americans.

Camp attended a meeting in 1873 that formed the Intercollegiate Football Association (IFA), initially composed of four Ivy League teams: Columbia, Rutgers, Princeton, and Yale. He played halfback at Yale from 1876 to 1882, coaching there afterwards, compiling a record of 67 and 2, while acquiring an astounding 12 national championships as a player and a coach.

Up until 1880, the game was essentially rugby, in which, once the opposing team stopped a player's progress, the player put the ball down, where there was a "scrummage" between the two teams for its control.   Camp proposed a line of "scrimmage," thereby commencing the evolution of football away from its rugby roots. Instead of the continuous action of rugby, play would stop after a player was down, with the opposing teams lining up on either side of a line for the next play.   He is credited with numerous innovations that would later seem commonplace, but were revolutionary at the time, such as the snap from the center, the system of downs with a first down after a prescribed number of yards (initially three downs to gain five yards). He also established the points system with 6 points for a touchdown, one for an extra point, and three for a field goal and the 100-yard football field with end-zones. Rugby players were not allowed to interfere with opposing players until Camp changed the rules to allow blocking.   He also introduced the eleven-man offense, with a seven-man line and a four-man backfield consisting of a quarterback, two halfbacks, and a fullback. Prior teams consisted of 25, then 20, then 15 players in a game that was more like a rumble.

One of the important aspects of any sport or profession's evolution is how an endeavor's leaders hand off their experience and inspiration to the next generation. This pioneering spirit of freedom, openness, cooperation, and opportunity permeating America helped facilitate football's evolution out of rugby—from Camp to Stagg, and then to Rockne, who would advance the sport beyond imagination.

Alonzo Stagg also coached the Chicago University track team and founded an annual competition for high school trackmen, providing a venue for him to promote the sport and recruit top talent to Chicago U.   His success in track mirrored that of football.   Spurred on by glowing reports of the university's exploits on the field, Knute planned to star for Stagg in both football and track. Rockne had been a bright elementary student, but by high school, due to his obsession with sports, his grades suffered.   Therefore, his athletic prowess would have to pave his pathway to Chicago U. and the esteemed coach.

Due to a growing number of casualties, football was seen as a brutal sport, especially due to the "flying wedge," in which ten players with hands gripping handles attached to the pants of their teammates, followed by the ball carrier, careened into the opposing line with bone-crushing force. Eight died in 1897. After Knute played in 1905, 18 were killed and 157 seriously injured.   Colleges throughout the nation banned the sport, with many calling for the abolition of football altogether. Hearing their pleas, President Teddy

Roosevelt called for reform. Camp and Stagg helped found the American Football Coaches Association and the Rules Committee. With Stagg and Camp playing major roles, they modified the rules to require leg padding, thin helmets, and the illegalization of the flying wedge.

As a concerned parent well aware of the news, Lars forbade Knute from playing football. Naturally, people assumed that Knute acquired his flattened nose in football, which would justify Lars concern, but this was not the case. After a key baseball game ended in a tie, it went into extra innings. With Rockne in the field, following a controversial play, possibly a player thrown out at home, the opposing bench stormed onto to the field where a fight broke out. During the melee, a player swung a bat that connected with Knute's nose. When the bleeding and pain subsided, Knute was left with black eyes and a flattened nose as a souvenir. When asked about his nose, Rockne would reply that is why he switched to football because baseball was too rough.

———

In 1896, Barron De Coubertin, established the Modern Olympics in Athens, Greece, inspiring youth throughout the world to "run faster, jump higher and throw farther." Fleet-footed Rockne became enchanted with the Olympics and track and field, hoping to compete in the exalted games. He joined the Park Athletic Club team where he was a half-miler and pole vaulter. Many sports at many schools at the turn of the century did not have coaches; thus, the school did not sponsor the team. Therefore, Knute helped organize the track team. In May of his senior year, shortly before graduation, the principal looked out his window and happened to see the team practicing outside. Unfortunately, this was during classes so the principal called all the boys into his office. To Rockne's dismay, he expelled the entire team. He was less than a month from graduation, but sadly would never be a high school graduate. Disappointed, Lars, who had hoped Knute would attend the University of Chicago, realizing their dream had been scuttled, told his son to, "Get a yob."

Discouraged with his lost college opportunity, Knute tried a variety of yobs, including being a ferryman, before settling in at the Chicago post office making $50/month. The post office's system for transporting mail fascinated Rockne, which consisted of thousands of pneumatic tubes routing the mail throughout the building to waiting trains and mailmen—a well-orchestrated symphony to move the items quickly. He applied for a position as a dispatcher, requiring an intimate knowledge of routes and train schedules tested in an examination. To become a dispatcher, he had to score above 94. Knute studied hard and scored a perfect 100. Over the four years at the post office, due to his industry and passion for the scientific system, his salary steadily grew from $600 to $1000 a year. He continued to compete in track over those years, joining the prestigious Illinois Athletic Club (IAC).

Thinking that he could not wait much longer, at 22, with $1000 in savings, Knute considered college again. He thought that if he did not enter college then, he would work at the post office for the rest of his life. He considered applying to the University of Illinois, but a couple of his IAC teammates, John Plant and John Devine, wanted to take a look at nearby Notre Dame College and invited him to join them on the train ride to South Bend.

Father Sorin, the French Holy Cross missionary who founded Notre Dame in the wilderness of Indiana back in 1842, when hardly any young men attended college, was not concerned with grades or standardized tests but was more concerned with establishing the struggling college and educating its young men, whatever their qualifications might be. He thought that any young man who wanted to attend Notre Dame should have the opportunity to do so, including Protestants such as Rockne.

In contrast to the crowded, grimy Chicago streets, Knute enjoyed the forests, open spaces, and grassy expanses of Notre Dame, which resembled his native Norway. As an industrial city, South Bend offered plenty of jobs to supplement his savings. Since he had not obtained his high school degree, he would have to sit for oral exams in his chosen major—pharmacy. Father Neuland, the chemistry and pharmacy professor who administered the test, was impressed with Knute's raw intelligence and accepted him into the school.

When Rockne arrived that fall, Notre Dame had only 700 students in the college, the Minim Grade School, and prep school, with perhaps 100 in his freshman class. Joe Collins, a member of the varsity football team, coached the Brownson Hall team where Rockne lived. Impressed by the 145-pound, 5'8" Rockne's speed and grit, Joe recommended he try out for the varsity team. Even though the season was underway, Rockne felt he could impress the coach and prove to be a valuable player. With little formal training and small in stature, Knute struggled through the routines and formations against the more experienced and larger players. He played terribly, and the coach assessed him as not being good enough to play, even as a scrub.

Discouraged and homesick, Rockne packed his bag and headed for the train station, intending to return to Chicago and the post office. Learning of this plan, his friends, Plant and Devine, headed him off and persuaded him to stay. His dismissal from the football team turned out to be a fortunate event, though. Knute turned his attention to his studies, becoming a superior student who garnered As in all his classes including the difficult science classes, scoring between 94 and 98 in each. Father Neuland, whom Rockne greatly admired, soon mentored him. That spring on the track team, Rockne competed in the shot put, pole vault, quarter mile, and hurdles.

With dark hair and movie star good looks, Rockne's roommate Gus Dorais had a similar stature—5'7" and 145 pounds and they soon became best friends. Gus remembered Knute as a serious student who could concentrate on his books despite the typical college dorm hijinks. He also remembered him trying any product that might save his thinning hair.

The 1911 team lost many of its starters and once again had a new coach, Jack Marks of Dartmouth, from the founding and predominant league in football—the Ivy League. Gus, previously a backup quarterback, encouraged Knute to try out for the team again. Faced with a lack of experience and size, Marks imagined a new strategy, concentrating on speed rather than brute force. He selected Gus as his quarterback and the speedy trackman Knute as an end, now a respectable 165 pounds. Marks' new strategy paid off that year: the speedy team racked up six wins, with no losses and two 0 to 0 ties against Pittsburg and Marquette.

Rockne's industrious father, Lars, died in May of 1912, a devastating blow to Knute, yet his dream of his son attending college and hopefully carving out a better life for himself was being realized at least up until his death. With his father departed, Knute decided to leave school and work at the post office to support his mother and four sisters. Anne, the oldest, was married; Martha (21) was a stenographer; Louise (17) and Florence (13) were still in school. Rockne's dream of becoming a pharmacist or possibly even a doctor suddenly vanished. After the funeral, Anne took Knute aside and insisted he graduate from college because his prospects would be so much brighter. His mother and sisters would find some way to get by. To support the family, they moved into a smaller house, and Louise, following Martha's example, learned stenography. Their sacrifice would prove to be immensely beneficial to Knute and fortuitous for Notre Dame.

———

Thanks to his sisters, Knute returned to Notre Dame in the fall of 2012. That year the team beat their first four opponents handily by a combined score of 270 to 20 before facing a stronger competitor in Pittsburg, who would soon win three National Championships under Pop Warner. Football was still primarily a grinding, running game. As an end, Rockne's role was to block for the four backs who attempted to crash into the middle or run around the end. The previous year's Pittsburg game was a defensive battle with neither team able to cross the goal line or kick a field goal, ending in a 0-0 tie. This year followed the same script with the fighting Irish able to score but one field goal that ultimately determined the outcome in a 3-0 victory. The Irish easily defeated St. Louis and Marquette at Comisky Park in Chicago. Brilliantly, Gus had led the team to a sterling 7-0 record.

In track that school year, Rockne set the indoor school record of 12' 4" in the pole vault, one of the top marks in the nation, less than a foot below the U.S. record and likely enough to qualify for the Olympics. The pole vault is the most difficult of all field events, in which the competitor must run at top speed with a long, heavy pole balanced in front of him, then plant the pole in a tiny wooden box and hope that he has enough momentum to carry himself up to the bar where, with his back to the pole, he uses his arms to push off the pole, hopefully clearing the bar. He then falls helplessly from an astounding height into a sawdust pit. These diverse actions require intricate coordination and execution by every muscle in the body. Later, fiberglass poles added flex that would catapult the athlete higher, but then the wooden poles were relatively rigid. Adding to the danger, the pole could snap in mid-air, with the vaulter falling helplessly to the ground, possibly outside the sawdust pit, where he might break a leg or arm.

While maintaining outstanding grades, Rockne became remarkably engrossed in campus life. He enjoyed most sports: rowing on the junior class's crew team, playing on the dorm baseball team, and of all things, winning the school's marble championship. In 1912, he served as treasurer of the Woodrow Wilson Club, campaigning for Wilson's successful run for President. Interestingly, Wilson, as a student, had been the coach of the 1878 Princeton's National Championship Football team. Rockne also played flute in the orchestra (badly) and was an editor of the *Dome* yearbook. Few students could match Rockne's frenetic pace.

Rockne developed skills that would later serve him well as an actor in theatre productions and helped found the Monogram Absurdities in 1913, which consisted of burly athletes dancing as if they were can-can girls at the Folies Bergere in Paris. He wrote most of the play, directed it, and also acted in it. All this activity would overwhelm most collegians, but Rockne thrived on it, and he still had time to star on the football and track teams. He was developing diverse skills and a philosophy of making the most of life that would serve him well, possibly too well.

———

That summer Knute and Gus decided to work at Cedar Point in northwest Ohio. Before air-conditioning, folks in the sweltering cities looked forward to escaping the oppressive, never-ending, bittering heat at the cooler, windswept beaches of the Great Lakes. The amusement park is located on a peninsula between Detroit and Cleveland that juts out into Lake Erie, barely connected to land by a narrow strand of sand. Now known as the roller coaster capital of the world, this, the oldest amusement park in North America, opened in 1870, adding its first roller coaster in 1892. By 1913, steamers brought people from cities around the lake to its beautiful white sand beach. The 1909 Irish football star Harry "Red" Miller had worked there, bringing along some of his fellow students. All four Ohio Miller boys, who were starters for Notre Dame, would work there.

The Grand Pavilion contained an auditorium, bowling alley, and bandstand, with a separate ladies' pavilion providing refreshments for them and their children. Bands held concerts playing the popular tunes of the day, such as "By the Light of the Silvery Moon" or "Let Me Call You Sweetheart." The beautiful Victorian Hotel Breakers (still operating) held 600 rooms; nearby stood the Crystal Rock Palace, which resembled a castle with an extensive menu. The park also boated the largest bathhouse in the world. The six-year-old midway featured various rides, games, fortunetellers, merchandise shops, a skating rink, and a massive Coliseum with a grand ballroom and other attractions.

Gus and Knute worked a variety of jobs to earn money for college, but the most pertinent one was as lifeguards on the expansive white sand beach. There, Knute, the captain-elect of the team, discussed the upcoming season with his quarterback Gus. For the first time, they were to play one of the eastern teams, routinely one of the best—Army. They knew they did not stand a chance against the much larger Army team's running game, so Rockne suggested they pass—a radical strategy at the time. The pass had been legalized in 1906, but it was utilized only as a desperate measure by the losing team late in the game—kind of a "Hail Mary" play. They spent hours passing the egg-shaped football, nothing like today's streamlined version, on the beach. Today, young collegians throwing a ball on the beach is a common site, but then it looked odd to the largely clothed bathers sunning on the beach, who even if they knew what a football was, rarely saw it utilized in such an odd fashion.

The few times a receiver caught a ball in a game, he stopped dead and let the awkwardly shaped projectile bounce into his chest, then ran. Rockne caught the oblong ball resembling a basketball, utilizing his fingers and softening his hands, cradling the sphere into his body, which allowed him to catch it on the run. Dorais learned how to arch the ball to him and lead him, throwing ever further, practicing various types of passes—fast, slow, lobs, etc. They practiced catching the ball with one hand and invented new plays and routes, running through these continuously. Perhaps Rockne envisioned the football as a cylinder in the post office's pneumatic system propelled by force following a predetermined route from the quarterback to the end's outstretched hands. They next practiced these plays against some of the beachgoers who had played football.

The beach and crashing waves of picturesque Lake Erie likely provided nourishment to Rockne's soul as he recovered from his father's loss. To the east, the sun rose over the expansive lake providing a spectacular scene. At the north end of the beach, you could see other Islands in the distance on the lake that were also popular destinations with resorts and hotels reached by ferry from the mainland, reminiscent of Nantucket or Martha's Vineyard off Cape Cod. (Today this area with scores of marinas boasts the highest concentration of freshwater boats in the world, a Mecca for perch, salmon and walleye fishermen.)

One of the girls on the beach, Bonnie Skiles, a 21-year-old waitress from nearby Kenton, Ohio, must have thought these two looked odd, relentlessly throwing that ridiculous-looking, oblong-shaped ball. Rockne was shy and self-conscious around women. Going to an all-boys school did not provide many opportunities to meet girls or develop social skills, especially for one with so many activities, but, with encouragement from Gus, he worked up the courage to talk to the fetching, slim, brunette, Ms. Skiles. After the summer ended, they corresponded.

———

Refreshed by the sun and sea breezes, Gus and Knute looked forward to another football season, thinking they might apply what they learned on Cedar Point's beach. A new coach started that year— Jesse Harper. Jesse coached at Chicago under the tutelage of aforementioned Alonzo Stagg, who learned the game from the Father of Football, Walter Camp. He was their third coach in four seasons, something not unusual at the time since Notre Dame had 13 coaches in the first 20 years of the program, with only one coach lasting as long as three years. Harper wanted to introduce a new brand of football, different from the bump-and-grind game in the East, where the teams depended upon size and strength. Following his mentor's example, he envisioned a game based on speed and maneuverability. Fortuitously, Rockne and Dorais's plans meshed perfectly with those of their gifted new coach.

The Irish's first four games were easy victories, but the next game would be extremely challenging. Up until then, the East Coast teams like Army, Harvard, Princeton and Yale, where the game originated, dominated the sport. The sporting world and press looked down on the inferior Western teams. On the rare occasions when they played the Eastern teams, they nearly always lost, usually by large margins. Notre Dame had played a few of the better Western teams but had never competed against a powerhouse like Army, who outweighed them by 20 pounds a man and included two All-Americans.

When their train rolled into West Point, few gave the Irish a chance. As the game got underway, Army massed in the center and as expected easily pushed Notre Dame back. Then, Gus started flipping the ball to a half back or end, who ran to the outside, taking advantage of their superior speed. According to plan, Rockne faked a limp as the plays unfolded, such that the defender soon thought he was not worth covering. On the next play, after he limped up to the line, the defender relaxed, after which Knute sped forward, leaving him in the dust. Just as they had rehearsed all summer, Gus threw the oblong ball an astounding 45 yards to Knute, who caught it on the run and sped to the end zone with no Army men in pursuit. With their mouths hinged wide open, the crowd stood aghast for nobody had ever seen such a play—the longest pass in football history. Rockne later said, "When I touched the ball, life for me was complete."

Imagine this play from the crowd's perspective, who went to the game expecting Army to trounce Notre Dame in a game of strength that was more like a rugby scrum with teams trying to push each other back, gaining but a few yards per play. It did not occur to them that anyone could throw a pigskin more than a few yards, let alone 45, and if it was thrown that far, that someone could be in the right spot at the right time and actually catch the ball on the run—unfathomable. One of those who witnessed this transformational event was an injured cadet on the bench, Dwight Eisenhower, future five-star General, commander of the Allied forces in World War II, and two-term President. Initially stunned, Army soon recovered, scoring two touchdowns in the next few minutes to take a 13 - 7 lead. Then Dorais threw a 25-yard strike to Rockne, followed by another spectacular 35-yard bomb to Pliska, the halfback who ran across the goal line for a TD. The score stood at 14-13 Notre Dame at the half.

After halftime, Army developed a strategy to control Notre Dame's shocking passing game, but Harper and the smaller Notre Dame team had another plan. When the cadets dropped back to cover the pass, the quicker Irish backs ran through the middle or around the ends. When the Army adjusted to cover the run, they passed, and soon, the mighty Army became thoroughly confused. The Irish ran for two more touchdowns and Dorais completed another TD pass to Pliska. The final score was Notre Dame 35, Army 13. Dorais was 14 for 17 with 242 yards passing— an unbelievable stat then.

The press went wild over the story, and the account of the amazing game appeared in newspapers throughout the nation. Not only was this an ascendant event for Notre Dame football, it was a transcendent event for Western football. Back in South Bend, students waited for news of the game over telegram at the News-Times office. They, too, were overwhelmed by what they heard, after which the 300 students snake-danced through the city back to Notre Dame, where they quickly spread the news throughout campus.

The Irish capped off their triumphant season with three more wins, including a 30 – 7 victory over Texas, ending up with an unblemished record of 7 and 0. Over the three years, Knute and Gus started, the Irish compiled a glorious, undefeated 20 – 0 – 2 record. Walter Camp selected Dorais as Notre Dame's first All-American. Rockne was a third-team All-American in football and later honored as an All-American in the pole vault.

In the spring, in addition to track, Rockne organized spring football practice for coach Harper, who was busy as the track coach. He graduated Magna Cum Laude with a B.S. degree in Pharmacy—not bad for someone who never obtained a high school diploma. His mother and sisters were incredibly proud of all he had accomplished. He was extremely grateful to them for all the sacrifices they made, without which he might still be working at the post office.

Rockne applied to St. Louis Medical School, hoping to earn his way as a coach, but was rejected because they thought no one could do both. He and Gus also applied for an athletic director position at Dubuque College in Iowa. Ironically, they chose Gus.

Father Neulan offered Knute a job as his research assistant and chemistry teacher at Notre Dame's prep school. Neulan was working on synthetic rubber, which would free the U.S. of dependence upon foreign rubber plantations—an exciting prospect for a budding chemist, one that would be vital in the event of a war. Rockne also talked to coach Harper about being his assistant, and having to choose between his two avocations struggled with his decision. Harper proposed that Rockne do both—coach and teach. Against Neulan's advice, the president offered him the chemistry and assistant coaching job for $1000 a year. Knute enthusiastically accepted the offer that would indulge both of his passions.

Soon afterward, Rockne married Bonnie on June 15, 1914 in a quiet ceremony in Sandusky, Ohio, across the Sandusky Bay from Cedar Point where they first met. Gus stood up for Knute as his best man. So, he graduated, started a new career, and married, all within a month. Their first son, Billy, was born shortly before Christmas on December 20, 1915.

That fall Rockne performed as the assistant coach and started to evolve his style of coaching. He learned the game from Harper, who learned from Stagg, who learned from Camp in a direct line of the great football coaches of football's first 70 years. Harper's new faster game, relying on shifts he learned from Stagg that he would improve upon and that Rockne would adopt and build upon himself. Rockne believed in strict discipline while developing a personal and varied relationship with each player, depending upon the player and what the player needed to become successful. One player might need specialized instruction in how to perform his position better. An unconfident player might need some praise, whereas a cocky player might need to be cut down a notch. Still, he never ridiculed a beginner. To earn extra money for his growing family, he also coached the Mussel Brewing football team in South Bend.

Rockne faithfully apprenticed under Harper for four years. Over that period, the Irish were 27 - 6 - 1, losing twice to Army in what became a featured annual national event, once to Yale where Walter "The Father of Football" Camp had coached, and twice to another foe, who was becoming a formidable rival—Nebraska.

After the 1917 season, five-year coach Harper, the longest-serving coach up until then, left Notre Dame to tend to his farm in Nebraska. He recommended Rockne for the job but the administration resisted having such a young and inexperienced coach take over the reins of their successful football program. Eventually, Harper prevailed, and Rockne assumed the head coaching position. The United States entered World War I in April, after which Rockne became the athletic director of Fort Sheridan, just north of Chicago.

Picture of Knute Rockne
From the 1920 Championship Football Team Book

Following a 26-6 victory against Case Tech in Cleveland, one of the few teams to have a winning record against the Irish, the 2019 season was suspended due to the Spanish Flu pandemic. With no games played in October, play resumed in November. They played five more games, winning two, losing one to Michigan State, 7-13, and tying the ever-tough Nebraska, 0 – 0.

One player stood out that year, showing great promise—George Gipp. The left halfback ran for 541 yards with two 100-yard games and completed 19 out of 41 passes for 293 yards. Rockne had reason to be pleased with his first season, but America was about to experience a football player the likes of which it would rarely see. Managing this temperamental and rebellious star would be immensely rewarding and dauntingly challenging for a novice coach.

As Rockne evaluated his prospects for the upcoming season, the largest player on the freshman team, 6'4" Gene "Kentuck" Oberst offered some promise. The big guy was very slow but seemed to be motivated and intelligent; perhaps he could play a role on the 1920 team. Kentuck was working a variety of jobs to earn his way through college, so Rock procured a position for him. Little did Rockne know how huge of a role this gangly tall fellow would play not only for Notre Dame but for the Rockne family and how surprised Rockne would be by his yet unknown talent.

9: Gene and The Gipper

In the fall of 1920, following an enjoyable summer spent with his family in Owensboro, Gene commenced his sophomore year, resuming his law studies and playing for Notre Dame's varsity football team. He relished the bucolic beauty of the campus on the bus ride back to school. A few of the leaves were already turning up north and he knew they would soon erupt into a brilliant canvas painted with reds, yellows and various hues of oranges and purples. Surely, it would be another spectacular fall.

Rather than working several jobs to scrape up enough money for tuition, room, board, and his modest expenses, Rockne found him a job as the prefect, coach, and athletic director for the Minims—boys from 6 to 12, taught by the Holy Cross Sisters. He would live with and look after them in the attic of St. Edward's Hall, just across the quad from Brownson Hall, where he lived during his freshman year. Both were adjacent to the main building under the Golden Dome, so he would not have to walk far for meals or classes. Brownson had a view of serene St Mary's and St Joseph's Lakes and the peaceful Grotto of Our Lady of Lourdes, which St. Edward's didn't, but these beautiful sights were only a short distance from his new dorm. He found walking around the lakes or stopping at the grotto relaxing after a particularly stressful day.

Gene's upper body became even stronger after lugging the heftier flour bags, but even with his metal braces, his club-like feet still did not allow him to run well. He hoped to be a starter, as he had been at Owensboro High. When practices got underway, Gene found it difficult to match the speed of the smaller linemen he competed against and Rockne was putting a premium on speed in his evolving offense. Therefore, prior to the opening game, Rockne listed him as one of the reserves—a step up from being a frosh scrub but still not a starter. There would be 11 starters, with the second string getting playing time. Lawrence "Buck" Shaw would be the first-string right tackle, with Bill Voss on the second string. Gene would be the third-stringer. Later, football teams from high school to the pros would have an offense, defense, and special team tackles and Gene would have played often, but they did not then. Still, as the season progressed, and as the tallest man on the team, he would surely play.

His major compensation that sophomore season was that he saw the spectacular performances of George, "the Gipper," Gipp from the best seats in the house—the bench. The Gipper's family emigrated from Prussia, about 40 miles west of the Oberst's home in Germany. His mother, Isabella Taylor's, family immigrated from Ireland during the potato famine.

His father, Matthew Gipp, worked as a carpenter in the mines near Laurium on the Keweenaw Peninsula of Michigan on the thumb of the Upper Peninsula, pointing up into Lake Superior and Canada. Mathew was also a deacon who preached at the Baptist Church. They had eight children, of whom George was the second youngest born on February 18, 1895. The Gipps were strict disciplinarians. Mother Isabella was known to be domineering with her children, which may explain George's desire to be free from rules and authority leading to his rebellious nature.

Copper County on the peninsula contained large deposits of copper and soon became a boomtown of 90,000 people by the 1910 census with 15,000 miners, most working for the Calumet & Hecla Mining Company that dominated the county. Calumet provided the high school named after it with excellent athletic facilities. George started on the baseball team, which had won 24 consecutive games, but due to his antics, he was frequently suspended. In his senior year, before graduation, he was expelled for smoking in the halls. Like Rockne, he excelled in numerous sports, including basketball, track, and baseball, but George oddly never earned a letter.

Working conditions in the mines throughout the United States were extremely dangerous, leading to the formation of mining unions and the bloody battles with mine owners. Company-hired thugs, like the Pinkertons, often tormented the union members, occasionally resulting in open warfare and shootings. In the previous six years, over 16,000 miners had died. The Calumet miners formed a union In 1913 and asked to meet with management to discuss better working conditions and pay, which the company refused to do, so the miners went on strike. Such a strike would have been devastating for the Gipp family and indeed, the entire county who depended upon mining incomes.

After being on strike for five months, on Christmas Eve, minors and their families gathered at the Italian Hall to celebrate the holiday, including a visit from Santa Claus bearing gifts for the numerous children, who, due to their imposed poverty, greatly looked forward to the event. Someone yelled fire, and a panic ensued. It must have been a horrendous scene as previously hopeful children, crying and yelling for their parents to rescue them were trampled maimed and their lives extinguished by those trying to flee the melee. There was no fire, but 72 people perished in the stampede out of the building. Tragically, the fatalities included 57 children, one of the worst tragedies for children in U.S. history, far worse than any of the horrible school shootings.

No Gipps were among the dead, but the calamity affected George and the entire community. He witnessed his father work hard at the treacherous mines, only to scrape up enough to barely care for his large family. He saw how the authoritarian mine owners treated their workers and how they rejected the miners' bid for fairer working conditions and pay. He saw many in the close community die in the stampede, which some alleged a company agent caused. He saw the strike drag on for nine months and the devastation it caused for mining families who lived paycheck to paycheck and for those who did not work at the mines but depended upon those regular paychecks to fund their businesses and jobs. With a natural independent streak following the strike and disaster, George was less likely to pursue a steady job. He was fiercely independent and did not like rules, routine jobs, authority, or schools.

After expulsion, his main source of income came from gambling, primarily on cards and billiards, at which he excelled. George played baseball on a semi-pro baseball team. In the 8th inning of the championship game, he smashed a home run further than anyone had ever seen, thereby winning the game.

———

At 21, he ran into one of his teammates, Dolly Gray, who attended Notre Dame and was aware of George's talents though he was good enough to earn a baseball scholarship. Notre Dame had outstanding baseball teams, sending a couple of dozen players to the pros. With his obvious talent, Dolly thought George could use Notre Dame as a springboard into the pros.

Like Rockne who also had not graduated from high school, George had to take an entrance exam, which he passed and subsequently started as a 21-year-old freshman. (Rockne was 22.) Like Gene, he, too, dreamed of a professional baseball career. George, Gene, and Knute all lived in Brownson Hall, Rockne three years earlier, Gene three years later. He soon found the pool table in Corby Hall where he might sink 80 balls in a row, something he preferred to do over attending classes or homework.

In the fall of 1916, George was punting to a fellow freshman on Carter field helping him practice receiving the ball. Rockne, the assistant football coach, happened to walk by when he saw George booming punts over 50 yards. Noticing his natural grace and athleticism, Rockne asked him if he had played football in high school. George said he had not. Rockne invited him to try out for the freshman team.

Quite handsome, at 6' 1" feet tall and a slender 180 pounds,

George had sandy blond hair with a sallow complexion from smoking and hanging out in pool halls. While playing on the freshman squad, he was soon elected their captain, demonstrating his popularity with the players. Late in a deadlocked 7 to 7 game versus Western Michigan, the Irish stalled out at their own 38 yard-line. On 4th down, quarterback Frank Thomas called for a punt. The Gipper lined up to punt, but when the center hiked the ball, he dropped the ball to the ground, which looked like a fumble. Then he kicked the ball.

A dropkick is the same as a field goal attempt, but with no holder to catch and place the ball on the ground. If the attempt failed, like any field goal attempt, the ball would have stayed at the line of scrimmage—Notre Dame's 38, granting Western Michigan incredible field position, where they could win the game with a field goal. You can imagine the shock on Frank Thomas's face when he saw the kick— "What the Heck?" Instead of disaster, the kick sailed 62 yards and split the goalposts for 3 points, which won the game. Frank was, no doubt, much relieved. This was the longest field goal in football history. The NFL would not post a longer field goal until 2012 when San Francisco's David Akers hit a 63-yarder. (Although rarely, if ever used, the drop kick is still legal in college according to the NCAA rulebook. Then, the upright was at the goal line.)

That spring George joined the baseball team. Late in his first game, Coach Harper gave him the bunt signal. Instead of bunting as required, he hit a long home run. When Harper asked why George had disobeyed the sign, he said that it was too hot to run fast. George had difficulty following orders and the next day he turned in his uniform.

True to form, Gipp missed the fall practices and did not show up until the third game of the 1917 football season. He injured his ankle in the Morningside, Iowa game and spent 11 days in an Iowa hospital before returning to South Bend, after which he was out for the last two games.

The 1918 season was Rockne's first as head coach. With Gipp's deferral expiring, rather than being drafted into the Army, he decided to go back to Notre Dame. He convinced a fellow Calumet resident, Hunk Anderson, to join him and play for the team, telling him that Rockne would find him a campus job. Even though they were devout Protestants, Anderson's father, a minister, was thrilled at the possibility of a college education for his young son. Hunk would soon become a prominent member of the team and a Notre Dame legend. In addition to kicking, George had many other talents that seemed to spring out of nowhere. The Gipper's best game came against Purdue, where he ran for 137 yards on 19 carries in a 26 - 6 victory. Due to the war and pandemic, the season was shortened.

———

Early in 1919, the papers played up a pool tournament that Gipp entered. He won all his matches and was pronounced the pool champion of South Bend. Afterward, he took his winnings and moved into the Oliver Hotel, where he played pool and hosted all-night poker sessions.

That fall, when Gene was a scrub, the Irish beat rival Nebraska 14-9, tying up the series at 2-2-1. They were down 9-6 to Army in the third quarter when the Gipper drove the team to a 12-6 victory. He gained 185 yards and 115 yards passing.

After the game, Gipp cut his classes and practices, not showing up until the next game with Purdue. Furious, Rockne suspended him for the 1st quarter but put him in for the second. In three quarters, the Gipper passed for 217 yards—a rare feat at the time, considering that Dorais and Rockne had introduced the passing game only six years earlier and college football was still primarily a running game. Thanks to the Gipper's performance, the Irish won 33-13.

The Gipper quickly became a legend with many pronouncing him to be the best all-around football player in college history. Able to run a 10-flat 100-yard dash, he could run as well as any back in the country and could pass the missed-shaped oblong ball 55 yards. He not only returned punts and kickoffs, but was Notre Dame's kicker, punter, and field goal specialist, able to propel the ball up to 70 yards through the air. Perhaps his greatest talent though, was as a defender, for throughout his college career he never gave up a single pass reception, but intercepted the ball several times for TDs. Today a college team would have up to six players performing the Gipper's various roles (quarterback, running back, defensive back, punter, field goal kicker, and return man)—amazing for someone who never played for a football team until college.

After the season ended, George concentrated on his avocation— gambling. His hometown teammate, Hunk Anderson said, "Every once in a while some of the hotshot pool players from Chicago would come to South Bend looking for action, and George would play them at $100 a game or more. They were crackerjack players who made their living shooting pool, but George would take them almost every time." He told Hunk he made at least $5,000 the previous year—five times Rockne's initial salary, the equivalent of $78,000 today.

The Gipper gambled on games too. The night before a game, the two teams would gather for a joint dinner. At the dinner, Gipp would bet the other team's players that the Irish would win the game. Since there was no TV, few knew what the burgeoning star looked like, so he frequently made bets with professional gamblers too. Sometimes he bet that that Gipper guy would score more points than the entire opposing team, which he would accomplish.

Oddly and atypically, the bets provided heightened motivation for this gambler to perform well. Running for 100 yards or completing ten passes in a game on the field was like running a rack of balls on the table. Perhaps his skill seeing difficult pool angles and combination shots translated to the ease with which he perceived Rockne's difficult plays. Perhaps he saw the players on the field as balls on the table—three-dimensional, moving objects to be mastered.

Kentuck thought the Gipper's behavior to be atrocious. As a highly disciplined individual, Kentuck could not understand why Rockne let him consistently miss practices. As a serious student, he could not understand why the Gipper cut classes and missed his opportunity to gain a college education. He was amazed by how well he played pool but thought spending hours smoking, drinking, playing pool, and gambling was a waste of time. Still, he liked the Gipper and his easygoing ways. He thought, *how could a guy who never practiced and who smoked a couple of packs a day be so adept performing the complicated plays and be so outstanding?*

Gene wondered how good the Gipp might be if he took it seriously, but then how could anyone be any better? The one thing that irked Gene the most was the Gipper's dirty mouth. Although he realized this was likely the product of growing up in a tough mining town, Gene was taught not to swear and could not stand being around those who did. To Gene, George was an enigma.

George's teammates, fellow students, coaches, and the South Bend townies all liked George. He hated rules and did not respect authority, perhaps a trait reinforced by the miner's unfair treatment by company executives. He might not come to practice until Thursday, but he was always ready to excel at game time. This undoubtedly caused the new coach Rockne, considerable consternation as he tried to form a well-disciplined team. But the Rock could not complain about his effort or the results.

George had no interest in promoting himself, avoiding interviews whenever possible, and never reading his headlines. When Notre Dame returned from a key victory, such as Nebraska or Army, throngs of students and townies would crowd the train station to cheer the arriving victors. George, the star, would slip out the back of the train, avoiding the adulation. If Notre Dame was on its way to a rout, George would pull himself out of a game to give the other players a chance. If he were concerned about records or statistics, he would have stayed in. If he won $500 playing cards, which he frequently did, he might buy dinners for the poor in South Bend. This would be the equivalent of nearly $8000 today, enough to buy five hundred steak dinners. On more than one occasion, he used his winnings to pay the expenses of needy students, which amounted to $500 a year. He never touted his charity. Even though he was supremely confident, he was shy and unassuming.

———

At a dance following one of the 1919 games, George met Iris Trippeer, a 20-year-old secretary visiting a friend at nearby St. Mary's College. She was attractive, possessing an upper-class, elite, classic beauty. George fell hard, exchanging letters with her frequently throughout the year. Her parents did not like the fact that George was not serious about his future and seemed unlikely to settle down. In the spring of 1920, Iris told George that she would no longer date him because he did not want to settle down. George was heartbroken and subsequently stopped attending classes.

George's disreputable behavior finally forced the Notre Dame President to act. On the one hand, he wanted to keep the alumni and business leaders happy and keep the star of the team, but he also felt he had to maintain academic standards and raise Notre Dame's reputation as a serious college. He expelled George. George was determined to prove to Iris that she could depend on him, so he acquired a full-time job at the Buick plant in Flint, Michigan. At night, he starred on the factory's baseball team.

Rockne, who had just finished an unbeaten season and whose team was the Champions of the West and National Champs on some polls, faced a clamor from alumni and South Bend businessmen to have the Gipper play on the 1920 team. They signed a petition and threatened to withdraw financial support for the school. With the help of the alumni, Rockne eventually persuaded the president to give the Gipper one last chance. Rockne went to Calumet to retrieve Gipp for one last season (his fifth including his freshman year—considered a red-shirt season today). George would have to pass a special examination, which he uncharacteristically studied hard for and passed.

———

The Irish easily won the first two games of the 1920 football season with a combined score of 80 to zip. In the third game, they faced their archrival, Nebraska, in which Gipp scored the cinching touchdown for a hard-fought win of 16-7 and the first lead of their series rivalry: 3-2-1.

Part of Rockne's strategy was to use smaller, quicker players as his mentor Harper, had done with him and Dorais. But the opponent's larger forces tended to wear his men down. Against Valparaiso, Rock started what he called his shock troops—the second string. This was another one of Rockne's brilliant strategies. Teams had always started their best players who slugged it out during the first quarter to prove themselves to be the dominant team, then as the contestants wore down or were injured, they put in the subs. In Rockne's new strategy, Valparaiso's first string wore themselves out against the shock troops, while Notre Dame's usual starters had a chance to observe their opponent's weaknesses. When the starters appeared fresh in the second quarter, the opposition's forces were already taxed.

Slow Gene did not fit into this smaller/quicker scheme, but he still got plenty of playing time, especially during the blowouts. As the tallest and one of the largest players on the team, Gene was a great shock trooper, particularly against a large and strong player who troubled the starters. He loved blocking for the Gipper. He might open a hole, blocking the opposing guard out of the way, then through his peripheral vision, see the Gipper scamper through that hole, then dance around the opposition's backs for a large gain.

Following a 28-3 victory over Valparaiso, the Irish faced their traditional rival, Army, who took a 17-14 lead into halftime. Rockne was furious with the way the team played and let them know of his displeasure. Even though Gene had not played and was not to blame, sitting in the locker room, he too felt extremely uncomfortable under Rockne's wrath. The Gipper was standing by a locker striking a typical nonchalant pose and smoking a cigarette while Rockne vented. The Rock turned to the Gipper and asked him if he was interested. The Gipper told him that he certainly was not going to blow it because he had bet $400 on the outcome.

On a punt early in the 4th quarter, the Gipper dodged and twisted his way through the entire Army ranks for a 48-yard return. George was deceptively fast and agile. One team member remembers him talking to some sprinters on the track team on the field. George, While George wore street shoes and pants, the three took their mark and sprinted for 60 yards. George handily beat them in the dash. The Gipper next went out and engineered two touchdowns for a 27-17 victory, gaining an astounding 480 total yards running, passing, and returning passes and punts. When he left late in the game, the cadets gazed at him with sorrow and wonder.

————

George still hoped that Iris would see that he had turned over a new leaf and was now more serious about life, so he wrote her passionate, surprisingly well-written love letters. He had moved out of the Oliver Hotel and now stayed at Sorin dorm too. She agreed to meet him in the Indiana hotel lobby before the IU game in Indianapolis. There, before the game, with his future in her hands, hoping she would see he had improved, hoping they would be together, she told him that she had married another man. Crushed, George went to the game in a daze. IU soon took a 10-0 lead. Rock wondered what was wrong with his star. To make matters worse, perhaps due to his lack of concentration, the Gipper suffered a separated shoulder, and Rockne took him out of the game, where, in pain, he shivered on the sideline during an exceptionally bitterly cold, windy day.

It looked like the Irish's 15-game win streak would soon end. Despite his pain, showing remarkable courage, the Gipper asked to go back into the game, where he soon ran for a touchdown. On a later punt return, after the Gipper caught the ball, the IU tacklers, seeing his pain, rather than tackling the star hard, gently lowered him to the ground. In the closing minutes, he completed a long pass to Anderson followed by a short run for a touchdown by Larson. The Irish eked out a 14-10 victory to keep their winning streak alive. With sore tonsils, a cold, a bum shoulder and a broken heart, George stayed in bed the entire following week.

It did not look like George would be able to play in the second-to-last game of the year against nearby Northwestern. Rockne went to see the Gipper in his dorm room and asked him if he could play. They agreed that he would join the team on the trip and see how he felt before the game. Obviously not improving, the Gipper did not start, but this was touted to be Gipper day by the Notre Dame alumni, and a crowd of 20,000 started chanting his name, "We want Gipp, we want Gipp." Eventually, Rockne relented and put the Gipper into the game. He soon threw a 35-yard strike to Hunk Anderson for a touchdown. Later, he threw a 55-yarder to the Northwestern 15 yard-line followed by a 15-yard scamper into the end zone by Barry.

Notre Dame won 33-7, registering its eighth victory of the season and 17th in a row. Now, they only needed one more to retain their Champions of the West title and possibly win a second national championship in a row. But would the Gipper be able to play?

Three days after the Northwestern victory on November 23, 1920, the Irish faithful held a banquet at the Oliver Hotel in honor of the victorious 1920 team. A festive atmosphere permeated the room, where the team sat elated in their success, talking about the glory they would accrue with just one more win.

Gene sat next to George and noticed that he looked terribly gaunt. The normally effusive Gipper sat silent as Rockne began to speak. Then Gene saw George coughing uncontrollably. He turned to Gene and said, "Excuse me Kentuck. I'm just too sick to stay." As George left the room, Gene looked around the table, noticing the concerned look on his previously elated teammates' faces. Their star and popular friend, who had given so much to the team, was obviously hurting. Later, Rockne checked him into the hospital, where they diagnosed him with strep throat and pneumonia. Both are curable with penicillin, but unfortunately, the wonder drug would not be invented for another eight years.

At George's request, Rockne sent for Iris, who, even though she was married, traveled to South Bend. While in the hospital, George heard of his teammate's astounding 48-0 victory against Michigan State—**they had won one for the Gipper**. Rockne soon told him that they were again the Champions of the West and that Walter Camp elected George as a first-string All-American, the second All-American after Rockne's roommate and quarterback Gus Dorais. After three weeks in the hospital, Rockne grew more concerned about his tough-to-manage but amiable star.

Towards the end, the Gipper told the Rock,

> *"I've got to go, Rock. It's all right. I'm not afraid. Sometime, Rock, when the team is up against it, when things are wrong and the breaks are beating the boys—tell them to go in there with all they've got and win just one for the Gipper. I don't know where I'll be then, Rock. But I'll know about it, and I'll be happy."*

George was not able to leave the hospital again. A group of students kept vigil outside the hospital, kneeling in the snow to pray. Three weeks after entering the hospital, he died on December 15, 1920. Practically the entire student body of 1,221 accompanied his coffin in a procession from the campus to the train station. Iris saved all of George's letters and, decades later, while giving these to her niece, told her that George was the love of her life.

The Gipper accumulated 2,431 rushing yards, a record that would not be broken for over 50 years—not until 1978. He still holds Notre Dame's record for average rushing of 8.1 yards and the total yards per game of 128 yards. Despite two seasons cut short by injury and the war, he generated 4,781 total yards of offense. The Gipper averaged 38.4 yards per punt, but perhaps the most amazing stat is that no one ever caught a pass against him. Considering the number of games he missed due to illness, injury, the war, and attitude, and the fact that Notre Dame now plays 13 regular-season games versus 6 to 9 when Gipp played, his is an impressive record.

Although he did not graduate, the George Gipp Award is given to the outstanding senior male athletes from Calumet High School. George is ranked #22 on ESPN's Top 25 Players in College Football History list.

Ronald Reagan, who later became the 40th U. S. president, played the Gipper in the 1940 film, *Knute Rockne All American*. Thereafter, he was known as the Gipper—during his presidential campaign, they adopted the effective slogan, "Win one for the

Gipper." That movie featured the 1930 game when Rockne's team, who looked whipped at half time invoked the famous, "Win One for the Gipper" quote. Two of Gene's best friends were in that locker room, Rock's assistant coach, Tom Lieb, and captain, Tom Connoly. Tom Lieb would play a significant role in Kentuck's success. Gene would send Tom Connoly to Rock who was an All-American end when they would win two back-to-back National Football Championships. Tom would later play a significant role in the Obersts' life and live with Gene and his family for a while.

The Gipper would be a tantalizing subject of an un-sanitized movie version of the enigmatic star (perhaps staring Bradley Cooper and Kristen Stewart).

Notre Dame was later selected as the NCAA's National Champions in 1919 and was the national champions on other polls in 1920, but the selection science was still developing at the time. They were the Western Champs both years. Gene accumulated enough playing time to letter on the 1920 championship team, but this was just the start of his athletic career.

Picture of 1920 National Championship Team
George Gipp 1st in the second row, Kentuck eighth in the top row
Notes by Gene

10: Back on the Field

That spring after Johnny Flynn accidentally discovered him and Rockne recruited him onto the track team, Gene started throwing the javelin for the first time. In his four competitions, he set records at Indiana University, Michigan State, and the Indiana College Meet and placed first to fifth at the first NCAA championships of any sport.

After Kentuck's sophomore year blocking for the Gipper and becoming an All-American in track, inspired by his sudden success in throwing the javelin, that summer he threw the projectile throughout Owensboro. He hoped to improve upon his previous distance, climb the ranks of national javelin competitors, and hopefully qualify for the Olympics. At the start of his junior year in 1921, Gene decided to change his major from Law to International Commerce, a new and exciting program at the university. Getting to know Fernando and the foreign students over the holidays and hearing about their families and their father's businesses, indicated to Gene that there would be immense potential in overseas trade, especially with his friends in Latin America. He continued to coach and direct the Minims athletic programs, which, meant arranging games with other schools, often with much bigger players. But whether it was football, basketball, track or baseball, his Minims were compiling an impressive undefeated record, and he grew very fond of the little shavers who gave so much of themselves.

He did not go out for the football team that fall. His back hurt and he was discouraged that he did not have more playing time, which he thought was likely due to his slowness, induced by his club-like feet. He was also disappointed in how Rockne let the Gipper miss practices and allowed his poor attitude to infect the team. The Gipper was the greatest athlete Gene had ever seen or heard of and he felt privileged to see him in action, but from his growing experience with the Minims, realized how important discipline was. Periodically, the little guys would slough off or display ill temper, but he immediately corrected their attitude. Afterward, he found that they respected him not only for his discipline but also for his fairness and kindness to them.

Gene received a telegram from Owensboro on Feb 2, 1922. He could not understand why they would spend money on a telegram until he read that his father had died. He had been to a church council meeting at St. Joseph's and argued with the directors. While walking home, he had a heart attack. He was 68.

Fellows at the school asked Gene how he was doing and he responded that he was fine. He finished his classes and coached the Minims basketball game as if nothing had happened. He was in denial and it wasn't until the train ride home that the death hit him. He had not seen his father since last September and he dearly wanted to see him one more time at Christmas, because this was his father's favorite holiday, always spreading joy throughout the extended family.

After thinking about his father's life and his family on the too-long, too-sad train ride, with a heavy heart, Gene finally arrived home for the funeral. He so looked forward to seeing his mother and siblings, but not under these circumstances. He was also worried that Albert would be disappointed about him changing his major and not joining his law practice. He soon learned that Albert's practice was thriving; he had joined many of the clubs in town and was becoming a civic and political leader. He was not too disappointed. After all, Gene had to do what felt right for himself.

Frank was living the high life as a captain in Panama with a string of polo ponies. To Frank, majoring in business would make sense because of the immense potential in Latin America, much of which was being controlled by the United States and its businessmen.

Paul, now Bonaventure, was rising quickly in the Passionate order and had started traveling around the world opening monasteries. As an adult now, Gene enjoyed talking to his older brother about his fascinating travels. Perhaps Gene would travel around the world too. Joe was the manager of an insurance agency in Atlanta and seemed to be doing well. Joe explained the importance of life insurance and considering how much the country was growing, getting into business would be a great idea.

Herman had just opened the grocery store near their house and managed a couple of farms that grew tobacco and corn for his mother on the outskirts of town. Herman was such a positive person; just seeing him always made Gene feel better. Mary worked as a deputy sheriff. At first, he thought this odd, but if any woman could do such a job well it was Mary—she was always in command. Louis was still struggling with his brain injury, had married Sadie Mae and they lived at the family home.

His father had been the first to die in his immediate family and he wondered what the funeral would be like and how he would be able to handle it. At the service, in addition to the huge family, he saw a surprisingly large number of Andrew's friends. He realized how good a man his father was and how much his life in his adopted land had meant to his church and community.

After the service and burial, they went back home and talked.

The talking was not somber, but rather about life. Going through the wake, ceremony, burial and reception helped to heal the wounds. While they honored their father, being together helped them connect to life and its continuous, ever-ticking cycle. Seeing all the grandchildren around was a testament that Andrew's legacy would continue. Gene worried about his mother but was glad that Mary, Josephine, Louis and Sadie were still at home to care for her.

Gene had not fully felt the weight of his father's death. He missed his dad terribly and thought of him often throughout the day. Like a typical stoic German, Andrew did not express his emotions much, but they were both youngest sons and Gene felt a special bond with him. He had known Andrew after the older sons had left home and started their own families when he was retired and was not busy with the daily grind of providing for the family of 13. Then he had been more easygoing and approachable. At first, Gene felt numb going to classes, but the daily routine helped him through his grief. Even though he had such great success throwing the javelin the previous year, he decided not to join the track team that March. He told those who asked that his ankles were swollen and since he changed majors, he had to devote more time to his studies and his job with the Minims, but it might have been due to his father's death. After showing so much potential throwing the javelin, he would miss a critical year of competition.

———

Over the summer, Gene considered participating in football again but discouragingly he thought his clubfeet and slow speed would continue to be an obstacle and source of ridicule. In preparation for football season, he worked out regularly in the shed using the equipment his father acquired from failed Columbia College when an idea occurred to him. His metal braces were heavy and the more he used them, the more the metal dug into his flesh causing pain. One morning, before the sun and intense heat hit the small wooden shed, as he lifted the dumbbells, he looked at the pile of Indian clubs in the corner and thought about a possibly better design. The clubs were tapered at one end and broader at the other. He sawed a club in half and shaved out the insides with the glass he used on his javelin to fit around his deformed foot and ankle, whittling the clubs into a shape similar to the bulky braces. He then used leather shoelaces and a shoemaker's last, which the family used to repair shoes, to strap the two halves together.

Gene tried the first one out and after shaving the wood more and several adjustments, it seemed to work well, so he made another for his other foot and ankle. The new Indian club braces were much lighter, more comfortable, and conformed to his swollen feet and ankles better. He next added an arch support. It took a while to adjust to them, but he found he could run, still slowly, but much faster than before—a Forest-Gump-like moment, when Forest being teased and chased by bullies, finally ran out of his braces and was free to run like the wind and conquer the world. This was a moment that would forever change Gene's life too, taking him along a course like Forest's. For someone confined by his painful metal braces for years, the new braces provided a huge relief. He was now able to work out more intensely and even run, bound to prove himself worthy of Rockne's consideration.

The previous year, the Irish had another winning record, only losing to Iowa by a score of 7 – 0. With a growing reputation, the number of prospects had grown exponentially and Gene faced more competition than he had two years earlier: nearly 150 went out for the freshman team. The Indian club braces gave Kentuck much more maneuverability and because he could run more, he acquired more leg strength too. Rather than hitting his spots late, he was able to complete his assignments efficiently and with force. A player who might have previously found Kentuck relatively easy to maneuver (a pushover) now found a more formidable, stronger foe.

Rockne encouraged walk-ons, attending intramural dorm games always on the lookout for potential talent. Those who were standout prep stars, because they had swelled heads often were not team players and he placed a premium on team play, emphasizing the importance of the line. Indeed, all the Notre Dame captains during the Rockne era came from the line.

Rockne was glad to see Kentuck back on the '22 team, spending time with him, teaching him some of the finer points to gain leverage over an opponent and how to tackle effectively. Earlier, coaches coached the team, whereas Rockne coached the individual, not just on the first team, but also on the second and third squad, where, over time, his future prospects would emerge. Rockne had become an excellent judge of character, instantly able to evaluate a player's motivation, strengths, and weaknesses. He did not demand that they fit his ideal mold in each position; rather, he worked with the player's strengths and helped him overcome his weaknesses.

Rockne had an excellent knowledge of physiology, partially due to his participation in the pole vault, which required intricate coordination of every muscle, joint and bone to make it over the high bar. He would show a receiver how to position his body and arms to be in the best position for a specific pass play or a lineman how to block an opponent. One of the things Rockne did want, however, was intelligence, especially from the line. His schemes were complex and required intricate coordination between all eleven teammates. If a big strong lineman could not remember his plays or was slow to reach his spot, he had no value to Rockne. After all, Rockne had been a lineman himself and appreciated their critical role in his offensive and defensive schemes.

Rockne was a stickler for details, especially blocking—everyone on the team had to be an excellent blocker, including all four backs. The press considered Rockne's teams to be the best at blocking and tackling. When he went up against Kentuck he realized that blocking the now-stronger 6'5" lineman would not be an easy task for opponents. Seeing much-improved play from the towering Kentuck, Rockne moved him up the depth charts to number two. Tom Lieb, one of Gene's track & field mates who threw the discus, shot put and javelin, would be the starter at right tackle with Gene as his backup.

When he came out onto the field, Rockne was now confident and in command. Gene was impressed by how much Rockne had grown since he played for the rookie coach two years earlier. Gene enjoyed the afternoon lectures where Rock would outline plays and tactics. These were finally starting to sink in and Gene started seeing the relationships between the interacting players and how their moves would impact the opposing forces. Rockne held the classes during a free period from 1:00 to 1:45 during the spring and fall where the skilled lecturer taught all aspects of football including equipment, offense, defense, plays, conditioning, strategy, and the various other football systems. There were exams and the seniors were expected to teach a class themselves. Rockne also continued to teach chemistry.

As a fervent student of history and its many battles, Gene started seeing the strategy behind the plays, especially the backfield shifts that would keep the opposing defense off balance. The formidable line composed the infantry, the speedy backs the cavalry, the fleet-footed, shifty receivers the air force, and the kickers the artillery. The quarterback was the general and Rockne the commander-in-chief. The game resembled a battle between two opposing armies. By teaching discipline, teamwork, and courage, Rockne knew football prepared young men for war, by providing leaders who could also take orders.

Rockne espoused the three Ds—dirt, drudgery, and discipline. Players had to get dirty, work through the drudgery of learning their plays and have the discipline to prevail in their games. He told his players that the three Ds would help them to prevail and compete in their chosen field too. Rockne had developed his famous backfield shift, in which any of the four players could perform any function— passing, lateraling, running, or receiving. Such moves prior to the snap were highly effective against defenses but required precision and much practice. Gene and the rest of the line wanted to learn the moves too, so Rockne indulged the big fellows, thinking that it would only increase their understanding of his system. Gene struggled with the intricate footwork but obtained a better appreciation of what

Rockne intended to accomplish. With his new braces, he was actually able to perform the shift, which he would not have previously been able to accomplish. It also helped him feel like an integral part of the team, not just a member of the line with a specific, narrow function.

In his classes, Rockne introduced his players to his 25 commandments, spending time on each one.

Rockne's 25 Commandments

- **Scholarship**: The player should first be a good student. Do not neglect your studies. Your first purpose should be to get an education.
- **Cooperation**: Everyone should work for the common good of the school and the squad. Everyone should boost everyone else; a disorganizer has no place on the squad.
- **Obedience**: The public holds the coach responsible for the team; his orders must be obeyed. He is responsible for the system and the carrying out of the system, not necessarily the winning of the game.
- **Habits**: Good habits are only doing those things which help and not doing those things that will harm or hinder.
- Ambition: Keeping an eye on the future, always trying to improve oneself. Interest and spirit sometimes outweigh natural ability.
- **Attendance**: Anything worth doing is worth doing well. Try not to miss a day of school or practice.
- **Earnestness**: The desire to make every minute count, always wanting to do the right thing for the team and the school.
- **Morals**: A high standard of living and thinking.
- Sportsmanship: Good sportsmanship means clean and fair play. Treat your opponent with respect.
- **Conduct**: Your school, family, town, community and yourself are judged by your conduct; you can make or break them.
- **Unity**: Actions on the part of every member of the squad are for the common good.
- **Service**: Students should always consider that they are receiving far more than they are giving. Their best efforts for their school are none too good.
- **Leadership**: The willingness to help, guide or direct, in the right way, be example, words or actions.
- **Patience**: The willingness to take and profit by the instructions received, although not a member of the first team.
- Loyalty: To give your best service to the team, school, game and coach.
- **Self-sacrifice**: Giving up some of the present things for the future.
- **Determination**: The mental quality of strong determination is very necessary to win in the face of strong opposition.
- **Confidence**: The belief in oneself, teammates, team and plays.

- **Remarks:** Be careful of your remarks about anyone; if you cannot say something good, say nothing. Talking too much is bad policy.
- **Responsibility:** Being dependable, the performing of one's duties, the desire to be known as responsible.
- **Concentration:** During school hours, think and prepare your studies; they must be of first importance. During practice, think only of playing; if you have studied, you will not have to worry about your schoolwork.
- **Losing:** You can be a hard but good loser. Any coach or team that cannot lose and treat their opponents with respect has no right to win; a poor sportsman generally tries to amuse the spectators with his self-styled clever wit by making abusive remarks, which act as a boomerang by intelligent spectators.
- **Winning:** If you are the rightful winner, be willing to take credit for it, but keep in mind that it was only your time to win and that your winning was probably due to conditions or a reward for your sacrifices; a kind word or a handshake goes a long way toward forming a lasting friendship, and does not change the score.
- **The Past:** It is history. Make the present good, and the past will take care of itself.
- **The Present and Future:** Give to your school the best that you have, and the best will come back to you. Your success in the future depends on the present. Build well.

Gene studied the commandments and thought that these were remarkably like *Pushing to the Front*, the foundation of his personal philosophy. He could see that Rock had learned much about what not to do by coaching the Gipper and would no longer allow such behavior, which Gene felt gratified to see. Inspired by Rockne's use of Marden-like principles, he planned to run through the 25 commandments with his Minims. Borrowing Rockne's classroom approach, but splitting it up over a few sessions so the younger fellows could absorb it better, he would walk through the principles, providing examples of each. He thought the commandments would inspire their lives too, especially since they came from Rockne, the man they idolized.

———

The first two games against Kalamazoo and St. Louis were easy victories with a combined score of 72 to nothing, in which Gene played much of the games. In the first quarter of the Purdue game on October 14, 1922, Tom Lieb broke his leg. Kentuck was horrified to see this happen. Even though Tom was the first-string right tackle, Kentuck wanted to win his position by playing, not through injury. He liked Tom and had immense respect for the versatile lineman.

He was likely shocked when Rock called him into the game and he lined up against the corresponding Purdue tackle. For the first few plays, he concentrated on getting into the right position, which he accomplished, but initially, his opponents had an easy time with him. He was going through the motions rather than being part of the game as if he still watched the game transpire on the bench. Then he lined up on defense, and, after the ball was hiked, he saw a direct line to the quarterback. He charged towards the ball carrier and was about to make the tackle when a pulling guard slammed into his left side throwing him roughly to the ground. When the successful guard got up, he had a smirk on his face. This angered Kentuck and from then on, he was in the game, performing his position well. It was no longer about Xs and Os—he was in a battle. Notre Dame went on to win 20 to zero.

Kentuck was now the starter. They easily beat a nearby team, DePauw, in Greencastle, Indiana 34-7.

Tall Kentuck in football uniform

Rockne was not only the football and track coach, but also the athletic director and one of his duties included scheduling games with other athletic directors. This was no easy task since the established teams had set schedules, the Eastern teams still looked down on Western teams, and the Big Ten teams did not want to play the stronger Notre Dame teams. To test his team's mettle, Rockne wanted to play the best teams, which took persistence, and pleading bordering on pestering to accomplish. Gene did the same for his Minims on a much smaller scale. For October 28, Rockne scheduled a game at an up-and-coming southern powerhouse, Georgia Tech. Rockne wanted to increase Notre Dame's visibility by scheduling a southern team, but due to their concern over expenses, the administration had refused to allow him to book the trip the previous year. Rockne argued that such games would increase revenues, and eventually, they relented.

The Southern press promoted the game as a clash between the North and South—a reenactment of the Civil War. In the Atlanta Constitution, writer Craddock Goins cast the game "As a contest between the skillful, keen, graceful and merciless Indianans against the spirit of the south."

In the week leading up to the game, Goins penned a column further hyping the North versus South aspect. He wrote: "The game between the Yellow Jackets and the great Notre Dame team will draw the eyes of southern football lovers from every gridiron in the nation Saturday, and the attention of football students throughout the land will be largely turned to what promises to be one of the greatest exhibitions of flash and fly in the history of the modern game.... It is Southern football's greatest opportunity.... It will mean the greatest possible impetus to football in this section." Football was just starting to become popular in the South and the West. Evidently, Goins saw the Notre Dame game as a way to increase its popularity. Judging by its influence in the South today and the near dominance of the Southern conferences, he was right.

Tom Lieb went to the station to wish his teammates well. Something not typically done for an injured player, Rockne invited Tom to join the team on the trip to Atlanta. The presence of the popular athlete inspired the team. The long journey south enabled Kentuck to spend time with Tom and receive valuable pointers on how to play their mutual position. They likely spent considerable time talking to each other about their lives, thereby forging a deeper friendship.

Tom, who would play a pivotal role in Gene's life, hailed from Minnesota, where he initially attended St. Thomas College. Recognizing a potential talent for his team, Rockne asked to meet Tom at a pool hall in Chicago. With trepidation, Tom entered the smoky room, a place his parents told the attractive, amiable, religious, Catholic young man never to enter for fear of being corrupted. He performed on the 1921 team as the backup left halfback before Knute converted him to a tackle and was a favorite to be an All-American. In addition, he threw the discus on Rockne's track team, placing first in the NCAA championships the previous spring when he became an All-American in track.

The South, like the West, was starting to produce some great teams, so this would be a good test for the Irish. For Kentuck, traveling south to his roots was a treat. Kentuck napped on the leg from Indianapolis to Louisville but awoke just as they crossed the Ohio River, and he started singing *My Old Kentucky Home*, then talked of the bluegrass, bourbon, fast horses, and refined ladies. The rest of the team enjoyed his enthusiasm for Kentucky. As the train pulled into the Louisville station, Rockne announced that they would eat there. Kentuck looked forward to having some fine southern cuisine, such as the fried chicken, greens, and grits he sorely missed while up north.

At the pre-game dinner the night before the game, the Georgia gentlemen were very gracious, and Kentuck felt at home talking to his fellow Southerners. Some of his teammates noticed how his southern accent seemed to regenerate itself. Before the game, Rockne turned to Kentuck in the locker room, "Kentuck, the whole game depends on right tackle, which is you!" Kentuck gulped but went to the field determined.

Even though it was 58 years since the Civil War and most of those present when Sherman burnt Atlanta to the ground had died, their children kept the memory of the tragedy and devastation alive. Atlanta now served as the headquarters of the Klu Klux Klan with Catholics one of their primary targets. The Irish had two strikes against them for being both Catholic and northerners. There were likely a few 75-90-year-old Confederate veterans among the 20,000 fans who continuously shouted the Rebel Yell, "YEAOW!," attempting to interfere with the Irish's signal calling. Of course, as a Southern sympathizer, this did not bother Kentuck, and the rest of the team soon adjusted. Kentuck did not really want the South to rise again since he was more a fan of Lincoln's than Jeb Davis's, but he enjoyed saying it would, especially to his northern pals.

Georgia kicked a field goal for a 3-0 lead. Later in the half, Stuhldreher passed to Castner for a TD. In the fourth quarter, Stuhldreher ran for another TD as the Irish prevailed, 13-3.

A couple of days later, when the train pulled into the South Bend station, Kentuck was stunned to see a mob of students whooping and hollering. After that, the cheering students carried the team on their shoulders for several blocks. He thought this was immensely enjoyable. The temptress, fame, had drawn his first adoration.

The next week, fullback Paul Casner scored all of Notre Dame's 27 points, including kicking the extra points to scorch Indiana University twenty-seven to zero. Many compared Castner to the Gipper due to his speed and kicking abilities. The Irish faced one of their two perennial rivals next—Army. Kentuck had not made the traveling squad for the Army game in 1920, so this would be his first trip east on the long train ride to West Point. As they chugged into

West Point, the Hudson River valley glowed in a patchwork quilt of fall colors.

Many of the senior cadet players fought in WWI and were grizzled veterans. The play at the line was fierce with both teams struggling to gain an advantage, more reminiscent of that war than modern football. Under Rockne's leadership, the game gradually evolved from a battle at the line of scrimmage to one of complex formations and plays, but in the 1920s, the battle at the line still dominated the game. Then, offensive players could grab a defensive man and throw him to the ground. Football equipment had improved, and the number of deaths decreased, but leg, hip, and shoulder padding was still very primitive, offering little protection. The flat leather helmet gave little cushioning against injury or concussions, and there was no facemask.

With little protection, football was a much rougher game. Kentuck played one game with a bloody nose, saying the red blood caking on his face made him look more fearsome. Twenty-first century, multi-tiered shoulder pads protect not only the shoulders but also the chest and ribcage, which the 1920s predecessors did not. Kentuck received a caved rib during the hard-fought scrums at the line but continued to play. He never told Knute of the persistent and painful injury, because Rockne would have taken him out of the game.

The backfield consisted of Frank Thomas at quarterback, Don Miller and Jim Crowley as halfbacks, and the amazing Paul Castner at fullback. Stuhldreher came into many of the games later to relieve Thomas at QB. Rockne's continuous backfield shift caused headaches for most defenses, including Army. The previous year, their coach, Charles Daly, had complained vehemently against its illegality. Rockne agreed not to use the plays in the second half and instead went into a shotgun.

Earlier, Daly visited Rockne in the off-season to understand the shift better. Rockne did not mind sharing his knowledge but rather thought of it as advancing the coaching profession in the still-evolving game. In the off-season, the rules committee voted to make the moving shift illegal, but in 1922, Rockne found a loophole and modified the shift by stopping for a split second before the hike. During the game, Army did a good job of defending against the shift, plus Daly, following Rockne's teachings, had adapted the shift to their backfield.

Elmer Layden entered the game after an unfortunate Castner injury and had his best game up until then. The rough-fought game was still tied towards the end of the 4th quarter when the Irish attempted a 55-yard dropkick field goal. Army blocked it. With seconds remaining, Army also attempted a more obtainable 40-yarder to win the game, which the Irish also blocked. The game ended in a

0-0 tie.

At West Point, there had been 20,000 fans in attendance, but the eastern Notre Dame alumni claimed that over 5,000 Irish fans had to stand without a view of the game and that they could not reserve seats. They contended that it was not fair that the Army game was played at West Point every year since Notre Dame, with a better record, was now equal to or even better than Army. There was much discussion about finding a larger venue like the Polo Grounds in New York City for this annual contest.

––––––

The Butler game contested the Indiana championship, after which Notre Dame fans complained of Butler's vicious play. For that game, with Castner still injured, Rockne started what would become the legendary backfield of Stuhldreher, Crowley, Miller, and Layden for the first time, destined to become the **Four Horsemen**. In the game, Don Miller was injured. At one point, Stuhldreher received a punt and shook off a potential tackler, then as two Butler players converged upon him about to make the tackle, Kentuck lunged forward, taking out both, freeing Stuhldreher to run 68 yards for the nail-in-the-coffin touchdown. After he scored, Stuhldreher likely ran to Kentuck shaking his hand vigorously, crediting him for the TD too. The Irish won 34-7.

Having won all their games thus far, Notre Dame became a favorite for the National Championship. One might wonder why tiny Notre Dame enjoyed such success. It was a small all-boys school with no fraternities where everyone lived in dorms; therefore, there was a spirit of cohesiveness permeating the culture that other schools lacked. Football games were not just the team's event, the entire school felt they were actively participating.

Five days later on Thanksgiving Day, the last game of the year pitted perennial rival Nebraska against Notre Dame in Lincoln. After the long trip back, there were only two days to prepare for the game prior to the Lincoln trip. The Nebraska student body provided an enthusiastic welcome for the Irish team as the train entered the station, cheering on good, old Notre Dame. At the pre-game dinner that night, Kentuck saw how big many of the Nebraska linemen were, likely from working hard on the farm. The large Cornhuskers line trampled the Irish in the first half. Despite his caved-in rib, Kentuck responded and the Notre Dame press called him the star of the line. Still the Irish registered a disappointing loss, 14 to 6. They would not be the champions of the West or the national champs that year, but they still had an 8-1-1 record to be proud of.

Kentuck proved himself to be an outstanding addition to the Notre Dame starting eleven. The one flaw he had was that, due to his disability, he was always the last one to run down the field on kickoffs and punts, but if an opponent escaped the other ten, he faced a sure tackler in Kentuck, providing safety for Rockne.

The season ended with another banquet at the Oliver Hotel. Kentuck sadly recalled the last time he had been there sitting next to the Gipper two years earlier, just before he went into the hospital never to return. He bowed his head and said a private prayer for George before eating.

After their highly successful football season, Kentuck looked forward to the spring track season. With only a year left to the Olympics and having only participated in a few meets, he had a long way to go. He showed so much promise back then, but he missed a critical year and had to improve his marks to compete with those aiming at the Olympics. Several athletes had thrown the javelin further than he, but one far-throwing competitor would prove to be particularly exasperating for Kentuck.

11: Back on Track

After the football season ended, with responsibility for the a large contingent of Minims, Gene had little time between his studies. Since he coached the young gentlemen in football, basketball, baseball and track, there was always a sport to coach. In his two years, despite being up against larger foes, the Minims had an unblemished record, winning all their games in all four sports, a testament to Kentuck's burgeoning coaching skills.

The Notre Dame Scholastic asked Gene how he accumulated such an amazing record, to which he replied, "I like the little shavers and I try to make them work for me just like Rock does with his teams. If they like you, they will do anything for you, and when they don't do what I tell them, I pretend that I am mad, and then they come around ready to do anything I say to make up again. Boys are just like men— you can't treat them all alike, but I find that kindness is the surest way to get results."

The Scholastic went on to say, "Big things are expected of Oberst in the javelin throw this season and on the football field next year, but his success will be nowhere appreciated as by the group of American orphans to whom he is almost as much a parent as an athletic coach. Rockne is the idol of the college boys, but Oberst is a king to the minims."

Gene learned much from Rockne about coaching during the 1922 season. Rockne believed in treating each player differently, according to his individual needs. Unless absolutely necessary, he did not belittle players. Gene applied these valuable lessons to his squads.

Gene learned that a coach's ego did not depend upon tearing down a player. Many coaches treated all of their players alike, scolding them no matter how experienced they were. They could be especially harsh on a new player, who might turn out to be a star, but leave the team because he felt belittled. After he was cut from the team, Rockne packed his bags, intending to leave Notre Dame, only to be talked into staying by his hometown friends. Because of his experience being rejected, Rockne empathized with his new players, not wanting to lose potential stars. Imagine what would have happened to Notre Dame's football legacy without those friends' timely action. Imagine what would have happened to Notre Dame itself, for the Rock led the way to a remarkable period of growth, recruiting and prominence for the old college.

Gene did not plan to be a coach, but he not only had a great coach to learn from but unlike any of his teammates, also had an exceptional opportunity to practice what Rockne preached with his Minims, including complicated shifts and trick plays. He was becoming an effective instructor, coach, mentor, and motivator. More than the ability to teach complex plays, Gene knew that being a coach was about becoming a good judge and builder of character.

Periodically, the Rocknes invited some of the boys to their home for dinner. Just as Rockne was like a father to the boys, Bonnie Rockne was like a mother to them. Since Gene could not afford to travel home during the school year, he greatly appreciated these visits. At home, Knute was more relaxed, approachable and easy to get to know, always willing to counsel his young men on the problems they might encounter, offering sage advice. There, Gene gained valuable insight from Rockne on how to coach his Minims. There, Gene also came to know Rockne's other children, including little, cute, blond Junie, who adopted the tall Kentuckian as an older brother. He enjoyed playing with them as he had with his nieces and nephews. These visits provided welcome relief for the boys cloistered in the dorms and campus, away from the institutional life.

———

Gene received his first letter in football in 1920, with his second in 1922, and his first in track in the spring of 1921, so the Monogram club invited him to join. In the winter, the club sponsored its annual Monogram Absurdities, a tradition that Rockne and Dorais started. The program listed the stars of the show, including Big Oberst and Tom Lieb. By now, the initially awkward southerner was having a lot of fun at Notre Dame with his friends, many from the football and track teams. During the minstrel portion of the show, the men sang:

> The march is on,
> No brain or brawn
> Can stop the charge of fighting men!
> Loud rings the cry,
> A grim defy,
> Of hard attack let loose again.
> Oh, it's the Hike! Hike! of victory.
> The call to rise and strike.
> For Notre Dame men are winning,
> Trit Tien Noti-e Dame hears "Hike! Hike! Hike!

In the winter, Gene spent hours in the gymnasium perfecting his snap at the end of his throw. Since he threw the spear over 175 feet now, the gym would not accommodate full-force throws. From his time as a pitcher, he knew that last motion is extremely important to gain speed. The same is true of football, golf, tennis, volleyball or any ball sport. He said, "I would throw the javelin a distance of about 25 feet, just to get that snap that enabled me to add a few extra feet to my distance"

As planned, Kentuck threw the javelin that spring. He had only thrown the spear in competition in four meets two years ago but had done extraordinarily well considering his relatively novice status. At Illinois on May 5th, he competed against the outstanding javelin thrower of the era, Milton Angier. Angier had flown for the Army Air Corps in World War I and would fly again in World War II. In 1920, he set the American record of 197' 5 ¼", becoming the U.S. champion. Angier finished 7th at the Olympics that year, the USA's best showing up to then, and had set another U.S. record of an astounding 202' 9" in 1922.

At the Illinois meet, Angier tossed the javelin an amazing 200' 3", with Kentuck finishing second. Flabbergasted, he had never seen anyone throw over 200 yards and thought to himself he had to up his game. Other football pals of Kentuck's did well including Tom Lieb, first in the discus, and Gus Desch, first in the 220 low hurdles. But Illinois had one of the best teams in the nation, outscoring the Irish 99 ½ to 33 ½. A week later, at Yale, he took another second place, throwing 181' 11".

Knute worked with Kentuck to try to help him improve his technique. "I had been a baseball pitcher in my hometown," Kentuck recalled, "and followed that general delivery in throwing the javelin. I sort of wound up, brought the spear down below my knees, then cocked my arm and let it go. As far as I know, I was the only man who ever used that delivery."

"Somehow, it made me throw a little off the course, the spear always going to the left. Since the rules called for the measurement to be made perpendicularly, I always lost between 15 and 20 feet on every throw."

"I used to ask Rock to watch me and see if he could correct my trouble. He was very patient but always came up with the same answer. He said I was getting good distance and not to change my style."

Against Michigan, Kentuck threw his best thus far with a toss of 187' 9", setting the Carter field record. Leon Moes, Kentuck's teammate, uncorked an unbelievable toss of 196' 5" to break Kentuck's minutes-old record. Kentuck finished second again. Moes was very competitive and the two challenged each other continuously, but Kentuck usually threw better, although sometimes everything aligns and you surprise even yourself with your result when

you are "In the Zone." Like a baseball pitcher, depending upon your
mood, your biorhythms, your rest, your physical condition, your
psyche, the weather, whatever, sometimes you have your best stuff
and sometimes you just don't. This is what makes flying javelins so
fascinating—with throws now approaching 200 feet, fans might expect
consistent results, but for the athlete, trying as hard as he can on
every toss, what they might achieve is often a surprise. Tom Lieb
was on that day, setting the discus record with 137', winning the shot
put with 43' 8 ½", and tying for second in the broad jump.

The Drake relays were held later in May. There Kentuck
witnessed Angier toss a new national record of 203' 9 ½". Kentuck
finished a respectable fourth. Since Angier competed for Illinois, he
would not be at the Indiana State meet, where Kentuck finally
finished first with a toss of 181' 2', setting a new state meet record.
Tom Lieb also set the record in the discus with 140'1" and came in
second in the javelin throwing 179'10".

The biggest meet up until then came on June 6, during the
Conference Championships at Michigan, which included 16 western
teams, nearly all from the Big Ten. There Kentuck faced the
outstanding athlete Milton Angier again, who threw the javelin an
astonishing 203' 9", just below his previous record. Gene was
somewhat frustrated that he always had to face Angier but admired
his ability and loved watching his form and far-soaring javelin flying
through the sky. Kentuck finished second again, congratulating Milton
on his sterling performance. On graduation week in June, Kentuck
took a first against the Illinois Athletic Club, throwing 179' 4" to
finish the year on a positive note.

After he graduated, Tom went on to win the NCAA discus title
that year as he had done in '22 and the American Athletic Union
(AAU) title. The track team was not as competitive as it had been in
'21, but had two outstanding prospects in Gene Oberst and Tom Lieb.
With the Olympics only a year away, both hoped to be on the
American team's ship headed for Paris in '24, just as Desch and
Murphy had done in '20. Even though he had performed well in the
first NCAA meet in 1921, Kentuck did not qualify for the 1923 meet.
Over the preceding two years, the marks had progressed, not just for
Angier, but for the others too. He vowed to train religiously during
the summer to improve his results in hopes of making the Olympics.

Inspired by the spring results, that summer, Gene worked out
with the Columbia equipment, whittled his javelin to perfection, and
tossed the spear throughout Owensboro in hopes of qualifying for the
Olympics. He knew he would have to throw significantly further to
compete with the likes of Angier, but, with more practice and
dedication, perhaps he could do so, perhaps.

Instead of working at the flour mill, to make some extra money,
Kentuck tutored Julian Adler, who was from a wealthy family

concerned about his grades and study habits, who wanted him to excel in life. His mother thought that, besides improving his grades, Gene's influence would help Julian in prep school. Young Adler was a Notre Dame sports fan who would soon visit him at Notre Dame and they would develop a "big/little brother" relationship, which would provide Gene with some unique opportunities over the following years.

12: Blocking for the Four Horsemen

Gene learned much about football from his mentor, which would benefit his performance over the upcoming season and that he could apply throughout his potential career. In a sense, Rockne was the fourth in line of the key coaches that evolved football from its metamorphosis out of rugby, through the times when players were dying, and the game was banned at many colleges, into the 1920s when the rules finally stabilized. Rockne would take the game to a whole new level, coaching and training an astounding number of the legendary coaches over the next 50 years.

Rockne played for and was the assistant coach to his mentor Jesse Harper who radicalized football with the forward pass and put tiny Notre Dame on the map. Harper apprenticed at Chicago under Alonzo Stagg, the director of the second stage of football's evolution, who created many of its famous plays. Stagg in turn, as one of the first class of All-Americans, learned the game at Yale from his mentor, the "Father of Football," Walter Camp, who grew football out of its rugby roots to the game we know today. If Gene decided to enter coaching, he would be in the fifth generation of great coaches who spanned the first hundred years of football.

That summer, Rockne began his football school. His first stint was at Brigham Young University in Provo Utah, which had fielded their first team earlier that school year. He had never been that far west and had never seen anything like the flat Salt Lake Desert flanked by 13,000-foot mountains—ironic that a Protestant, from a Catholic University, taught at a Mormon University, highlighting the ecumenical nature of sports. Of course, with its newly instituted football program, the university had an incredible opportunity to learn so much from one of the best.

On August 20, Gene received a telegram from Rockne to motivate him for the upcoming season, offering him a scholarship:

My dear Gene:

Just a line to remind you to be on hand for the opening practice. As we play the Army and Princeton so early, it is necessary that all men report on time and in good shape. We are playing a hard schedule so get on your mark. You are all set for next year and you need not go to the minims at all unless you want to .... I confidently expect that you will make a name for yourself this fall at tackle. Trusting you had a good summer, I am.

Cordially,
K.K. Rockne

Rockne's letter inspired Gene. Accepting the offer would mean that Gene would not have to coach and care for his Minims, which would save him much of his time so he could concentrate on his studies and sports and maybe even socialize a little. Gene considered the offer but thought that a college athlete should attend college to obtain an education not just to play sports. Participating in sports should be an extracurricular endeavor, like any other, such as singing in the glee club or playing in the band. Gene thought college athletics should be strictly amateur and therefore declined Rockne's generous offer. These days, when college athletes are paid, it might be difficult to imagine someone turning down a scholarship, but sports were still evolving in this, the Golden Decade of Sports. He would play his heart out for the team but without any financial consideration. Rockne, who felt he was building character, likely appreciated Gene's decision.

Nearly all the athletes on Notre Dame's team played multiple sports in high school and college when there was less emphasis on size. Gene's friend Tom Lieb was not only an All-American candidate in both football and track but was a standout in hockey and baseball, too, lettering in all four sports at ND. In the early 1900s, college sports were limited to a three-month season with two-hour practices, giving plenty of time for study, other sports, and other pursuits. There were no August two-a-day sessions, and the Irish's first games were not held until late September. Since all the colleges generally followed the same patterns, the competition was roughly equal. An average-sized student like the Four Horsemen (5'9, 155 lbs.) could compete in sports at the college level, for it was not just something reserved for exceptional physical specimens.

Then, the equipment, especially the thin leather helmets, offered little protection, but when the largest player on a top college team might be 200 to 210 lbs, the hits were not as forceful. Imagine the impact that a 300-pound highly conditioned college or even high school lineman delivers and all the concern there is today regarding life-altering concussions. The force a 330, lightning fast, NFL tackle delivers is close to that of a ton falling on a quarterback, nearly twice what it was in the 1920s. For the first time in over a century, numerous parents, such as Rockne's father, Lars before, have serious concerns about allowing their sons to try out for football.

Before intensive recruiting and conditioning, the Golden Decade was an innocent era in sports when a walk-on like Rockne or the

Gipper, with no intention of playing football, could become a national hero, or a crippled young man like Kentuck could pick up a spear for the first time at the end of his sophomore year and in only one full season become an Olympic contender.

The athletes enjoyed their sports, fought hard, and acquired an increasingly larger fan base, but other than baseball, there was no real entrée to professional sports where you could earn a livelihood for you and your family. They went to college for the education, connections, and a degree that would help them commence a career. Many schools did not even offer scholarships and if they did, did so only to their star players. For the first time, people had time to indulge themselves in the joys of sports with multiple daily papers and the new radio media serving as a blaring megaphone calling attention to the latest amazing teams, athletes and their unbelievable feats—an unassisted triple play, a no-hitter, a 90-yard kickoff return, a massive upset, a last-second win, an undefeated season, a new home run record, the longest hitting streak in history, the fastest man, the highest pole vault, a sub-4-minute mile, a world record javelin throw... Interest in sports would grow exponentially, eventually becoming a mega-billion dollar industry with multi-hundred-million dollar contracts, but that was all in the future, which highlights how truly special this time of innocence was.

———

Gene enjoyed being at Notre Dame, his home, for the previous four years. He looked forward to seeing his teammates and friends. Walking a little taller, he stood out, not just for his height but also as a respected athlete. The underclassman's awkwardness had vanished. He belonged, and he could not wait to get back on the field and perform for Rock.

As he settled into the hot attic of Edwards Hall, where the Minims lived in a long dorm room with two rows of bunk beds, adjacent to Gene's room, he saw that one new student attracted much attention from the young fellows—Rockne's 7-year-old son Billy. Perhaps because his father was the famous football coach and the most famous man in South Bend, Billy became spoiled and extremely disrespectful to his mother, ignoring and disobeying her.

The neighborhood kids found Billy's bragging and attitude insufferable, and one day, while playing cowboys and Indians, they strung him up to a post surrounded by split wood. Billy had told them in no uncertain terms that he should be a cowboy rather than an Indian, so the Indians danced and chanted around Billy at the stake. The game got out of hand when they lit the wood on fire. Perhaps they were just trying to scare Billy, but fueled by dry wood, the fire soon burned fiercely out of control. Badly burned, poor Billy spent several days in the hospital.

It is not clear why Rockne enrolled Billy in the Minims. It might have been to get him away from the kids who burned him, or it might have been to try to straighten out his bad attitude. As a master motivator, one wonders why Rockne could not straighten out his eldest son himself, but parent-child relationships are not always that clear. Billy showed no respect for the nuns or any respect or affection to his mother. Regardless of the reason, Rockne sent Billy to Gene, whose character and motives he trusted. Rockne had seen how much the Minims, who showed up at the games and practices, adored Gene.

Gene not only coached the Minims but also looked out for them at night, nursing those who were sick or wet their beds.

As recommended by the doctor, Rockne asked Gene to massage Billy's legs nightly to keep the scarred, burnt flesh from tightening so he would be able to walk. When he did this, Billy swore like a sailor, something Gene could not condone, especially when it affected the other Minims in the large dorm room, many of whom had never heard such foul language. So, Gene told Billy, "If you swear one more time, I will never massage your legs, and you will never walk again. Act like a man." Stunned, Billy never swore again in Gene's presence and started to become a more disciplined human being. After a year, young Rockne's legs healed, and he was able to walk without pain. His mother came to visit Billy at St. Edwards, and Gene saw the boy tip his hat to her, saying, "Hello, mother." She burst into tears. Gene was proud of Billy. Bonnie Rockne was eternally grateful to Gene for turning her son around. Afterwards, they developed a close relationship.

Rockne was highly pleased with Billy's recovery and changed attitude and was grateful to Gene. Gene was glad he was able to help the man who had taught and done so much for him. Ironically, if Gene had accepted Rockne's scholarship offer, he would not have been able to help Billy, because he would not have been with the Minims.

———

The 1923 backfield featured four juniors. Although they did not start at the beginning of the previous season due to injuries, they proved themselves to be an effective starting unit by the season's end. These four, Stuhldreher, Miller, Layden, and Crowley, would soon be dubbed The Four Horsemen. Rockne looked forward to molding these quick, young men, who might do well if they did not sustain the types of injuries the Irish endured the previous season. This year, he managed to schedule a game against Princeton, the phenomenal team that had won numerous national championships and currently holds that lauded distinction.

Two of the dynamic foursome hailed from Northern Ohio—Harry Stuhldreher of Massillon and Don Miller of Defiance. Harry weighed in at a mere 5'7" and 151 pounds and had become an All-American the previous year as a quarterback and return man. Rockne had coached the Massillon Tigers pro team where Harry Stuhldreher resided. As a teenager, Harry met Rockne, who was coaching there, and snuck him and some of his pals into a game. Massillon and nearby Canton were early football powerhouses at both the high school and pro level. These two cities followed their teams religiously, and the games they played against each other became legendary.

The backup right tackle behind Gene, Edgar "Rip" Miller stood out at Canton McKinley. Rip and Harry, growing up so close together, met during freshman registration and became best friends. (These two Ohio cities are still crazy for football. Whenever a boy is born in Massillon, he receives a football autographed by the high school football team before he leaves the hospital. The NFL was founded in Canton, where it would later house the $700-million Football Hall of Fame Village near McKinley High, where the Hall of Fame game is played every year)

Don Miller, who grew up less than 100 miles from ND, was the fourth of the famous Miller brothers to play for the Irish. Creighton "Red" Miller, a halfback like Don, captained the 1909 team. His second older brother Gerry started at halfback the previous year until he was injured in the second game against St. Louis. As a sophomore, Don beat out the other older competitors to assume his brother's position. Don stood 5' 11" and weighed 151 pounds. Rockne said that Don was the greatest open-ended runner he ever coached.

At 5'11" and 162 pounds, hailing from Green Bay, Wisconsin, Jim Crowly occupied the other halfback position. Known as "Sleepy Jim" for his drowsy-eyed appearance, Crowly outmaneuvered opponents with his clever open-field running and ball handling.

At 6' 160 pounds, Elmer Layden completed the backfield as a fullback from Davenport, Iowa. Gene knew Elmer well from the track team. With a 10-flat 100-yard dash, he was lightning fast, able to outrun anyone on the field.

Nearly all the initial starters from the 1922 team had graduated, and Rock was glad to have Gene and Harvey Brown, the left tackle and captain, back anchoring the line. Although he did not expect another great season, he would rely on a group of talented former sophomores for any success they might achieve. Since the inexperienced backfield only averaged 156 pounds, they, like previous Irish teams, would have to rely on speed and maneuverability versus size. Before the start of the play, the four would shift, stop and be in motion when the center hiked the ball. Such plays confounded the other larger teams, who still relied on brute strength and frequently complained about the shifty Irish.

Rockne enjoyed the theatre and thought of football as a form of entertainment.   He encouraged nicknames like "Kentuck" and "Sleepy" Jim Crowley because it added interest to the team for the fans. Players at any level, whether in a Pee Wee league or the NFL, know they are playing a game, but they also sense in the back of their mind that they are playing for an audience, who they want to perform well, seeking their cheers and adulation. In contrast to the earlier grinding running game, Notre Dame football was spectacular. Rockne utilized theatrical movements and gestures not just because these looked stunning but because they worked.   Because of his games' entertainment value, he played in the largest cities: New York, Chicago, Philadelphia and Los Angeles.

The nature of the game was changing. After the war, America's young men became heroes, and the public wanted to see them play football. Attending a football game had been something only a man would do. Partially due to Rockne's showmanship, husbands started bringing their wives, young men started bringing their girlfriends, and couples went to the games in groups, vastly increasing attendance.

After the loss to Nebraska, Rockne had taken the team, including Gene, to see a show in Chicago to celebrate a nearly unbeaten season. While there, the dancers fascinated him, not just their long legs and beauty but their precise movements and coordinated steps. They inspired him to rethink his backfield's motion, which he drew up on a napkin. Much of Rockne's education and experimentation in chemistry consisted of diagramming elements with electrons buzzing around, the nucleus in elaborate structures, like football plays. His four years mastering the intricate routes of tubes through the post office also provided him with a subtle metaphor to imagine football plays. With his adept mind, fierce intelligence and training, he could see relationships that had eluded other coaches.

The standard diamond formation for college backfields had the quarterback behind the center, the two halfbacks a half-step back on either side of the quarterback, and the fullback a full step behind the quarterback. This is, after all, where the names came from—quarter, half and all the way or the full back. Rockne's new formation gleaned from the dancers was a box with a halfback next to the quarterback.   The other halfback and fullback lined up directly behind the quarterback and halfback. The four men would be in continuous motion until the hike.

Walsh, the center, might hike the ball to the quarterback, who might pass, run, or hand the ball off. Walsh might also hike the ball to the halfback who might run, pass, or kick the ball. Potentially any of the four backs might end up running, passing or receiving the ball. Rockne choreographed and rehearsed his plays to music relentlessly with his backs as if they were dancers until the four could run these in their sleep. With so many possible variations, the other teams could not set their defense and were constantly off balance. Underscoring Rockne's attention to detail, since Layden and Miller were faster than Stuhldreher and Crowley, he fitted them with lighter shoes and thigh pads, so the four could be more in synch.

Defenses in the 1920s were a mirror image of the offense with seven on the line and four backs. Some schools pulled the center back to become a linebacker with six men on the line, but the classic 5-2-4 formation with two linebackers would not come into play for 25 years. Rockne instituted a balanced line with the same number of players on either side of the ball and the ends slightly off the line, making it easier for the ends to maneuver around the opposing end to catch a pass. In what was still primarily a running game, controlling the line of scrimmage and closing gaps constituted the emphasis for most defenses, which Rockne, with his lighter, faster team, endeavored to confound.

Although the press often credited Rockne for inventing the shift, he always deferred to Alonso Stagg. Jesse Harper assisted Stagg at Chicago prior to coming to Notre Dame, bringing the shift with him, where Rockne learned it as his assistant. Rockne did, however, perfect the shift into a highly effective offensive weapon. According to Stuhldreher, the shift master, the object consisted of finding an opponent's weak spot and then concentrating men at the point of attack. The shift made it difficult for an opponent to set their defense before the snap so that they were constantly off balance.

Rockne worked well with the backs but as a former lineman, he also spent time coaching each member of the 7-man line regarding their form, position, tackling, blocking, and gaining leverage over their opponents. That year, Kentuck was stronger and more experienced. He adapted his braces to hold a piece of metal under his foot, helping him simulate a natural arch to overcome his flat feet so he could build leg strength, speed, and gain leverage on the line. In a picture showing him practicing against a smiling Rockne, Gene said, "Sometimes he (Rockne) would run away from me," which caused the rest of the team to laugh.

Since Tom Lieb graduated the previous spring, Gene would have been pleasantly surprised to see his fellow trackman on the field that fall. Tom had enrolled as a graduate student in psychology and would be Rockne's assistant coach taking charge of the line, so he would coach Kentuck on how to perform his old position.

Rockne continued the daily classroom lectures, in which he would invite comments and laughs. Rockne felt that humor was an important aspect of the game, helping to release tension and build camaraderie, which his boys quickly adopted and applied themselves. He did not want them to take themselves too seriously. As one of the few seniors, Gene would teach one of the daily classroom lectures.

Gene also coached groups of players on the field as part of the practice, which not only helped the younger players and built team spirit but also helped the seniors to understand the system better. In addition, it helped teach them leadership, valuable as a coach or in any field of endeavor.

Rockne purposely scheduled the season's first games in late September and early October against two less competitive teams, Kalamazoo and Lombard, to allow his relatively inexperienced team to gain confidence and perfect the box shift. They beat Kalamazoo 66 to 0. The Lombard game proved to be more challenging, only beating them 14 to zero. The next five games would be much tougher, though, starting with Army and ending with Nebraska—their two major rivals.

The inexperienced squad's first challenge would be against their traditional rival, Army. Since West Point's stadium was too small for the epic rivalry, the game would be played outside of West Point in New York City for the first time. Originally scheduled for the Polo Grounds, the Yankees and Giants were competing in the World Series there, so neither field would be available. Therefore, the colleges agreed to meet at Ebbits Field in Brooklyn, later the home of the Dodgers.

Ten years after Notre Dame first upset Army, when Rockne was a player on the team, the eastern papers still did not cover the upstart Western teams, preferring to focus on their traditional favorites. The frugal ND administration wondered if they would be able to recoup train and hotel expenses, and again Rockne had to persuade them to let the team travel to New York. When the cadet corps marched into the stadium, it overflowed with 35,000 anxious, primarily Fighting Irish fans, with another disappointed thousand outside unable to obtain seats.

———

Why did the Eastern Irish in cities such as Boston, New York, and Philadelphia identify so closely with little, Midwestern Notre Dame, with its French name founded by a French missionary with only 1/3rd of its players actually Irish? After all, Rockne was a Norwegian Protestant, not a Catholic. The answer has to do with Irish history and Ireland's centuries-old struggle for independence. In the 1600s, the British took over the Irish lands. Large Anglican landowners, many of whom lived absentee in England, controlled huge estates tended by poor Irish peasants, who essentially had no rights and could not vote. In essence, five percent of the populace controlled the property, legal system, and government, inducing a sense of injustice like what black Americans or South Africans had to endure. They were treated little better than slaves.

At the end of the mini-ice age in the winters of 1841-42, 400,000

Irish died in the potato famine. Even while the wealthy landowners exported and sold their crops, more succumbed to the famine in the latter half of the decade. Estimates showed that a million died in the potato famine with another million migrating to the U.S. The population of Ireland had dropped from 8 million to 4.4 million by 1909, with a continuous stream of Irish immigrants sailing to the U.S., living primarily in Northeastern cities such as Boston, New York and Philadelphia.

To a lesser extent, the Irish in the U.S. were suppressed by laws that prevented them from voting and by prejudice that extended to employment and housing. Rooting for Notre Dame throughout the struggle for independence in Ireland and for justice in the U.S., lifted the long, downtrodden Irishmen's spirits. Even though they lived in the East, they saw upstart Notre Dame's victories against the established Eastern teams as their own. The Irish finally won their independence from Britain less than a year earlier, in December of 1922. It was not until 1927 that Notre Dame officially adopted the Fighting Irish label, although in spirit and because of their fan base, they were always the Fighting Irish.

Gene was excited to learn that his brother, Father Bonaventure, had just returned from Europe and would be in New York while his younger brother played there. Bonaventure not only came to the game, but Rockne arranged to provide the esteemed priest a sideline pass. Whenever he could, to Gene's delight, Bonaventure would attend Gene's games, appearing at Princeton, St. Louis and Notre Dame. Bonaventure likely remembered when Gene spent months with him at the St Louis monastery while his legs were being operated on. After seeing how the operations did not cure his disability, Bonaventure would have been pleased to see how well his youngest brother performed.

———

Roars from the excited Irish fans greeted Kentuck and his Irish teammates as they entered the stadium. While conducting their pre-game stretches, he likely looked over towards Army's undefeated Black Knights, who outweighed the Irish by 15 pounds a man. As the largest starter on the Notre Dame team, Kentuck stood a little taller, puffing up his chest to add some gravitas to the Irish side.

As the game proceeded, the battle at the line was rough, resulting in injuries to players on both sides. At one point, an Army player was penalized 15 yards for throwing a punch. In the first half, Stuhldreher hit the speedy Layden for a TD, the first Army had given up all season. The only way Notre Dame could gain an advantage over Army was through their speed, box formation, and shifts. Army had a new coach that year, John McElway, who was not as experienced as Daly against the shift.

Kentuck and the team performed well on defense and the game became a struggle to gain advantage with frequent fourth down punts. More injuries slowed down the struggle. Halfway through the pitched 4th quarter, Crowley intercepted a pass, running the ball back to the Army 24-yard line and, on the next play, ran for 17 more yards. From the 7-yard-line, after shifting and receiving the hike, Miller faked a pass and then scrambled his way into the end zone.

Notre Dame won the well-fought game 14-0, the first game the superb Army team had lost in two years. The sold-out attendance generated $19,500 for Notre Dame, a princely sum at the time, enough to pay for nearly 40 students' annual expenses. The president, Father Walsh, was pleased. The administration now saw that football could be more than just an expense and could even be a substantial revenue generator. In the future, the Army game would be played at the even larger Polo Grounds and the newly built Yankee Stadium that held 80,000. Irish fans and alumni would no longer complain about the small West Point field.

During the long train rides back to South Bend on Sundays, people from small towns seeking entertainment would go down to the tracks to watch the trains come in. Zany Jim Crowley, as if he were running for president, sometimes went to the back platform and started talking about some of the topics of the day, such as farm subsidies. The boys would gather on the tracks behind the train and clap as he went on, attracting a crowd who would join in on the applause.

After their premier New York trip, the jubilant alumni treated the team to a night on the town in Manhattan on a double-decker bus with the second level open. When the bus was stuck in Times Square's traffic, Jim stood up and started speaking about Prohibition, attracting a crowd of mock cheering fans. This stopped traffic with cars honking their horns until he completed his remarks, thanks to an Irish cop. They hit some of the clubs, including seeing the Ziegfield Follies, where Will Rogers, the popular, down-home comedian, and satirist, talked at length about the Irish team. Kentuck was starting to feel less like a country bumpkin and more like a sophisticated man of the world.

Encouraged by their stunning victory, The Irish looked forward to their next game against the National Champs, a game Gene had been preparing for all year and indeed all his life.

13: Exaltation and Deprivation

Next up was the game of the year against the National Championship team, Princeton, who had won 21 such championships, more than any other college before or since. From 1869, when college football started to evolve, until 1914, the game had been dominated by three Ivy League schools—Yale, Princeton and Harvard. Contributing to their prestige, over a third of the presidents (15) and four of the last seven, came from the "Big Three." One of these three, usually Yale or Princeton, won the National Championship in all but two years—an astounding 41 times. It wasn't until the 1900s that other teams, such as Michigan, Chicago, and Army, started appearing in some of the selections.

Not unlike today with over ten selection entities, there was a lack of consistency. For instance, Notre Dame's undefeated teams in 1920 when Gene lettered and in 1921 had been selected by three selection groups, but there were four other national champions elected by other groups in each year. Adding to the confusion, sometimes a selector had two colleges tied for the honor. A win against Princeton would greatly enhance Notre Dame's image and probably lead to its first undisputed national title.

Rockne focused on the Princeton game like no other, the most important challenge of his career up until then. Borrowing from his experience teaching chemistry, he held daily lectures at lunchtime, requiring all team members to attend. There, he would joke with the players and detail plays and assignments on the board, constantly repeating these so they would remember. In the afternoon, after warm-ups, during 90-minute practices, they would run through the previously discussed plays. Expecting an easy victory against an inferior opponent, Princeton who at one time had been coached by the previous president, President Wilson (1913-1921) barely practiced.

Four days after their return to South Bend from New York, they would repeat the long trip back east to Princeton, New Jersey. It might have made sense to stay east, but the administration wanted the players back in class.

Thirty-five thousand fans filled the stands that day, mostly Princeton alumni used to seeing their team be victorious, thinking this game would be a rout against an inferior Western team. At 2:30, Emery kicked off to Layden. The Irish lost yards on their first possession and had to punt. On the second down of the second possession, Kentuck opened a hole for Layden, who scampered for 39 yards. He loved blocking for these four talented backs and watching them run like antelopes. Don Miller ran for a 20-yard touchdown. Layden kicked off to Van Gerbig, who was tackled at the 20. On the next play, Kentuck tackled Dinsmore for a yard loss stalling the Tigers' drive.

In the second quarter, with passes by Layden and Stuhldreher, Notre Dame scored another touchdown. Later, Smith of the Tigers blocked a Crowley punt for a touchback, and the half ended with a score of 12 to 2, Irish. In the third quarter, Miller had a couple of 40+ yard runs, with Crowley picking up numerous yards but no points.

Down by only a touchdown and field goal, the loyal Princeton fans still expected a comeback. In the fourth quarter, Notre Dame's Maher scored a touchdown and Layden dropkicked the extra point. Late in the quarter, as the clock ran down, Princeton began passing until- speedy Layden intercepted a pass and scampered for a 45-yard TD. Notre Dame won by a stunning score of 25 to 2. Kentuck made numerous tackles and was featured in the *South Bend Tribune*.

The papers printed a photo of the "Perfect Play" with all the linemen, including Kentuck making "perfect" blocks against their Princeton opponents and Harry Stuhldreher running around end. The perfect play would later occupy a place of honor in the Notre Dame Hall of Fame. Fifty years later, in 1983, TRW, a Fortune 50 aerospace company, had a picture of the '23 team on its annual calendar. Gene's son, Rob, worked at TRW's corporate headquarters at the time and was surprised to see his father when he flipped the calendar over to October.

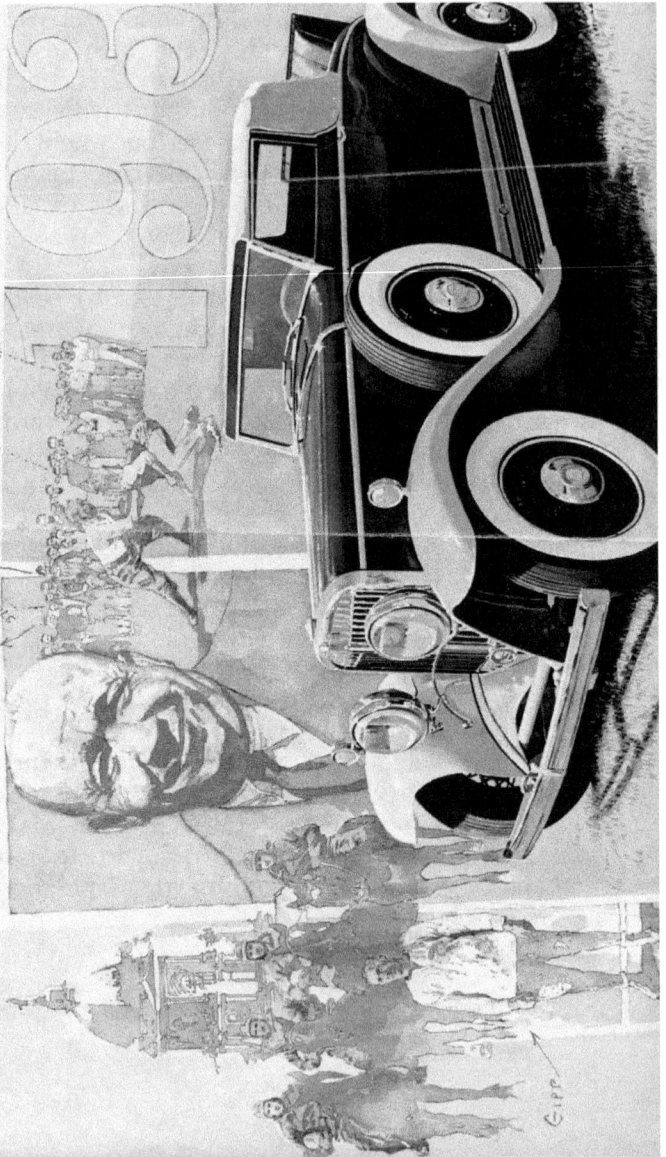

1931 Mercer

TRW-CALENDER 1983

... University of Notre Dame football coach Knute Rockne, who'd popularized such offensive plays as the forward pass, died in an airplane crash. ... Mercer introduced a striking tan and blue convertible coupe at the 1931 New York National Automobile Show.

The flaws expected of a prototype didn't appear in this model. With coachwork by Merrimac Body Company, the Mercer was comfortable, powerful, and well designed. It seemed Mercer's new president, Harry Wahl, would see his dreams fulfilled. But the

economic crisis threatened the stability of the new Mercer Company. There wasn't enough capital and the factory up for production and operating at a loss proved imprudent. Wahl had no prototype to exhibit Auto Show. Out of desperation, he displayed water of projected styles. But the depression obscured his automobile's potential.

F. BACH   GENE OBERST   WEIBEL   CROWLEY

GIPP

TRW Calendar, October 1983
Rockne coaching 1923 team middle of picture
Kentuck is the tallest in the forefront of the team, just behind
Rockne, with annotations by Kentuck

Back at Notre Dame, the students gathered at the field house to follow the game over the gridgraphie, a remarkable device that ahead of its time, showed players' progress on the field as points of light, with each play based on telegraphed input, similar to following a game on an ESPN app on an iPhone. Students and fans would gather at a pool hall downtown or at the fieldhouse to "watch" the game. When the team arrived at South Bend, a huge crowd and band greeted the conquering heroes at the station. They cheered the team as they exited the train. The fame and notoriety began to affect Kentuck—it felt pretty good to be a key member of such a fabled team—a team of destiny.

In a time before the Internet, smartphones, and TV, most sports fans learned of the games through the multiple editions of the papers throughout the day. The first radio station broadcast occurred in Pittsburg in 1920, but New York did not have its first station until 1922. They broadcast 1923 games against Army and Princeton, but it is doubtful few other than the wealthy had the expensive radios to hear the first sports broadcasters. The previously silent Eastern press, which paid little attention to Notre Dame, or any Western team for that matter, went wild over the Irish, heaping praise upon the eleven and especially the dazzling backfield of Miller, Layden, Crowley, and Stuhldreher—"The finest backfield seen in the east for over a decade."

Later in the week, they held a huge celebration in South Bend for the victorious Irish with one of Indiana's senators speaking at the rally. Rockne had the team stand to receive the cheers of the assembled, jubilant students and teachers. Throughout that week, students in Kentuck's classes patted him on the back, engaged him in conversations about the game, and encouraged him to greatness throughout the remainder of the season. He tried to remain humble, but all the attention was starting to swell his head.

Extremely pleased with his young team's results thus far, Rockne could not have expected more of them. The Irish confronted Georgia Tech next at Carter Field. During the game, Rock heard fervent cheers whenever Kentuck made a tackle. "Go Kentuck, yea Kentuck—Kentuck, Kentuck, Kentuck." He looked over to the section that held the rambunctious Minims, including his son, whose hero was Kentuck. He had never heard a lineman attract so much attention. Gene was a little embarrassed but waved and smiled meekly to his fledglings. No one loved the team more than these lads did, and the team appreciated their young admirers, often spending time with them after practices. Unlike the previous hard-fought battle against this premier southern team, Notre Dame easily won, 35 to 7.

After the game, Gene walked out of the fieldhouse behind two students whom he happened to overhear. One said that the team was made up of a bunch of dumb jocks, especially the big linemen. The other replied that not all the players were that dumb for that Kentuck was one of the best students in his class. Gene felt proud.

During the following game against Purdue at Carter Field, a referee overheard a lineman talking smack to Kentuck saying, "I hear you pray before each game."

"Sure," answered Kentuck.

"What do you pray for—victory?"

"No," replied Kentuck, "I just pray that I won't hurt you fellows too much."

They beat Purdue 34 to zero.

————

For games, Rockne, with cigar in hand, sat on his camp chair with his manager, assistants and quarterbacks sitting next to him. As the game progressed, he coached each of the 11 players individually, calling out directions to them, like a juggler with 11 balls in the air or a computer server managing 11 users simultaneously. The manager would record his constant stream of comments. On the surface, he was cool and collected, but underneath his mind constantly churned. In later years, coaches would review the game on film and go over it with their players after-the-fact, Rockne did this in real time. Kentuck would receive instant feedback on how he blocked or tackled, enabling him to constantly improve his performance, play after play, game after game. His criticism was not cutting but rather constructive and positive. Yelling at Kentuck accomplished his ultimate goal for he wanted Kentuck to learn, think, and constantly improve his performance; he wanted him to collaborate with him, not be afraid of him. Eventually, he lit his cigar, which he continued to twirl.

With a sparkling 6-0 record and growing national reputation as the best team in the nation, the "wonder team," faced their tough archrival Nebraska next, the only team who had beaten them the previous year.

In the 1920s, the influence of the KKK and their attitudes stretched into the Midwest. A headline in a Lincoln Star article read, "The Horrible Hibernians Arrive Today." At a supposedly private pre-game practice, Nebraska freshmen wearing green caps as if they were Notre Dame students snuck into the stadium and yelled anti-Irish epithets. Thirty thousand people packed the stands for the game, yelling Irish and Catholic slurs, like "Mick, Mackerel Snapper, Paddy, and Potato Nigger."

Klan activity had died out by 1900, but the Klan enjoyed a resurgence after WWI. Prejudice extended not only to the blacks, but also to Jews, Irish, immigrants and any Catholics. On several occasions, Notre Dame tried to gain admission to the Big Ten but was denied because some of the universities such as Nebraska, did not want a Catholic college among its members.

The rumble and tumble first quarter resulted in a standoff with frequent kicks, and neither team was able to gain an advantage, as the Irish struggled against the much bigger line.

Kentuck faced a worthy opponent, the Cornhuskers' left tackle and captain, Ed Weir, the team's first two-time All-American. The Omaha World-Herold later would name him one of the best athletes in Nebraska history. Kentuck outweighed Weir by a few pounds, but as a champion high hurdler, Weir was much quicker. Their other tackle, Bud Weller weighed in at a hefty 250 pounds. After mesmerizing Army, Princeton, and Georgia Tech, Nebraska diagnosed Notre Dame's shift well, and the four backs struggled to gain ground against the much larger foe.

On fourth down, the fourth play of the second quarter, the right halfback, Dave "Big Moose" Noble ran for 24 yards off the left end for the TD. Noble was 6'2", 195 pounds outweighing the Notre Dame backs by 30 to 40 pounds and all the Irish line, except for Kentuck. If a back was that big, imagine the size of the line. Frequently outweighed, Notre Dame relied on their shift and runs to confuse opponent defenses. With their running game stagnating, they turned to the pass, but Nebraska thwarted the passing game too.

At the beginning of the fourth quarter, Noble caught a 15-yard pass and ran 5 yards with an Irish player draped over his back for the touchdown. On its last drive, Stuhldreher mounted a successful passing attack that ended with a 20-yard touchdown pass to Cerney, but it was too late. Nebraska beat the Irish 14 to 7 in one of the biggest upsets of the year. The Cornhuskers had defeated the preemptive favorite for the National Championship.

After the game, Rockne praised Kentuck's play at the line. The Scholastic called him the star of the line. The Associated Press wrote, "The Notre Dame line led by Captain Brown and (O)Berst battled fiercely, but the Nebraska forwards were too heavy and too shifty." This deservedly loomed as one of the top victories in Cornhusker history, with Lincoln erupting in a jubilant celebration.

The statistics tell the story of the game. The Irish gained ten more yards, 238 to 228, but Nebraska eclipsed them with their running game, 208 to 48. With their hope of a national title crushed once again by another devastating defeat at the hands of the Cornhuskers, the train ride back to South Bend was a solemn one.

The Irish accumulated two more victories against Butler and Carnegie Tech. For his last game at Notre Dame, Kentuck was the featured player on the Carnegie Tech postcard. Each week featured a star on the card, sold by students at the exit gates. Other postcards featured each of the Four Horsemen and Maher. Kentuck's last game would come against St. Louis, with the Irish being heavy favorites. On the dining car on the train ride to St. Louis, many on the squad became sick and experienced diarrhea just before the kickoff. According to Gene, "We weren't feeling well and it showed in our play. There was no score at the half and Rock was seething. We knew we'd get a rousing final prep talk and we did," Gene recalled.

— FOOTBALL —

AT PITTSBURGH, SATURDAY, NOVEMBER 24

19 | N. D. | 23

GENE OBERST

FINAL SCORE
NOTRE DAME, - - - - 26
CARNEGIE TECH., - - - 0

FOOTBALL

HOME-COMING---NOVEMBER 3, 1923

DON MILLER

19 | N. D. | 23

FINAL SCORE
NOTRE DAME 34
PURDUE 7

FOOTBALL

SATURDAY, OCTOBER 20

ELMER LAYDEN

19 | N. D. | 23

FINAL SCORE
NOTRE DAME 25
PRINCETON 2

FOOTBALL
SATURDAY, OCTOBER 27

19 | N. D. | 23

FINAL SCORE
NOTRE DAME, · · · · 35
GEORGIA TECH., · · · 7

HARRY STUHLDREHER
"The Little General."

FOOTBALL
SATURDAY, OCTOBER 13

19 (ND) 23

FINAL SCORE
NOTRE DAME, · · · · 13
ARMY, · · · · · · · 0

JAMES CROWLEY

Player postcards for Kentuck and the Four Horseman

"He pulled out all the stops and even tossed in a few cuss words, which was unusual. However, his young son, Billy, (Gene's charge) a precocious kid, had sneaked into the locker room and was in a corner where we could see him but his dad couldn't."

"Billy kept grinning and covering his mouth so he wouldn't laugh out loud. None of us was paying any attention to the coach. We all were watching Billy."

"Finally, Rock looked around the corner and saw his son. He thumbed him out of the room but the speech was ruined. We won the game 6-0, but Rock's speech for once had nothing to do with the victory."

Over Kentuck's five years, the team's record was 45-3-1—a 94% winning record against some of the best teams in the nation. (He didn't play in 1921 when they won all their games.) Over Rockne's nine seasons as a player and coach, he had only lost 4 games versus 70 wins (95%). New York Times columnist and United Press Sports

Editor Henry L. Farrell listed Gene as a second-team All-American when only eleven were selected to each team.

Minims

Called the "Rockne of the Minims," Gene continued to coach the juniors throughout the winter and spring. His little men were undefeated over three years in four sports despite sometimes being outweighed by 20 or 30 pounds a man.

In football, they outscored their opponents 233 to 13. The last game of the season was played against the Hebrew Eagles, who outweighed them by 30 pounds per player. Down 6-0 at the end of the game with the ball on their own 10-yard line, the team bravely fought back. Utilizing three trick plays Gene borrowed from Rockne, they carried the ball 90 yards to score and then kicked the extra point to win the game. With this final victory, they won the All-Western championship again with a record of 27 and 0 over Gene's tenure.

The basketball season started with players who had never played before, but with expert guidance from Kentuck, they beat teams like South Bend Junior High. Practically every game was won against freshmen and sophomores in high school.

Earlier in the summer, as part of his duties with the Minims, Gene had become the troop leader of one of the first two Boy Scout troops at Notre Dame formed with the Minims. Both troops were founded at the same time. During the Christmas break, he took the troop on a two-week winter campout to the wilds of Michigan, a welcome change from lonely Christmases spent away from family at the college for he was with his boys.

———

Bothered by his initials, EWO, standing for Eugene William Oberst, Gene thought he might change his name. EWO sounded weak and did not match his estimation of himself formed when he first read *Pushing to the Front*. The remarkable performances in track and football in 1923, the team's successes, the headlines, and the adulation from fellow students all went to his head. He had been baptized Eugene William George Oberst but had always gone by Eugene William, dropping the George. He decided to change his name to Eugene George Oberst, EGO, which better represented his assessment of himself. Many athletes become egotistical and Gene was no exception, but it is doubtful many changed their initials. So, after the football season ended, he went to the South Bend court and legally changed his name.

That winter Gene acquired his fifth letter and joined the

Monogram club for their annual Monogram absurdities extravaganza. The shows that Rockne and Gus Dorais inaugurated provided welcome relief from the rigors of sports and an opportunity for the players to bond outside of the practice field and hard-fought battles. He played "Big Orchestra" in the "Wild Bull on Campus" scene along with Tom Lieb. The four backs were featured in the show with Jim Crowley the star, dancing in an immensely well-received minstrel number. The students and athletes in the crowd rolled on the floor with laughter especially when the big linemen danced in skirts.

The club awarded Rockne a watch as an expression of their regard for their outstanding coach. Rockne, never short on words, was a little choked up, as was Gene when his mentor received the award. Gene was in the chorus as they ended the show with a song about Rock.

> *Gaboon, Gaboon, Gaboon.*
> *You are mine from September till June,*
> *What tales you could tell*
> *Of this place where we dwell*
> *Gaboon! Gaboon! Gaboon!*

Students could be overheard singing the catchy song as they left the auditorium.

Time passed quickly as the Minims basketball season gave way to their baseball and track seasons. He organized a "state" track meet for the Minims, which included bicycle events.

The Minims

For the closing pages of this athletic section, nothing is more fitting than a story of the little fighting men of St. Edward's Hall. Under the name of Minims and Minim Specials, they have made a record during the past three years which will make them famous in the world of boys and which will add glory to the name of Notre Dame athletics. Fighting against odds such as would discourage any Back Yard League, sometimes outweighed thirty pounds to the man, and playing against lads several years older than themselves, the little Minims have added another undefeated year to their record, making three consecutive years of victory.

In football, the Minims played six outside games and were victorious in every game. The season's figures of 233 points scored to their opponents 13, tells the story of their great offensive and defensive power, and the consistent winning of twenty-seven consecutive games within the last three years, marks them as the boy All-Western champions.

The last game of the season was played against the Hebrew Eagles, who outweighed the Minims thirty pounds to the man, and this game was characteristic

Minim's Special '23

"Rock" and his men

As spring approached, Kentuck hoped to prove himself a worthy competitor in the javelin—worthy for a steamer ticket to Paris. Based on last year's performance, he would need to substantially improve his distances. Could he do it?

14: Records Shattered

The spring track season would be a critical one for Gene and the fulfillment of his Olympic dreams. He and his buddy, Tom Lieb, hoped they would both make the team, which their coach, Rockne, would revel in. Tom had won the NCAA discus championship in 1922 and 1923, making him a favored contender. On the other hand, Gene had done well the year before, but due to Angier, had finished lower in the rankings and had not even qualified for the NCAA championships. He would have to improve, consistently throwing further, if he wanted to make the Olympic team, for there were several athletes throughout the nation who threw the spear further than he did, including Frieda of Chicago, Priester of Mississippi, Whelchel of Georgia and Neufeld of California. He had practiced relentlessly during the summer, but then he was working out for football too. His new braces enabled him to run better and throughout the football season, he had grown stronger. Blocking and pushing against some of the best tackles in the nation helped him build leg and upper body strength that would aid in tossing the javelin. Although the term had not yet been coined, he had been cross-training, continuing to work out in the gym throughout the winter. Finally, as the weather improved, he was able to go outside and throw long.

Gene's best throw in competition the previous year was nearly 188 but most of his other tosses were around 180 feet. He knew he would have to throw 10 to 15 feet further to qualify for the Olympics and beat the competition. He still struggled with his accuracy, with most of his javelins landing far to the left, losing 10 to 12 feet on the arc. Like any athlete in any sport, he also struggled with consistency. His teammate, Moes, uncorked the amazing Carter field record of 196' 5" the previous year, a good 15 feet further than his usual result. Moes would also be a contender and he hoped they could both qualify.

The season's first meet came at DePauw on April 7th. There, Gene set the field record, recording a distance of 195'7", substantially farther than before. He was definitely heading in the right direction.

A major test would be the upcoming Kansas Relays on April 17 in Lawrence, Kansas, the second such annual meet. Over 1,000 athletes from nearly 100 universities, colleges, and prep schools competed in the carnival, as they called the major relays of the year, with colleges from

15 states, including those as far-flung as Texas, California, Oregon, and New Hampshire. This would serve as an early test for Olympic hopefuls. The weather was cool, so the coaches did not expect to break many of the records. Since the javelin is the lightest and flies the furthest of the four field projectiles launched at such meets, the shotput, discuss, hammer and javelin. Traveling up to 200 feet, weather and atmospheric conditions impact it the most. Like a homerun with the same amount of force, the javelin would travel further during a hot, dry day than a cool, wet one when there is more air resistance. But wind creates even more challenges. A stiff headwind drastically decreases its flight path, and being so long, a side wind would throw it radically off course, making it difficult to stick in the ground, leading to a possible disqualification.

Despite the cool conditions, Gene launched the best toss of the day – 197'6", ten feet further than his best the previous year. With this mark, he took first place, setting the meet and field records, something that would surely garner the attention of the Olympic committee

———

The prestigious Penn relays occurred the following week in Philadelphia. Because there were so many renowned participants and the odds of winning were so long, looking to save expenses, Rockne had sent only one of his best trackmen to each year's meet, sending Gene's buddies Gus Desch and Tom Lieb each of the previous two years. When he asked Gene if he would like to attend the hallowed meet, Gene felt highly honored and enthusiastically accepted. Traveling to Philadelphia on the train seemed odd to Kentuck since he was accustomed to being with his teammates on such long trips. This would be his first venture to historical Philly, a city that would later play a major role in his life.

Rockne accompanied Gene to the meet. Gene had spent hours scraping his javelin with glass to gain proper weight and balance. When appropriately whittled, he would guard it carefully. Rockne would carry Gene's suitcase on such trips, so Kentuck could carry his precious javelins. The long trips would have enabled Gene to get to know his mentor even better. They likely discussed Billy's progress and coaching, which, given his experience with the Minims, was a natural fit as a career. Gene would consider a coaching career, but since he had changed his major to commerce, following the example of the great entrepreneurs he studied, he was anxious to get into business.

Forty thousand fans packed the stadium with an astounding 600 colleges planning to attend. With teams from Cuba, Canada, and Britain, the relays became an international meet containing numerous Olympic stars and hopefuls. Gene would face some of the best in the nation, including Harry Frieda of nearby Chicago, who won the 1923 NCAA championship. During the qualifying rounds, Harry had the best toss of 176'11'. But Gene performed remarkably well with a launch of

196' 6", eclipsing the old record by nearly nine feet. Frieda took second place, 20 feet short of Gene's astounding mark. The third and fourth-place finishers were less than six inches behind Harry's mark.

Rockne told Gene how proud he was. Several articles in papers throughout the U.S. featured his record-breaking performance. With marks fewer than six feet below the American record, Gene now warranted more attention from the Olympic committee, especially Frieda's illustrious coach Alonzo Stagg, who would be the coach of the American track team. Stagg was likely there to appraise prospects for the upcoming Olympics and support Harry from his team. He and Rock, who in high school had wanted to play for coach Stagg, likely talked to each other about track, football and their hometown, Chicago.

Gene's friends back at South Bend saw him at the movies that week at the local Palace theatre. *Pathe news* showed excerpts of the relays including Gene tossing the javelin with an account of his remarkable record-slashing performance.

The Penn relays also included a preview of the Olympic competition for the world's fastest man, featuring Britain's speedster, Eric Liddell, the Scot from Edinburgh University. Louis Clarke of John Hopkins narrowly beat Liddell in the 220-yard dash. The Cambridge relay team, which featured another of the fastest men alive, Harold Abrahams, competed in the medley relay, where they finished third to Penn State and Georgetown. (Liddell and Abrahams would be the main characters in the Academy Award-winning film *Chariots of Fire*.)

On his victorious trip back from the Penn Relays, Gene stopped by in Connecticut to see his cousins, the Eisenmans. His father and aunt Christene stayed with their aunt Elizabeth Oberst Eisenman in Poughkeepsie when they first arrived in America. Earlier they had visited Gene's family in Owensboro. The Eisenmans later moved to Connecticut. Gene also stopped at Niagara Falls, which even at the end of April was still frozen. There he stood on the precipice of the frozen falls, looking like a 170-foot multi-tiered, glistening, white frosted wedding cake, forming a spectacular scene.

———

On May 3rd, Gene once again faced his nemesis, Milton Angier, in ND's meet against Illinois. Angier had beaten him every time they faced off, but Gene had worked hard since then to build up his body and improve his form and distance. He looked forward to their competition. In addition to Angier, Illinois boasted another Olympic javelin hopeful, Fred Schildhauer. The wind was howling that day and it would be difficult to let loose a respectable throw.

There is no detailed record of the competition, but it might have transpired as follows. Each athlete is allowed up to six total attempts. During large meets, such as the relays, each athlete receives three initial throws with only the top competitors advancing to the finals with an additional three attempts, but in a dual meet, each participant throws the full six tosses.

By now, Gene's awkwardness had dissipated, becoming a well-disciplined and confident athlete, but as he grabbed his carefully whittled javelin and approached the field, his nervousness took him by surprise—perhaps competing against Angier meant more than he thought. He shook it off, ran to the line, and let the javelin soar, but like a hooking golf ball, the crosswind grabbed the spear sending it far to the left. Both Illini field-men easily beat his mark. He fouled on his second toss, and his third was little better than the first, again carried off course by the fierce wind. Instead of landing and sticking in the ground, the errant projectile fluttered, fell aimlessly, and landed flatly on the grass—a disqualification. Now he was worried that he might not get off a good toss, not even finish in the top three. Lose points for the ND and be embarrassed. Before the fourth attempt, he took a deep breath to calm his nerves. He ran up to the line, twisted, crossed over, reached back, lunged forward, and let the spear fly. As the projectile crested then arched downward and stuck with a twang, he could see that he registered a respectable distance that bested the other two worthy competitors.

On the fifth round, Schildhauer let loose the farthest mark of the day—over 190 feet. Then Angier let loose an even better toss. Considering the wind, this was an amazing feat. The Illini stood at first and second with Gene third, but at least he was on the board. Gene approached the line for the final throw and took a deep breath. This time it felt effortless as he let if fly. The javelin soared and kept flying, nearing Angier's flag. It was impossible to tell who won from so far away, so the three ran to where the far-away javelins landed to ascertain the winner. It was close. After careful measurement, the referee confirmed that Gene had won by a mere foot with a distance of 192' 11". Gene had finally beaten his archrival and the American record holder. He felt incredible, thinking that he had a great chance at the Olympics now.

Unfortunately, the Notre Dame team did not fare well against the Illini, perhaps the best team in the nation. Gene took the only first place with the team losing 102 to 24. Rockne was not pleased but congratulated Gene on his performance, "Finally got him Kentuck, great job. I think you just might have earned a chance at a berth on that boat to Paree."

The next meet on May 17 pitted the Irish against the Michigan Agricultural College's (M.A.C.) Aggies, who the following year would change their name to the Michigan State Spartans. That day the javelin competitors faced a light wind but Gene was able to register 190' 9 3/8". Rockne felt much better as his team beat the Aggies 81 to 45.

The Klan comes to South Bend.

In the ongoing struggle between the more established rural population and growing immigrant-based cities, Prohibition passed while the boys were away fighting in World War I. After the war, due to patriotic fever, religious bigotry, and anti-immigrant tendencies, racism reared its ugly head once more. Many traditionalists were upset by what the Roaring 20s, exemplified—flappers in scandalously short skirts, liquor-infested speakeasies, and sexually arousing jazz. The lax morals of the "lost generation," coined for those who had endured the horrors in the muddy, hellish trenches of WWI where you could die in an instant from a well-aimed shot or artillery shell and their cohort felt disoriented, directionless, aimless. Like the Viet Nam vets, they suffered from shell shock or what would later be called PTSD.

This version of the perennial conflict was nothing new since America had been dealing with such divisiveness for over 100 years. The hostility tended to reemerge whenever a new wave of immigrants washed up upon America's Shore. Earlier settlers were concerned that their power and control over the political levers of the nation were being diluted by these newcomers or, in the case of blacks and women, these new voters.

Such strains first appeared in the 1840s with the Native American Party, which was followed by the Know-Nothings in the 1850s, who beat or killed numerous people for trying to vote and controlled numerous state and local governments throughout the country. Then, following the Civil War, when blacks accrued the right to vote, the Ku Klux Klan was hatched. Up until the 1900s, the southern whites were able to pass Jim Crow laws that vastly restricted black liberties. A new version of the KKK reappeared in the 1920s. Recently a new incarnation of the nationalist movement reappeared in the 2010s in reaction to the illegal immigration of Hispanics and Asians and the black lives movement.

D.C. Stephenson went to the KKK's leadership in Atlanta to start a chapter in Indiana, hoping to organize the state against these corruptive influences. The Klan blamed Jewish bankers, Wall Street tycoons, blacks, and the secretive Roman Catholic Church for the ills that plagued the country. Not surprisingly, Notre Dame became a prime target of the Klan's conspiracy mongers. D.C. soon recruited 250,000 members, one-third of Indiana's male population. Grand Dragon Stephenson soon became a millionaire from his share of the membership fees and sales of white hoods and robes to newly recruited Klan members.

Notre Dame's recent athletic prowess not only represented much to the downtrodden Irish and Catholics but also to the Klan, who saw their success and growing confidence as a challenge to their rightful dominance. Some thought Notre Dame's priests conspired with Rome against the United States. Klan members or sympathizers soon occupied nearly all of Indiana's political positions, including the governorship, senators, congressmen, and state and local representatives, with

Stephenson becoming the most powerful man in the state.

Notre Dame stuck like a thorn in D.C.'s foot, so Stephenson decided to hold a Klavern in South Bend for a week with meetings, rallies, marches, and a cross-burning or two to teach those "cat lickers" a lesson. He hoped to instigate a fight with the students, which would stir outrage against the Catholics, cause a backlash, and recruit even more members, thereby making him that much more money.

Gene had a growing interest in politics and heard about the upcoming rally. Off-campus students spread the word that Klansmen in full regalia were directing traffic downtown. A large group of students gathered at the train station and got into a fight with the first of the arriving Klansmen, in which the Klan endured the worst of it. The police broke up the fight and restored order as other Klan-laden trains arrived. Afterwards, 500 students marched to the Klan's office in South Bend, where they threw potatoes at the red lights of the Klan's symbolic cross. Quarterback Harry Stuhldreher connected with the last light to cheers of his fellow students. Gene thought this was entertaining but not constructive. The students were enthralled with their symbolic victory.

Rumors spread that a cross was burning on campus and that a student had been killed, neither of which were true. Hundreds of students rushed downtown to confront their enemy in their territory. Gene joined them, but even though he was nearly the largest man on campus, he would not fight and was more likely to break up a fight than start one, as he had frequently done with his Minims. Even though he was a Southerner where those he knew had some of the same attitudes, he could not condone the Klan. But like a moth to light, he felt drawn to the events, for this was real-life history happening in his little corner of the world.

The County Sheriff, who was a member of the KKK, deputized several Klansmen. These "deputies" met the first students with billy clubs cracking several stunned students' heads, the blood streaming down their faces, dripping off their chins. Horrified by what he saw, Gene urged his classmates to go back to school. Next to him, a fellow student had a bottle he was about to throw at one of the pseudo-sheriffs. Gene envisioned the bottle hitting the man and igniting a round of deadly gunfire. Gene grabbed the student's arm on the backswing, telling him in a deep voice he used to control an errant Minim, "You really do not want to do that, do you." The student faced with the half-foot taller Kentuck, whom he rooted for at the games, let the bottle drop softly to the ground.

The scene began to look ugly with enraged students having red angry faces gearing up to fight the Klan members, who looked equally enraged, ready to crack more student heads. The Klansmen, now holed up in their headquarters, peered out the window where Gene thought he saw a pistol.

Gene then heard that the president would speak. Father Walsh, who thought the situation had been defused following the initial confrontation, went to the courthouse hoping to end the bloodshed. He thought some of the Klan may have guns and, if threatened, might use these against the students. He called the students over to hear him and attempted to calm them down saying:

> *Whatever challenge may have been offered tonight to your patriotism, whatever insult may have been offered to your religion, you can show your loyalty to Notre Dame and to South Bend by ignoring all threats. The constituted authorities have only the desire to preserve order and peace and protect everyone. That is their duty. Others can well leave to their hands the maintenance of peace and the punishment of anything that is wrong. If tonight there have been violations of the law, it is not the duty of you and your companions to search out the offenders.*

> *I know that in the midst of excitement, you are swayed by emotions that impel you to answer challenge with force. As I said in the statement issued last Saturday, a single injury to a Notre Dame student would be too great a price to pay for any deed or any program that concerned itself with antagonisms. I should dislike very much to be obliged to make explanations to the parents of any student who might be injured—even **killed** in a disturbance that could arise out of any demonstration such as has been started tonight.*
> *There is no loyalty that is greater than the patriotism of a Notre Dame student. There is no conception of duty higher than that which a Notre Dame man holds for his religion or his university. I know that if tonight any of the property of the university or any of its privileges were threatened, and I should call upon you, you would rise to a man to protect it. It is with the same loyalty to Notre Dame that I appeal to you to show your respect for South Bend and the authority of the city by dispersing.*

Father Walsh, pointing a finger at the building in which the Klan had holed themselves up, said: "I know that if I told you boys to go back there and show the Klansmen of what stuff you are made of, you would tear that building apart, leaving no stone upon a stone!" There was an instinctive surge toward the building, a movement which Father Walsh stopped in his next sentence. "But I know, too, that you have confidence enough in me so that if I tell you to go back to the college, you will obey me, and you will leave to my judgment what is best to be done. And so, I tell you: Go back to the college!" With a roar, the students formed ranks and, in columns of four, as if they were an Army battalion, marched back to Notre Dame.

No doubt, some of the Klansmen, who saw the angry, jeering mob of outraged, athletic young men outside, were afraid for their lives and grateful to Father Walsh for saving their necks in the tense situation that they intentionally initiated. Others wanted to escalate the conflict into a gang fight. The KKK considered this a victory for the Klan for they had successfully provoked the Notre Dame students and inflated the actions of the "anarchistic" Catholics in their publications. Afterwards, Father Walsh received anonymous mail from Klan members, threatening to blow up the school. The campus was on edge the rest of the school year, with students walking guardedly at night for fear of white hooded knights jumping out of the bushes.

Within a couple of years, D.C. Stephenson was indicted for sex crimes and attempted murder. The Klan quickly declined in membership and political power.

––––––

The state meet immediately followed the Klavern on May 24th at Carter Field, so Gene turned his attention once again to his javelin. Other than the results, the details of the meet are not available, but here is how it likely transpired. He practiced relentlessly until Thursday. His routine included exercises and repeated mock throws, in which he went through all the motions of the first two launch stages, but instead of throwing the spear, held on to it at the end. He would then practice his release throwing the spear 10 or 20 yards at a time. Finally, he would throw the javelin for distance, but since it flew so far, it would take him time to retrieve it. Rockne would not let him practice on Friday since he wanted his star fresh for the Saturday meet and did not want his hard-working. star athlete throwing his arm out before then.

Prior to the meet, Gene honed his new javelin, shaving off the mud and just a little to ensure the right balance and weight. The wooden javelins would frequently break, so he would have to repeat this process throughout the year on new javs. This ritual helped him relax and focus on the upcoming competition. Saturday turned out to be a beautiful hot day, with a blue sky and mercifully no wind—ideal for flying javelins. After setting records at the Kansas and Penn Relays and finally beating his nemesis, Angier, Gene felt confident he would do well on this gorgeous, sun-filled day. Of course, as he learned from the Nebraska football game, victory was never assured, especially with the finicky javelin.

He went through his warm-up drill, stretching, running, and loosening his arm; then he discarded his sweats. He now had a full uniform, but he kept the football spikes that he was accustomed to wearing. His braces were in place, tightly laced, and working well. His javelin was perfectly honed and balanced, and he felt confident! His first throw was a respectable one, and although it might not win the meet, it would guarantee him a spot in the finals. Gene had to wait as a couple dozen others threw their javelin, trying to keep his arm loose and stay relaxed. Elmer Layden, who also tossed the javelin for Notre Dame, stopped by to encourage Gene, saying, "This is not my real event, Kentuck, but I want to see you throw it out of the stadium today."

On his second of the final three throws, he uncorked a beauty. Concerned that he again threw it to the left, he saw the spear keep climbing before it finally reached its pinnacle far above the field then arched its way on its reentry back towards Earth. The other athletes stopped and marveled at Kentuck's wooden shaft flying through the air, set against an azure blue sky as if powered by a propeller. To them, it looked like it would never reach the ground. When it finally stuck, it was far beyond any of the other participant's flags. It had sailed 202' 10", setting the Indiana and Carter Field records—a remarkable result that would stand for 35 years. The distance was less than a foot below Angier's American record set the previous year. Since it had flown so far to the left, Gene surmised its actual flight distance to be seven feet further. If they measured on the arc, as they did later, he would have beaten the U.S. record by up to six feet. As it was, he still set both the NCAA and AAU records for that year. Gene had broken nine records that season including those at the prestigious Drake, Kansas, Penn relays, and Indiana meets. For each, he received a grand medal or watch as a keepsake.

The javelin competition was one of the first, so Gene went up into the stands to watch the remainder of the contests and root for his teammates, whom he enjoyed seeing compete. Watching the others perform and analyzing their technique also helped him understand the other events, which he would use to instruct his Minims. Two of Gene's friends from the football team also fared well. He cheered for Elmer when he broke the 10-second barrier in the 100-yard dash with a remarkable time of 9.8 seconds, taking first place, a tenth of a second better than the NCAA Championship record. His fellow lineman and next year's captain, Adam Walsh, won the grueling quarter-mile with a time of 49.6 seconds. Rockne's Irish team ended up winning the meet racking up 53 ¾ points to Butler's 45.

––––––

Graduation commencement occurred on June 15, 1924, but Gene would be at the Olympic trials by then. Before leaving, Gene likely walked around campus one more time, around the two serene, restorative lakes, stopping by the peaceful Grotto to say a prayer to Our Lady of Lourdes, seeking her support of his quest. Next, he walked onto Carter field, where he played with the Gipper, the Four Horsemen, and all his other teammates whom he felt a strong bond with, for this is where he came into his own, excelling on the line and at the javelin as he first dreamed of when he stepped off the bus when he first saw the picturesque campus and golden dome.   He likely visited the main building, enjoying the dark halls, cool relief from the intense summer heat, and looking up at the inspirational painted ceiling under the dome one last time.   He had spent five years on this beautiful campus and, since he stayed there during the holidays, was there longer than nearly all of his fellow classmates.   He would miss it all.

Earlier, he would have said goodbye to his Minims.   One of his charges, Tighe "Tiger" Woods (the first Tiger Woods) would become the housing secretary under Truman in 1949.   The Minims told him they would never have a coach better than him and to come to their games when they starred at Notre Dame.   They told him they would follow his exploits at the Olympics and thought he would easily win a gold medal—there was no doubt of it in their teary eyes and shaky voices.

He would miss Rockne most of all for he greatly admired his mentor, whom he learned so much from.   He said goodbye to Rock, and they talked about possible coaching positions.   He had never planned to be a coach, but Rockne and his experience with the Minims got him thinking.   Rockne said there might be a position in Louisiana, which Gene said he might be interested in.

Rockne had once dreamed of going to the Olympics to compete in the pole vault.   Until 1920, Rockne's best vault was only 8" short of the American record, and he was an All-American pole vaulter—one of Notre Dame's first.   With this proficiency, Rockne could have well made the 1916 Olympic team in Berlin; unfortunately, that Olympics was canceled due to war, and afterward he was so busy coaching he did not have time to vault.   He told Gene that all of Notre Dame would be there in spirit, rooting him on.   Rock looked into his eyes and told him, "Gene, remember life is just what you make it; you'll get out of it just what you put into it."   Rock fervently shook Gene's hand, patted him on the back, and wished him well at the trials and in Paris.   Gene felt a lump in his throat as he left Rock's office; more than being his coach, Rockne was the man he looked up to, the highly intelligent, caring, moral man who inspired him and would be the model for his future life.

Gene received his Bachelor of Commercial Science (BCS) in Foreign Commerce.   The certificate was even bigger than the huge ones he received in grade school and high school measuring 18"x 14".   It was from the University of Notre Dame du Lac. (of the Lake).   When he started, it was more of a college; now, it was truly a university.   He graduated Cum Laude (with high honors) and had enough credits for majors in History and English too.

EUGENE G. OBERST, *B.C.S.*
OWENSBORO, KY.
Monogram Club; Varsity Football, 3; Varsity
Track, 3.

To those strict and accurate judges of
men, the Minims, Gene has ever been
a big brother. Big of body, big of
voice, big of heart, he has distin-
guished himself both as a varsity ath-
lete and as a coach of Notre Dame's
future athletes. Gene leaves Notre
Dame with the respect of everyone.

1924 Notre Dame *Dome* yearbook

The 1924 Dome yearbook pictured Gene along with five others on a two-page spread: Don Miller, Elmer Layden, Jim Crowley, Harry Stuhldreher (the Four Horsemen), and Adam Walsh, captain elect. All six would be All-Americans, although Gene was an All-American in track and second team in football. Captain Joe Bach, who was the only other starter graduating that year, was an All-American too. Therefore, 7 of the starting 11 were All-Americans— how remarkable!

The endearing caption under his yearbook picture said, "To those strict and accurate judges of men, the Minims, Gene has ever been a big brother. Big of body, big of voice, big of heart, he has distinguished himself both as a varsity athlete and a coach of Notre Dame's future athletes. Gene leaves Notre Dame with the respect of everyone."

Also in the Dome was a page-long, heartfelt tribute to Gene as the "Rockne of the Minims."

"To big Eugene "Kentucky" Oberst is due the credit for the success of these teams. Oberst is a varsity man in football and track and under his coaching, the Minims have gone through three seasons undefeated. He is the hero and the idol of every lively Minim and it can be safely said that they fought to victory in so many hopeless contests just to win the regard of this big fellow. When vacation time rolls around many hearts will be saddened at the loss of Gene Oberst who has been a coach, a father, and a hero to the lads of St. Edwards's Hall."

Gene would have loved to attend graduation with his friends and teammates, but although it is hard to imagine, he had something more important to do – qualify for the Olympics.

1924 Yearbook: Oberst, Captain Elect Walsh,
Stuhldreher, Miller, Layden & Crowley - The Four Horsemen

15: The Olympic Trials

With his remarkable performance that spring, Gene looked forward to fulfilling his dreams of sailing across the broad Atlantic to Paris and the Olympics. He felt that he was certainly living up to his ideals formulated when he read "*Pushing to the Front*. Since the Olympics were that year, there were no NCAA championships. Much of Alonzo Stagg's thinking in establishing the championships was to serve as a predecessor to the Olympics, testing the best college athletes in the nation and building support for track in the intervening four years. Befitting his role in helping to promote the sport in America, Stagg would be the coach of the U.S. Olympic Track and Field team.

In the regional qualifications held at Ann Arbor, Michigan, on May 30th, 1924, Gene captured first place, and Alonzo likely congratulated him on his stellar performance. Gene was thrilled to see that Tom Lieb also captured first place in the discus. The final trials would be at Harvard in Cambridge, Massachusetts, on June 13 - 14.

Tom joined Gene on the trip, leaving on June 11th. The long train ride to Boston gave the two friends plenty of time to talk. Tom had blue eyes, brownish blond hair, a square jaw that complimented his square face, and a slightly busted nose similar to Rock's, although he was acquired as a hockey goalie rather than in baseball like Rockne's. From head to toe, he looked extremely athletic—tall and strong with a well-balanced physique. With a pleasing personality, all the athletes liked Tom.

The two had a fascinating history together. Gene and Tom were both All-Americans on Notre Dame's track team. Gene was the backup right tackle until Tom broke his leg in 1922, after which Gene took over Tom's position. In addition, Tom earned letters as the goalie on the Irish hockey team and on the baseball team—four sports altogether. After graduating in '23, Tom enrolled in graduate school at Notre Dame. As the athletic director, Rockne recognized that Tom had a marvelous head for sports and invited him to be his assistant football coach for the 1923 season. Tom coached Gene on the line and helped him to be the outstanding tackle he was. In addition, Tom coached the hockey team and helped the Rock coach the track team, so Tom likely coached Gene in the javelin, too, and may have been partially responsible for his remarkable success.

On the long train ride to Boston, Gene had an opportunity to discuss coaching with Tom. Although he was not sure where to start, he had just earned his degree in business and had planned to launch his career in that direction, but he also enjoyed coaching. Tom likely thought that with the experience he gained coaching the Minims and their unblemished record in four sports, he would make a fine coach. The trip might give him some perspective to help him make the decision, and that he should do what felt right to him.

They no doubt talked about what had happened that year in football and track and the prospects for the football team the following year. With so many players coming back, including the outstanding four backs, they might finally overcome their nemesis, Nebraska, and take the national championship. As Tom had personally experienced, anything could happen, especially with respect to injuries, but the team should win nearly every game. If they were undefeated, they had a good case to finally win an undisputed national championship, for over the last four years, they were selected twice on some polls and would have won except for the darned last games against Nebraska, but that was a big "if."

There was still a bias towards the established eastern teams. With last year's victories against Army and Princeton, in no small way thanks to Kentuck's performance, they had finally cracked the perception of the East's football dominance. Notre Dame had earned its national reputation over the last ten years, and if it played well, it should get a fair shake at the national championship. Gene would follow the team's progress religiously and all the players he knew so well, wherever he ended up.

Besides NCAA championships in '22 and '23 in the discus, Tom held the AAU title for '23 and also for '24. Tom was very strong, but he owed his outstanding performance not to his strength but to his innovative technique. Since the first Olympics 2,500 years ago, athletes would swing the discus back and forth, bending their entire torso, and then hefting the heavy disc up into the air. Similar to what the backward Fosbury flop did for the high jump in the 1968 Olympics, Tom devised a new method of spinning that increased his distance—a technique that would revolutionize the event. In Tom's technique, the athlete started at the back of the circle facing backwards, then spun around one and a half times, cocked his torso, then released the disc. The motion was like the three stages in throwing the javelin—spin, cock, throw. Like the javelin, the most important aspect was at the end when you snapped your wrist and flicked the disc off your middle finger, inducing spin that would reduce air resistance. The discus flew like a spinning flying saucer or Frisbee gliding over the air at an approximately 45-degree angle. When the disc landed, it landed with a thunk, often sticking into the ground where the distance would be measured.

Tom knew Gene still struggled to keep his throws straight, and he, as his coach, had tried to correct it to no avail. They hoped they would both make the team and, as national champions, had good reason to believe that might come true. Arriving at 7:30 on the evening of June 12th, they settled in at the Lenox Hotel. Gene's initial impression of Boston, whether justified, was that "it was a queer, staid old city, very cold to strangers."

Tom took first place in the discus with his best throw to date – 153'6"—a remarkable 5 feet better than his toss at the NCCA championships the previous year. He went to see how Gene was doing. It was a rainy day with a stiff headwind, so the distances would be limited. The preliminaries were on the 13th with the finals on the 14th. Gene did not fare well. He only managed to fly the spear 180' 3", finishing a disappointing fifth. William Neufeld finished first at 191'2", followed by Lee Priester, Homer Whelchel, and William Healy with a throw of 181'7". Illinois' Schildhauer finished 6th after Gene. Gene's nemesis and U.S. record holder, Milton Angier, the preemptive favorite at the start of the season, suffered an injury and was not able to recover completely.

After the competition, the two met for dinner at the regal Lenox's elegant dining room. Tom likely tried to console Gene, but he was understandably, highly distraught. He had worked so hard all year, done so well and had been so consistent. How could he do so badly when it counted most? His were the best distances of the year and he was the national champ, yet he would not be joining Tom on the ship to Paris. His dreams went up in smoke, he would not be able to see Paris or tour the WWI battlefields he so longed to see. He was no doubt pleased that his companion and coach, Tom, did well and had made the team He would root for him and wait for his return to hear all about it. Tom might send him a postcard or even write him a letter telling him what Paris and the Olympics were like. Oh well!

Tom, the psychology grad student, suggested that there might be a way Gene could make the team since the Track and Field committee would make the final decision on the attendees. After all, he was the best javelin thrower in the nation, possessing the NCAA record that year: therefore, they should want to have their best competitor in Paris—right? Alonzo Stagg might play a role, and since he was from nearby Chicago, he was well aware of Gene's success. At first, Gene would have thought Tom was trying to make him feel better, but the idea had some merit.

They anxiously waited around the hotel until 10:30 P.M. when the announcement of the Olympic Team took place. After disclosing all of the running and jumping events, to the elation and deep disappointment of those assembled, they finally listed the four javelin competitors to go to Paris—Neufeld, Priester, Whelchel, and...

Oberst. He could not contain himself. This was the best news of his entire life—his Olympic dream would come true—YEA! He would be going to Paris with the rest of the team—"Paris, WOW!" We can imagine in all the excitement that Tom gave him a big bear hug lifting Gene above his head. Gene had not been manhandled like that since he was a kid by his eight bigger brothers. Few could do it now, other than Tom. They would be going to Paris together after all. Rockne would be proud. He went to bed at 12:00 A.M. but was so excited he could not sleep for hours.

The next morning, they went to mass and toured the area. As a student of history, Gene was thrilled to see the sites where the United States was born, such as Bunker Hill and Concord, where the patriots fought their first battles for independence. Boston was so much older than Indiana and Kentucky. They toured the Granary Cemetery, where the famous patriots John Hancock, Samuel Adams, Thomas Paine, Paul Revere, and members of Ben Franklin's family were buried. It was stunning to think that people he had read about all of his life actually lived and died there hundreds of years ago.

Gene sent a telegram to his mother and family to let them know of the fabulous news. All of Owensboro and Notre Dame would be rooting for him. Rockne would have two Olympians at this Olympics too, like their pals Gus Desch and Johnny Murphy, the first in 1920.

Following a train ride to New York the next day, they settled in at the ritzy Park Avenue Hotel. In the morning, he, Gus Pope and Harry Frieda went to the American Express office on Broadway to secure Travelers' Checks. Gus was tall, dark, handsome, and looked very strong, an outstanding discus thrower from Washington University who won both the discus and the shot put in the 1921 NCAA championships. Harry had blond hair, blue eyes, and Nordic good looks. He won the javelin competition in the 1923 NCAA championships and was from the nearby University of Chicago. Harry had come in second to Gene at the Penn Relays. In Paris, he would compete in the grueling decathlon rather than the javelin.

Gene had picked up a 3" x 6" black diary in South Bend to record his trip. Later, on New Year's Eve of that year, on the first page, he wrote, "I want to read this book in 1974. What will the earth be in that day? Just fifty years from this hour this December 31st, 11:17 PM, I may be floating over the North Pole in an airship driven by atomical power." He could not wait to get on with his exciting adventure—across the Atlantic to Europe, to Paris, to the glorious Olympics.

16: Olympic Voyage

In his Olympic diary, Gene recalls his impressions as they set off on the adventure of a lifetime.

> *At 11 A.M., we arrived at pier No. 4 Hoboken and caught our first view of the S. S. America on which we were to sail to France. After looking over our cabin, which is one of the best on the boat, we went back up on deck. At 12 A.M., we slipped anchor and steamed away from the pier. The throng gathered upon the pier gave us a roaring send off. As the tugs were pulling us out into the harbor, the whistles of other boats, bidding us a bon voyage, drowned out the sounds of bands playing on nearby boats.*
>
> *Everyone stayed on deck to watch the ship slip by the maze of sky scrapers heaped up on the lower New York. Then we passed Ellis Island, and finally passed the Statue of Liberty green and beautiful in of all its glory, fame and significance. Emotions choked me as I looked at this statue. I was steaming away on a voyage that offered new sights and adventure, but, I am willing to wager that I will be anxious to see that statue several months from now.*

After a fine lunch, Gene explored the ship, becoming familiar with its layout and meeting his fellow passengers, 350 of whom represented the 1924 U.S. Olympic team, some of the best athletes in the world. The 30 women on the team would be the first true women's team to compete for the U.S.A. As might be expected, it was an extremely fit, good-looking group. They and their coaches were not the only ones onboard, though, for the huge ship held 2,500 passengers in four classes and a complement of 577 crewmembers – over 3,000 souls afloat on the broad Atlantic for days. Extroverted Gene soon met some of the outstanding athletes assembled on the grand ship.

WOMEN SWIMMERS OF AMERICAN OLYMPIC TEAM SAIL WITH COMRADES ON S. S. AMERICA FOR GAMES IN FRANCE   —Photo from Wide World Photos.

The first U.S. Women's Olympic Team
Onboard the USS America
(Few American women previously competed.)

Notice the short, bobbed hairstyles and how the prescribed, fashionable hats of the day covered most of these athletic women's heads down to their eyes. That night there was dancing at the ballroom, but with 30 women for 350 men, the odds were not in the young men's favor, although the women would have plenty to choose from.

The contingent included two notable male swimmers, who at 6'4" were nearly as tall as Gene, Johnny Weissmuller, and the Hawaiian Duke Kahanamoku, who won the gold medal in the 100-meter freestyle in both the 1912 and 1920 Olympics. Duke also won additional gold and silver medals in the relays. He could not compete in the 1916 Olympics, scheduled for Berlin, because it was canceled due to World War I. His father and, subsequently, he was named after the Duke of Edinburgh, Queen Victoria's second son, who had visited Hawaii in the mid-1800s. Duke was tall, dark, and handsome, ripped with a classic Greek-statue physique. Despite his fame and good looks, he was shy and easy-going.

Riding waves on a board twice his height, he became the "primus inter pares" (the first among equals) of American surfing—the "Father of Surfing." When he started surfing, boards could be 10 to 15 feet long and weigh up to 100 pounds. Duke would later preach surfing along the East Coast at Atlantic City, Coney Island, and Long Island as well as along the West Coast at Malibu, Redondo Beach, and Long Beach, gaining a growing following for his sport, especially in California, whereby the 1960s with the Gidget movies, Franky Avalon and Annette Funicello and the Beach Boys it would come to symbolize the rapidly-growing, sun-kissed state and idyllic, beach culture. He also took surfing to Australia's Bondi Beach, where it quickly garnered nearly religious zeal. Like Johnny Weissmuller, Duke also became a Hollywood actor.

The Harvard eight-man rowing team included James Rockefeller, a member of the prominent Rockefeller clan, who would become president of Citigroup, and Benjamin Spock, who would write books on how to raise children by being more flexible and affectionate—used to raise a generation of American children.

Since there were only seven women present at the 1920 games, this was the first large contingent of U.S. female Olympians, such as Gertrude Ederle, the famous swimmer who became the first to swim across the English Channel. They would be confined to the expansive ship for eight days, out of sight of land, floating over the broad, deep North Atlantic. During that time, they would work out to keep their bodies toned and fit, and they would find interesting ways to amuse themselves. They were literally all in the same boat—a select, young, enthusiastic, educated, attractive group eager to meet each other on their long voyage.

Besides the athletes, Hollywood royalty graced the expedition with their presence—Mary Pickford and Douglas Fairbanks, who were there to entertain and inspire the athletes. At the time, they were the most famous actors in the world. From 1909 until 1924, Mary completed an astounding 174 films (nearly one a month).

To succeed as an actor or an actress, you had to be under contract to one of the major studios, such as Metro Goldwyn Mayor, which was headed by Louis B Mayer. The studio would direct nearly every aspect of your life: your publicity, your image, your look, your clothes, who you dated. If there were a scandal, they would work to cover it up. You had no choice regarding the movies you made or the parts you played and as the number of your fans increased and your corresponding value skyrocketed, you would still be paid your initial salary dictated by the years-long contract. For big stars such as Mary and Douglas, they cast you in what seemed like an endless string of movies with rarely a break or chance to catch your breath—why the trip to the Olympics would be such a treat for them.

Along with Charlie Chaplin, they founded United Artists Pictures to thwart the stifling control movie moguls exercised over their lives.

United Artists endeavored to free the actors from the repressive studios. Together, Fairbanks and Pickford also founded the Academy of Motion Picture Arts and Sciences, which sponsors the extravagant Oscars every year.

As one might not think up until the recent mega-ships, cruising then did not differ vastly from an early 21st-century cruise. There were dining areas, lounges, bands, theatres, entertainers, movies, a pool, and decks for walking and sunning on deck chairs. Of course, the recent mega-sized cruise ships with numerous restaurants and amusement park-like attractions eclipse the earlier versions. There were, however, no other options for traveling to Europe since Lindberg's monumental flight across the Atlantic would not occur for three more years.

1924 Men's United States Olympic Team
At Prince Murat's Chateau in Rocquencourt

———

Feeling tired from meeting everyone, Gene headed for his cabin, which after living in the St. Edward's dorm, he thought to be luxurious. There he shared the room with the three other javelin participants. As he recalled,

> The cabin which I am in is nothing less than beautiful and comfortable. We had four beds, two above and two below in a straight line. Beneath the port holes there is a large and inviting sofa. Two wash basins with running water help make things seem rich while above each bowl is a large looking glass which conceals a cabinet behind it. Each bed is separated from the rest of the room by curtains that are of a pink Chinese variety and draw back like a stage curtain. There is drinking water in three bottles hanging on the wall. There is but one chair and one small cabinet. And either end of the sofa there is a clothes closet. The room is about 12 ft by 14 ft and has besides ten electric lights, an electric heater and fan. The floor is covered with a light brown cover.

Lulled by the swaying ship, like a baby's crib rocking by the ocean's gentle hands, listening to waves slapping against the ship's side, it did not take long for Gene to fall asleep. A bugle woke him from a restful sleep at 7:00 the next morning. After breakfast, they attended a meeting where they were introduced to the coaches, rules, and given uniforms, tracksuits, and sweatsuits. The uniforms consisted of a blue coat with an American emblem on the left pocket, a pair of blue pants, a pair of white pants and white sneakers. Gene's was too small, so he exchanged it with another athlete whose was too large and the new suit fit perfectly. The tracksuit's pants, however, were six sizes too small, which he was not able to immediately exchange.

At some point during the voyage, Gene met coach Alonzo Stagg from nearby Chicago. Perhaps his friend Harry Frieda introduced his illustrious coach to Gene. Besides Midwestern track, Alonzo and Gene had football in common. Alonzo impressed Gene, who like Rockne exuded the air of a great coach. Rockne would later say, "All football comes from Stagg." The press often credited Rockne for creating the backfield shift, but he would always defer to Stagg. Besides inventing many of football's iconic plays, attesting to his prominence in the sport, Stagg, one of the first eleven All-Americans, co-founded the Big Ten, the American Football Coaches Association, and the Rules Committee. Having seen Gene win the prestigious Kansas Relays and

Penn Relays, and living only 60 miles from South Bend, as Chicago's Track and Field coach, Alonzo may have been the one who pushed for Gene to make the squad.

Gene then went to the well-equipped gym where he worked out with its superb equipment and a medicine ball, then ran laps around the 220-yard track made of cork circling the deck. He went to the aft deck where he practiced his throws. All around the ship, athletes were working out and practicing their events. From the passengers' perspective, the ship resembled a beehive of activity, with young, well-built athletes busy buzzing around everywhere. After another wonderful dinner that night, he went to the movie theatre, where he saw a newsreel and *Fighting Blood*, a boxing movie.

––––––

The next day, Wednesday, June 18th, Gene watched the swimmers practice in a small canvas pool where they attached large rubber bands to their ankles so they could swim for distance in the restricted area. While gazing at the splashing, shimmering water, he became infatuated with the lovely Gertrude Ederle, her rhythmic strokes pushing the water and feet kicking up spray while she stayed stationary. She obtained her first world record at 12 in the 880-free style, the youngest to ever do so, and by then held nine such records with more to come.

The swimmers' rubber bands gave the javelin men an idea. Until then, all they could do was practice their approach and throws while holding onto the javelin, but they felt without actually tossing their spears over the week they would become rusty. So, they drilled a hole in the tail of a javelin, through which they attached 300 feet of light string with the other end tied to the railing at the aft end of the ship. Carefully timing their motion to the ship's ups and downs, each man would run along the wooded deck and throw the spear that flew up into the assure, thin cirrus-veiled sky far out over the deep blue waters, landing like a whaler's harpoon with a distant white splash. Then, since it was made of wood, the shaft bobbed up to the surface and floated. Afterward, they would reel the spear in like a thin fish and start over. They joked about the tip of the spear being red from hitting a shark or whale, and all claimed to have broken the world record. But the coaches humorously said that because they were throwing from 50 feet high while the ship sped along at 20 knots, they could not honor such records. Moreover, they would not swim out to measure the result and leave the ship behind.

Later, Gene saw a huge fish leap out of the water, perhaps a sailfish. Good, they were not throwing then. With the thin line, if they speared the fish, he would have made off with their javelin, perhaps with a javelin man in tow.

Besides being vital to their success, sailing the javelin 200 to 250 feet into the bright blue sky was fun. Several other athletes gathered around to watch the javelin flying over the ocean. Having taken a spot from another competitor, at first Gene felt a little out of place, but his throws were as far as the others, and now he felt worthy of these highly accomplished, good-humored men.

In contrast to Gene's reserved personality, Bill Neufeld was out to have fun. He hailed from sunny California and attended UC Berkeley, where he was the captain of the track team, regularly winning the javelin, discus, and shot put. Bill scored the most points at the ICAAAA (Intercollegiate Association of Amateur Athletes of America) national meet helping the Bruins to win the meet, while becoming an All-American in the discus.

Bill came from a truly international family. While he was born in the Ukraine where his father was a professor of history and music, his mother hailed from Prussia and his father from Switzerland. He was first at the trials, which he attributed to his ability to throw low in the wind that day. Like a golf shot, if you toss it high, the wind could knock it back considerably, and it might land without sticking in the ground, which would disqualify the attempt.

Tall and exceedingly handsome with wavy dark hair, Lee Priester hailed from Mississippi A&M, later known as Mississippi State. An outstanding pitcher with a lightning-fast fastball, recognizing his potential, the track coach asked him to throw the javelin. Like Gene, for his first meet, he wore his baseball uniform and spikes, where he finished second to Homer Whelchel of Georgia. He became an All-American the previous year, finishing 2nd at the NCAA meet. Prior to the preliminaries on Saturday, Lee was stricken with malaria and could not get out of bed to compete. With his Olympic dreams shattered, because he held the American record, the officials let him compete in the finals on Sunday, where he again finished second. Lee's home was in Louisiana. Based on Rockne's efforts, Gene told him he might have a position as a coach in Louisiana and therefore he peppered Lee with questions about the Bayou State, of which he knew little about.

Handsome Homer Whelchel, who, as another nearby southern boy, Lee knew well, was the captain of the Georgia Tech team and had finished third in the trials. Gene recalled his trip to Georgia Tech, saying how much he enjoyed being in the South again. These four constituted the USA javelin team. Ranging in age from 21 to 24, all were attractive, over six feet tall and in impeccable shape. Bill had an impish grin to match his personality. With their telltale accents and gentlemanly manners, he felt a little outnumbered by all the Southerners. But Bill was from Southern California so in a way, he too was a Southerner.

The head field coach, Walter M. Christie, commented in the

Olympic Committee's Report to Congress on how well the four javelin men got along with each other. "The four Americans were an object lesson for all traveling groups. Never in all my career in any field of activity have I ever met such a group of four splendid personalities as America's four entries in the javelin—Oberst, Neufeld, Whelchel and Priester. Even in our wonderful array of great personalities and splendid types of athletes, these four were noticeable and stood out."

On the ship, after working out together and showering, Bill noticed that Gene had what he called clubfeet. Gene had the condition before his months-long stay at the Passionist monetary in St. Louis with his brother Bonaventure, where they operated on him. He never spoke about what they did, he never complained about his pain or his difficulties, and he never told anyone about it. He did not want sympathy, and he would not make excuses; rather, he wanted to prove himself despite his handicap.

Bill could see that Gene's feet were totally flat and his ankles were three times a normal size. Indeed, to him, it looked as if Gene had thick clubs hanging from the bottom of his legs. Whenever they went up on the deck to work out or throw their javelin off the stern, Gene would lace up his Indian club braces. When they went to meals together, Gene wore his orthopedic black boots—specially made, with high laces. Being smaller, Bill depended upon his speed, during the run to obtain his spectacular distances. Gene, on the other hand, could not run much and instead depended upon his upper body strength.

Picture javelin men
Oberst, Neufeld, Whelchel, Priester
In front of their cabin at Rocquencourt, Paris

————

That evening they saw a large passenger ship all lit up passing through the darkened night with melodic music playing. couples likely dancing. It was Lusitania. The transatlantic voyage would take eight days, with the SS America steaming at 17 or more knots an hour or about 480 miles a day. Gene adjusted quickly to the ship's routine, eating regular meals, working out, running around the deck, throwing the javelin off the aft deck, reading, taking naps, and watching movies at night. One night he went up to the first-class salon and watched men in tuxedos, women in cocktail dresses and short dresses dancing to the rhythmic beat of the Charleston. During meals, he would have stimulating conversations with athletes from throughout America. He also watched others working out. The boxers practiced relentlessly, wanting to keep their weight down. Gene also enjoyed watching the fencers whose motions seemed balletic to him.

He especially enjoyed watching the sprinters practicing their starts and dashes on the cork track. Two were among the fastest men on the planet: Charlie Paddock, who won the 100-meter dash in the 1920 Olympics and was the first to be named the "fastest man alive," and Jackson Scholz, "the New York Thunderbolt." The press highlighted the dashes as a competition for the world's fastest man, the premier event of the upcoming Olympics. They were favored to win the sprints, but there were two Brits, Harold Abrahams of Cambridge and Eric Liddell from Edinburgh, who might make it a race. Because of their blazing speed, they were called the "Chariots of Fire." Gene had seen them race at the Penn Relays just last month and could testify to their lightning-fast speed.

While walking around the deck, Gene met a handsome, tall, affable Irishman named Jack Kelly, who hailed from Philadelphia and recalled Gene's outstanding performance at the Penn Relays. Jack was also a fan of the fighting Irish football team. He had briefly played professional football in Philly, winning the city championship. Jack worked in construction as a bricklayer. Gene told him that his family owned a brickyard for two generations, and he had helped make thousands of bricks. What an amazing coincidence.

Much of their initial discussion revolved around Gene and Notre Dame—Gene always enjoyed talking about his athletic exploits. He did not learn much about Jack though, other than he competed in the skulls—rowing. Nearly as popular as football, rowing events could remarkably draw over 100,000 fans.

Afterward, while eating lunch with Tom, Gene heard that Jack was the greatest sculler in U.S. history, winning every title, including World Championships in both the single and double skulls. He won an amazing 126 straight races in the single skull. In 1919 and 1920, Jack won the national single sculls title over both the sprint distance (¼-mile) and the longer 1½ miles. He won gold in both skulls at the 1920 Olympics and would likely win gold in the 1924 Olympics competing in the double skulls with his cousin Paul Costello.

Testifying to the evolution of sports during the golden decade, even though he was the best rower in the world, Jack faced stiff resistance because he was a bricklayer. The premier rowing event in the world was the Henley Royal Regatta Cup in Great Britain, which prevented him from competing because he was a common laborer and because his rowing club raised money to cover travel expenses. They thought that such sports should be reserved for those with an upper-class background, those who had leisure time to indulge in such activities and pay their own expenses. Initially not planning to enter the Olympics, angered by this royal snub, he went on to win the gold medals.

His stunningly beautiful daughter, Grace Kelly, would become a famous movie star and the princess of Monaco. Considering his stinging rejection, it is interesting that his daughter would become a royal, as would his grandson, the current Prince of Monaco, Prince Albert. Gaining a measure of retribution, Jack's son, Jack Kelly Junior, would go on to win the singles at Henly twice. He would also compete in four Olympics, winning a bronze medal in rowing in 1956, and would become the president of the U.S. Olympic Committee. Possessing Jack's athletic prowess, the prince would compete in five Olympics and be a member of the Olympic Committee for over 35 years.

On Friday evening after learning and attempting to sing the Marseillaise, the French National anthem, with the rest of the team, Gene went out into the black night and peered over the deck. There, with a sky whitewashed in stars, he saw a fascinating sight of phosphorescent lights glowing in the deep dark sea. "Some would twinkle like a star and then disappear; others would expand and then break up into smaller particles. How they were formed, I don't know."

The seas grew rough on Saturday with waves of 15 to 20 feet, and they were issued emergency kits donated by Johnson and Johnson. It would be impossible to practice that day. Some of the runners tried running slowly around the deck but kept hitting the rail, providing a comical effect. At 10 A.M, all athletes assembled on deck, arranged by height and weight for drills. Gene was the tallest, and Matt McGrath, at nearly 250 pounds, was the heaviest. Matt set the Olympic record in the hammer throw during the 1912 Olympics in

Stockholm and won a silver in the 1908 Olympics in London. After injuring his leg in 1920, he finished 5th. Matt had been 33 at his first Olympics and was 47 in this one—the senior statesman of the group. With the severe pitching of the ship, Gene finally felt seasick, but when he left his room and took in some fresh air up on deck, he felt better.

On Sunday, Gene went to mass in the beautifully furnished, splendid, first-class drawing room. Here are his thoughts on the experience, "Mass upon the ocean is very inspiring. One needs no urging to realize the vast significance of self when compared to the magnificent size of the ocean and the rest of the creator's handiwork." Later he saw the Lusitania sail by, named after the ship that was sunk in 1915 by a German sub with Americans aboard—a major reason for the U.S.'s entrée into the war.

After mass, they assembled on deck for drills, and, at three o'clock, all members of the Olympic team met on the front deck for pictures. The rest of the day was spent signing numbered autograph books for both the athletes and the passengers. This craze started several days ago and soon engulfed three-fourths of the passengers. While he had no desire to have such a book, thinking it was a moneymaking scheme, Gene thought it was a wonderful time to secure the names of the famous athletes. At 8:30 PM, Col. Thompson, the team manager, gave the team an excellent talk on the behavior expected of the athletes in Paris. He dwelt upon good sportsmanship, especially in defeat. Following his speech, he led the assembly in a rousing cheer, "Ray! Ray! Ray! U-S-A... A-M-E-R-I-C-A!"

Monday was the last day before they would see land. The fierce storm had finally abated as brilliant sunshine filled the decks above the smooth blue sea under a serene cerulean sky. Gene settled into one of the deck chairs, where he felt a tinge of anxiety mixed with excitement. The long passage was a marvelous experience, offering the opportunity to meet, enjoy, and bond with the rest of the team. He had a similar connection with his Irish teammates on the long train trips to the East, but the long voyage over the vast sea seemed to engender an even deeper bond. Even though they were from a variety of sports, there was a kinship with all the team, for they were representing their country—the greatest country in the world. Going to college at Notre Dame certainly expanded his horizons. Although most were from the Midwest, he met men from throughout the nation too. Competing with so many men from the U.S. and dining with them regularly gave him an even broader appreciation of our diverse country. On the ship, he had the opportunity to see and get to know these famous athletes daily. Soon they would be competing against the best in the world as a team.

He felt they would all do well, but that remained to be seen since they would be competing against 44 other nations. He felt close to the large contingent of track and field participants, especially the members of the throwing events like his – the javelin, discus, shot put, and hammer throw—the **"men of steel."** They weren't as flashy as the runners were but represented the stouthearted, strong working men of America who built the country with their hands, hearts, backs, and sweat.

He liked his fellow javelin throwers most, against whom he would have to compete. The Finns and Swedes dominated the sport, so any one of them would be lucky to place in the top six and garner a point or two, let alone win a medal. Over the last three Olympics, eight of the nine medals went to Norsemen with only one bronze going to a Hungarian. In the last Olympics, the Finns swept all three medals. The four Americans were a team, and he would be proud if he did not place as long as one of the others did. When they practiced off the back of the ship they encouraged each other in the true spirit of sportsmanship, heightened because spears tied to a line piercing the Atlantic could not be measured.

Gene reflected on his education. Even though he majored in commerce, he was glad Notre Dame provided a broad education in the arts—philosophy, literature, history, and languages. This education helped him to become a more complete man, like the Greeks, or a Renaissance man, something he had aspired to since his readings as a youth, to become a citizen of the world. Making the Olympic team confirmed the dreams he had when he first stepped off the bus onto the Notre Dame campus. He was not sure what his next step in life would be, but he felt prepared for whatever fate had in store.

Gene had an intimate knowledge of French history. Soon he would be in France, the epitome of European culture, the home of Napoleon and Josephine, Louis the XVI and Marie Antoinette, and the French Revolution. Less than six years ago, France was the main battleground in the largest war in world history, and he wondered how much devastation would still remain.

Paris was also the home of perfume, fashion, the Follies, and art, especially the Impressionists. He was not sure he would like Impressionist paintings, but he wanted to see them. Then American artists flocked to Paris to learn their trade and live a libertine lifestyle. An early expatriate, Gertrude Stein, said Paris "Was where the 20th century was." In addition to Stine, Hemingway, F. Scott Fitzgerald, James Joyce, and Ezra Pound flocked to Paris.

Gay Paree was home to the Moulin Rouge, where Toulouse Lautrec painted, but the most popular club of the time was Revu Negee, which featured American jazz with black bands and incomparable singers like Josephine Baker. Paris was a center of American jazz, where blacks were treated well and accepted. So close to France now, Gene could barely contain his excitement. He could taste it.

That evening, members of the Olympic team entertained their compatriots and passengers with a talent show in the lounge. The Hawaiians performed some of their stunning native fire dances. Caroline Kelly, a beautiful, young, tall blond who looked like Cinderella, danced as well as if she was in the Follies, after which the crowd stood up and clapped furiously. She would soon win the first diving gold medal off the 10-meter platform. Later, she would become a dancer, model, actress, and, presciently, a cruise director. Other Olympians performed magic stunts, juggled, sang, and played the piano. The entertainment was a rollicking success. Afterward, according to Bill Neufeld, Johnny Weissmuller jumped on a table, swung on a chandelier, scratched his armpit, and let out a yell like the one he would later do as Tarzan. Perhaps one of the passengers was a producer, who would later cast him to play the role—maybe Douglas Fairbanks? Gene went up on the deck and saw the lights of six different vessels in the distance. They were close.

17: Paris

At 11:00 A.M. Tuesday, June 24th, sketchy, ghost-like islands appeared in the distance, the first land in a week. That evening, the team packed their clothes to be prepared to disembark early the next morning.

At 11:30 P.M., Gene heard shouts above and looked out the porthole where he saw Cherbourg Harbor. As he recorded in his diary,

> A large ship was perhaps a mile from us with all her lights lit, making her look like a huge floating palace. Lights on shore and the dim outlines of hills in the background struck up a feeling like Xmas produces within me. To know that land was just a few furlongs away, gives a feeling of security to all aboard, I believe everyone aboard got up for at least a few minutes to look around the harbor. The chains were dropped, the anchor took hold and we came to a dead stop; for the first time in 8 days, we could rest without moving; but I was almost sorry because I learned to like the sound of the water beating against the side of the vessel.

Even though breakfast would not be served until 6:00, Gene woke at 4:30, charged with excitement. Soon, like a dimmer switch illuminating the darkened world, it gradually became lighter. Then as a blue sky began to appear, a brilliant sun shone down upon the warming ship as a refreshing breeze blew. Like a child on Christmas morn, he could barely wait to be on land, to see France, to see Paris, to see Rocquencourt. What would this foreign land be like? How different would it be from America?

General Douglas MacArthur, the famous leader in World War II and Korea, commanded the military members of the team, who primarily competed in the saber and foil. He cautioned the Americans prior to their departure: "Now remember, you are ambassadors of the United States, and we expect you to behave accordingly." After checking their passports, they boarded tenders that transported them to the landing pier.

———

According to Bill Neufeld, "We were told that on arrival in France, we would be met by beautiful French girls that would greet us with flowers and give us a kiss on each cheek... We looked forward to that very much. Actually, what happened is that it was raining, and all we saw was a bunch of bearded men to greet us." He hoped these men did not want to kiss him and was highly disappointed.

It may have been because he had been at sea for over a week, but Gene had never seen such green trees and foliage. He had no idea what a foreign land might look like, but seeing the quaint and picturesque stone, mortar, and slate houses of Cherbourg was a curious sight. The automobiles looked like those in America twenty years ago. The trolley cars were duplicates of the Toonerville Trolley—a popular cartoon of the day whose conveyance resembled a warped, colorful, smaller version of those in San Francisco.

Gene saw his first European train, exclaiming, "And my what trains." When he entered their 2nd class cabins, he could not imagine that the 1st class cars could be any better, for these were so luxurious compared to those he roamed around the U.S. in. The Americans exchanged their dollars for francs, after which a slew of vendors descended upon them, selling telescopes. Induced by the bargain, Gene bought a pair of binoculars for $2 that would have cost $8 back home. He could use these at the Olympics to see the action up close.

It seemed that all of Cherbourg came to greet them. Never before had he seen such a worn-out, bedraggled, tired-looking bunch. Small boys with dirty patched clothes begged for pennies, a few of whom endeavored to earn the money by pulling off stunts, such as walking on their hands.

One rugged, rough-looking, middle-aged man asked several of them if they wanted wine; all he could say was "Cognac! Good Cognac—Big!" and then he would point to his muscles as if the liquid could produce strength in the Olympians. They told him that there was, "nothing doing," since they were American athletes in training. Not relenting, he insisted they purchase some. Finally, when the athletes acted threateningly, he walked away.

At 9:15 A.M, they embarked to Paris. As the train pulled out, they threw pennies, nickels, and French coins out of the windows to the throng of people gathered below with pleading faces, who, as the coins rolled upon the cobblestones, scrambled to grab them.

He could not believe that Cherbourg had advanced much over the past centuries. There were few autos; rather, the popular method of transportation consisted of one-horse carts and a few two-horse carts with the horses pulling one in front of the other. Fresh water must have been scarce because he could see several kegs and barrels of water transported around the town. So, there was no municipal water system.

He wondered if Cherbourg had a washtub. Where a small stream flowed towards the ocean a hundred or more women were leaning over the water washing piles of clothes. Some were rubbing garments together while others used clubs or stones pounding the clothes to get the dirt extracted.

After a short ride, they were served dinner, "French style." According to Homer Weichel, "We had eggs boiled and then put some sort of sauce over them, (perhaps Hollandaise) which was not good. Then a piece of duck, which was better. Then the dessert which was ice cream and you never tasted anything just like it. They gave us Cherries and black coffee, which none could drink." Evidently, French cuisine did not stack up against the hearty American, meat and potato cuisine. Of course, this was long before the proliferation of international restaurants that would appear in nearly every city and town, when it would be difficult to find Mexican or Chinese food when nearly all restaurants were American.

The countryside appeared rugged, with every strip of available land in use, divided into small plots marked by trees, bushes, or a stone wall. Cherbourg's main crop seemed to be hay, eaten by the numerous herds of dairy cattle.

The villages en route to Paris were so quaint Gene felt he had been transported back to the 15th century. Each picturesque house had a yard encased in vines and flowers. They passed hundreds of straw-thatched homes, many with flowers or small trees growing on the apex of the roof. Other trees had branches cut off for firewood, which the trees would continue to produce. There were long, dark tunnels along the route, some a mile or more in length. Sometimes, the train would be high on the hillsides, and he could look down into the verdant valley below where villages appeared as if they were in a framed picture. Gene pinched himself to see if it was all a dream. A church appeared in the center of every passing village or town. In the larger towns, the cathedrals were magnificent to view through his window. A few impressive, multi-turreted, fairytale castles passed by too.

At about 2 P.M, the train reached the banks of the Seine, a narrow but beautiful stream, small compared to the mighty Ohio River.

They reached the environs of Paris at 3 P.M. arriving at the Saint Lazare station shortly thereafter. Thousands of people lined the streets surrounding the station cheering for the Americans, which reminded Gene of his arrivals in South Bend following a Notre Dame victory.

The U.S. committee did not want the athletes to stay closer because they did not want them spending too much time touring Paris or being tempted by Parisian ladies of the night. This backfired since they would spend more of their time traveling back and forth to Paris and the Olympic venues and less time practicing.

Paris looked extremely old to Gene. All the buildings were five stories high and close to the street. They passed the Arc de Triomphe and saw the Eiffel Tower in the distance. Then they drove through a Parisian park, which gave him an appreciation of the beauty of the city of light the downtown section failed to impart. The park had trees close together in manicured grounds that looked cool and inviting in contrast to the hot air of the steaming city streets.

The athletes boarded private autos for the trip to Rocquencourt, about ten miles west of Paris, where the U.S. Olympic Committee had rented a chateau, in which most of them would stay, but the driver became lost and went about 20 miles out of the way. The chateau originally belonged to handsome Prince Joachim Murat, who married Napoleon's sister, Caroline Bonaparte. During the French Revolution, Joachim had helped Napoleon seize power and became Napoleon's aide-de-camp, commanding the cavalry during the campaigns in Italy and Egypt. Napoleon rewarded him by appointing him as the King of Naples and Admiral of France. The estate bordered Versailles, where Napolean and Josephine ruled so that the siblings could be close to each other. After Napolean lost the war, Murat was executed and his son emigrated to St. Augustine, Florida. Joachim Murat, the 8th Prince Murat, is the current head of the Murat family. Gene greatly appreciated that the magnificent estate in which they stayed had such a strong connection to Napoleon and French Imperial history.

———

Murat Chateau

When they finally reached the expansive walled Rocquencourt estate, they drove down an exceedingly long driveway with carefully trimmed beautiful trees lining the route. As they approached the stately chateau, they may have thought they would be living in the sumptuous quarters for the month. Instead, the officials assigned them to rooms in newly built, unpainted, plywood cabins—eleven cabins in a row. As Gene walked into the assigned cabin, he saw a hallway with five doors on each side and two beds in each room. The accommodations were Spartan, but with no less space than the ship or a college dorm room; besides, they were at the Olympics, and such concerns were unimportant. (After being bombed in WWII, the historic estate is currently an arboretum and park)

Gene roomed with Lee Priester, a Southern boy from Louisiana. He never knew this, but Gene's fifth great-grandmother's name was Priester, perhaps making them distant cousins, which may explain why they got along so well. The other rooms in the cabin contained the two other javelin competitors, Tom and the discus men, the shot putters, and hammer throwers—all "The Men of Steel." Similar cabins accommodated the women housed in a separate section of the huge estate. In contrast, the dining hall and showers were very spacious and comfortable. The coaches and officials dwelt in the magnificent chateau.

U.S Men's clapboard Cabins
Ten rooms to a Cabin, Two men to a room

Many thought the first dinner was terrible, only eating bread and butter. They could not drink the awful-tasting water either. After dinner, Gene and the javelin men sauntered down to the nearby village, where they noticed a great disturbance. As they approached, they smelled the fragrant odor of burning wood and saw red, yellow, orange and blue flames shooting out of the walls of several burning houses. When the lights in the dozens of rooms at the makeshift clapboard village had turned on for the first time that night it likely overloaded the town's primitive, thin electrical gap, causing the current to jump across the wires, spewing hot sparks, igniting the close-set houses. In an attempt to save the village, one courageous villager grabbed a pulsating wire to tear it down, immediately being electrocuted. For an hour or more, no life was safe near the houses until Jack Kelly and two of his heroic rowing teammates used axes to chop down wires and save the grateful village.

Later, Gene and the Americans took up a collection for the widow, raising $1000 - $2,000, which a hundred years later would be worth about $37,000. According to Bill Neufeld, "We received any number of invitations to weddings and parties after that, and it helped establish good relationships ..."

———

The next day, Gene toured the small charred village of

Rocquencourt. With fewer than 20 closely knit houses, perhaps in anticipation of an economic boon from the nearby Olympians, many served liquor. He knew from his French history studies that the town was famous as the site of the last major battle Napoleon's forces won against the Prussian Calvary on July 1, 1815, two weeks after his defeat at Waterloo and three days before the signing of the armistice and Napoleon's subsequent exile to the island of Helena.

Gene then conducted a tour of inspection of the chateau's high-walled property: "The place was not well kept but from the looks of decaying beauty, it must have been marvelous in its prime." He sat, mesmerized on a bench on a hillside overlooking a picturesque pond fed by a stream that flowed out of a nearby cave. "Beautiful little bowers of flowers and shrubbery made it appear as a paradise." Thus far he had only seen a small portion of the expansive estate.

That afternoon, not wanting to forget his main purpose, he worked out on a large field well suited for javelin throwing.

Newsmen were taking pictures of the athletes' practice that day. Not realizing how far some of the projectiles traveled, they placed a couple of their cameras on the far end of the field. One of the outstanding hammer throwers, big James McEachem, the largest man on the team, practiced throwing his hammer half a football field away. An ancient Scottish weapon, the hammer is basically a cannonball tied to a four-foot chain, weighing 16 pounds. To throw the hammer, you spin around several times, releasing it at the end of a rotation. Gene had a difficult time throwing the javelin accurately, but imagine spinning around several dizzying times and then releasing such an unwieldy device. Unfortunately, one of McEachem's errant tosses took out two of the newsmen's cameras, something they would not have been pleased by.

After dinner, Gene, Tom, and two others walked to the city of Versailles. They toured the town, noting the dilapidated houses while admiring the fine structures located on the road to Paris. They found numerous beer houses and gardens there. In the evening, the proprietors placed benches, tables, and chairs in front of their establishments as the villagers assembled to drink and talk over glasses of French wine and foaming beer.

———

The indifferent French cooks were not used to feeding highly tuned American athletes' appetites, especially the hefty men of steel like Gene and his cabin mates. At first, they served hors d'oeuvres, tomato salads, cucumbers, and other French fare, like horsemeat, that seemed indigestible. They only had croissants and coffee for breakfast the first day, not what young, hard-training, calorie consuming American athletes were accustomed to. Fortunately, the committee had planned for this eventuality, and by afternoon, they had transported hundreds of boxes of cornflakes, puffed rice, and shredded wheat along with ample supplies of fruit to Rocquencourt from the S.S. America. Replacing the French cooks and waiters with Americans, they changed the evening menu to include steak, potatoes, and dozens of loaves of bread with butter. The ravenous athletes must have been highly pleased.

On the morning of the 27th, his muscles were tight from the two-mile walks to Rocquencourt and Versailles. The sun was hot so he worked out in the morning, trying to perfect his form.

That afternoon, Gene joined a group of athletes heading to the Colombes Olympic stadium for the first time. About two miles from the chateau, five of them got off the bus and paid one and a half francs to ride to Paris on the trolley. The party stopped at the towering, substantial Arc de Triomphe and walked along the broad boulevard. Then they hailed a taxi and drove several miles to the American Express office where they exchanged American dollars for French francs—18.87 per $1.

Tom Lieb wanted to buy some "high-class" perfume for his girlfriend, so the group joined him at the perfumery. The store also featured Olympic memorabilia so they all purchased Olympic handkerchiefs and badges. The athletes passed Vendome Square with a huge bronze column engraved with war figures.

Next, the young athletes visited the Opera and the Madeleine, which Napoleon designed to look like the Parthenon. The building was surrounded on all four sides by tall Corinthian columns. Inside they saw monumental sculptures and inspirational frescoes by 19th Century French artists on the domed ceiling that reminded Gene of Notre Dame's golden dome.

They toured the Place de la Concorde, Paris's largest public square. At the eastern end of the Champs-Élysées, Louis XVI, Marie Antoinette, and Maximilien Robespierre were guillotined during the French Revolution, something Gene, although gruesome, with his love of history would have appreciated. After sauntering up the broad Champs-Elysées, they had dinner at an Italian restaurant.

That evening back at Rocquencourt, several entertainers, including longtime comedian Marie Dressler, pianist-composer and racial activist John Powell, and Nora Bayes, entertained the Americans. Nora was a famous singer and vaudeville performer who recorded over 160 popular songs. She is credited with co-writing one of Gene's all-time favorites, "Shine On, Harvest Moon." Other famous songs, which the Olympians likely enjoyed and may have sung along with, included the rousing WWI anthems "Over There" and "How Ya Gonna Keep 'em Down on the Farm (After They've Seen Paree)?" which considering where they were seemed most appropriate.

On Sunday the 29th, Gene attended an inspirational mass at the marvelous St. Louis Cathedral in Versailles. Although he could not follow the French sermon, the rest of the mass was in Latin, which he could understand and respond to. About halfway through the service, the ushers circulated the customary collection basket, to which Gene generously contributed a few francs. Then another basket circulated, and again, he contributed. By the fourth collection, he thought he had contributed enough.

That evening they watched the *Thief of Baghdad* starring Douglas Fairbanks. The black and white epic film with its stunning opulent settings, is widely considered one of the great silent films and Fairbanks's greatest work. who along with Mary Pickford remarkably were in the audience and addressed them afterwards. In this recently released 1924 film, the swashbuckling thief, Fairbanks, performs amazing gymnastic feats in extravagant settings—a movie that would have been thrilling for the athletes to see.

When he first saw them on the ship, he was surprised to see how small they appeared in person but following the movie was taken by their charm and thought it was no wonder why they were so well-liked on this well-earned sabbatical from their frantic movie making.

Monday afternoon, he and several companions journeyed to Versailles, a half-hour walk from the adjacent Rocquencourt, to tour its glorious palace and grounds. He had read about Versailles, the grand palace of Louis XVI and Marie Antoinette, the regal palace of Emperor Napoleon and Empress Josephine.

Gene had long looked forward to seeing it, but what he imagined could not compare to the magnificence of what he beheld:

> *I was surprised to see its great size. Surely the palace is 1200 feet in width* (four football fields). *I was astonished at the beauty of the fountains and gardens in back of the palace. Never in all my life had I beheld such a large building as this. It is said that Louis XIV almost bankrupted France in its construction, and his work was added to by his descendants. Thousands of fountains, wonderfully constructed, are placed around the grounds, while flowers in cleverly arranged designs tend to beautify the whole.*
>
> *An extensive park runs back more than a mile alongside of an artificial lake or canal that runs in perfect straightness a half mile in back of the palace. I walked several hours through these parks, looking at splendid fountains, beautiful marble statues, vases, and columns artistically arranged at intersections of the geometrically planted trees. I saw*

perhaps a tenth of all that was to be seen on this day. I also walked to the Grand Trianon, Petit Trianon, and through Marie Antoinette's Swiss Village. The grounds and palace of Versailles impressed me so profoundly that I fairly shook with admiration for the artificial beauty that could be seen on every side.

I felt as if I was in Paradise. The magnificence of it all forced me to say to myself that I would like to live there in its shadows forever. I don't think man could possibly construct anything more grand than this place. Millions and millions of dollars must have been spent in its construction, and I believe a billion dollars could not reproduce it today. 'Tis no wonder that the burden of taxation upon the people led them to revolt when their masters threw millions of dollars away to satisfy their whims.

Gene had the right idea for it might cost $300 billion or more to rebuild Versailles today, especially when considering the voluminous priceless art by famous artists. The chateau has over 700 rooms, many decorated from floor to ceiling with fine works of art that include the ceiling. The palace has an astounding 2,143 windows, 1,252 fireplace chimneys, and 67 staircases. The massive building is set on 1,200 acres of manicured grounds having 400 magnificent sculptures and 1,400 peace-inducing fountains.

All these statistics are overwhelming, which is how Gene felt when he beheld its magnificence, the reaction the French royalty and Napolean sought. Unfortunately for the royals, their extravagance caused the people to rebel, which would be concerning to dominant royal families throughout Europe.

The main house appears to have about 750,000 square feet of space, but it is not clear how many bathrooms there are. In addition, there is a 130-foot-high chapel with a four-balcony opera theatre that holds up to 1200 people and a separate smaller Queen's theater. The grounds are graced by a picturesque mile-long pool, intersected by another three-quarter mile-long pool, which would have been ideal for long-distance swimmers.

The grounds also contain a separate guest house occupied by visiting family and celebrities, the Grand Trianon. This house is set within its own park, lake, and extensive gardens, which also have its own guest house, the Petite Trianon, with amazing gardens, pools, and fountains.

———

Later that week, he witnessed the Grand Prix at Longchamps—his first horse race with a crowd of 200,000 in attendance to watch the action on the grass course. The women dressed in their best Parisian couture of many colors and wore elaborate hats for this was, in effect, the grandest fashion show of the year. He knew of the 50-year-old Kentucky Derby back home in Louisville and how well people dressed for that race, but could not imagine it to be as grand as the splendor he saw at Longchamps. The prestigious race was run over grass turf with perhaps 15 horses closely bunched at the finish.

On Wednesday, they had luncheon at the Trianon Palace Hotel, a grand hotel with a regal dining room that had 200 feet of two-story-high windows overlooking Versailles' picturesque grounds. They had to leave the room for a committee meeting of 42 nations. The hotel is a Waldorf Astoria today.

After lunch, the young Olympians toured the Palace of Versailles again and wandered through its galleries and rooms for several hours. It contained the greatest collection of paintings he had ever seen, some 80 ft. long and 30 ft. high, practically all portraits and war scenes. Louis XIV's statues and portraits occupied over half of the rooms and galleries. The Hall of Mirrors was truly exquisite, but the chapel was the most stunning creation Gene viewed in the entire building. Treasures of gold, carpets, tapestries, clocks, tables, chairs, etc., were scattered throughout the building. "Magnificent carvings and statues of uncountable worth lend charm to the surroundings."

He also went to the Grand Trianon with Joie Ray and another friend in an old-fashioned Victoria automobile. Joie competed as a distance runner and would soon win a gold medal in the 3000-meter race. The Grand Trianon structure was clad in beautiful pink marble. The bedrooms were the very essence of beauty. Several have canopied beds where Napoleon slept. "The most extravagant articles money could afford furnished the lounging rooms, library, etc."

They next toured the Petit Trianon, built for Marie Antoinette and her lovers. Gene found the building to be much smaller than the Grand Trianon and not nearly as pretentious. Its most striking feature was the dining room, where the table containing the meals rose through a trap door from below. Perhaps it also hid a lover when someone from the court unexpectedly called upon the Queen.

They visited the carriage house containing the state carriages. Gene had never seen such marvelous vehicular creations before: "The largest carriage seemed to be 15 feet in height and 20 feet in length, richly upholstered within its glass sides. The doors were marvelously painted. Gold leaf covered the wheels, springs, and carriage. Surmounting the whole was a huge crown of gold." These vehicles were highly important during the centuries the French monarchs ruled France: "The ostentatious luxury was meant to dazzle and awe the subjects wherever the king showed up." "An extension of the throne, the royal carriages were made by France's best craftsmen and artists." Napoleon III continued to use the carriage until his regime ended in 1870.

On Friday, July 4th, there was a disagreeable cold rain, so they could not practice and spent much of the time inside their crowded plywood cabins conversing. That evening, General Pershing, commander of the Allied troops in World War I, General Gouraud of France, and Senator Reed addressed the athletes. Marie Dressler and her performers entertained again —the best show Gene had seen.

Gene was highly impressed by the other Notre Dame, the Notre Dame Cathedral of Paris, "awed by the number and queerness of the stone figures, posed in freakish positions, as if they were suffering from the ages of time leaning out and glaring upon the passers-by below. It looked like there were nearly 200 of the ghastly four or five-foot creatures." These were part of the visual message for the illiterate worshipers as symbols of the evil and danger that threatened those who did not follow the teachings of the church.

Gene was impressed that they started building the cathedral in 1163 taking nearly 100 years to construct the magnificent structure that by his time was 750 years old. Since nearly all the parishioners were illiterate, the church presented depictions of bible stories, such as the central portal on the west façade, which vividly illustrates the Last Judgment, with figures of sinners being led off to hell and good Christians taken to heaven. In 2019, the great church that had lasted 850 years by then succumbed to a horrific fire, toppling the iconic 226-foot-high steeple. Thanks to generous donations from around the world, following medieval construction techniques, at a cost of $ 767 million, it should be restored by December 2024.

That night before he dozed off, Gene considered all he had seen in Versailles and Paris. He felt very lucky to be granted such an amazing experience, a wonderful extension of his college education. From his reading, he knew that some of the children of wealthy families would conduct a European tour, but he never imagined he would have such an opportunity. He thought every student should endeavor to do so because one could learn so much by being there in person and experiencing European history, culture, and art up close. He had diligently read about these sites throughout his life, but their reality surpassed his imagination.

And yet, the real excitement was still to come—the Olympic competition. How well would he do? How well would his new American pals and ladies do? That remained to be seen.

18: Chariots of Fire Olympics

The 1924 Olympics were the most heralded sports spectacle of "The Golden Decade of Sports," the press obsessing over the event with its unprecedented coverage. The *New York Times* featured 397 headlines on the 1924 Olympics versus 218 for the 1920 games. The *Washington Post* would have 137 Olympic headlines versus 17, and the *Chicago Tribune* would double its features. With the antenna on top of the Eiffel Tower this would be the first Olympiad to be broadcast heard around the world over the radio. Gene and Tom's families, friends, teammates, and coach Rockne would receive multiple daily reports of their exploits and experiences through the papers.

According to historical records, the ancient Olympics spanned nearly twelve centuries, from 776 BC to 393 A.D., enough time for 283 Olympics to transpire (CCLXXXIII Olympiads). Following a fifteen-hundred-year hiatus, in the spirit of international cooperation, competition, and sportsmanship Baron De Coubertin founded the modern Olympics in 1896. This was to be the 8th, VIIIth Olympiad, but there was none held in 1916 due to the war, so technically it was the seventh. The Baron and the organizers hoped that young allies and foes, who fought so vehemently against each other, would get to know each other better and be less likely to wage war in the future, thereby serving as a release valve for the world's tensions. This was the first Olympics where numerous women would compete and the first to use the motto "Citius, Altius, Fortius" (Faster, Higher, Stronger).

Not enough time had passed since the war; therefore, the Germans were not invited to France, although Germany's allies Austria, Italy, Turkey, and Bulgaria were. Shortly after the communist revolution, the Russians did not attend either, but China joined the opening ceremony.

Interest in sports had grown exponentially over the preceding 50 years, as evidenced by football, baseball, and basketball's rapid evolution in America—why this was called "The Golden Decade of Sports." In the 1800s, when the average workweek encompassed 60 to 80 hours, and children started working on the farm or factory at twelve or as early as seven, there was little time or energy left to participate in or watch sports. Then, such pursuits were reserved primarily for the leisure class. The Olympics patterned itself after the British ideal of amateur sports—the concept of a gentleman sportsman who participated in sports to develop a balanced mind, body, and spirit.

With the advent of universal education in the United States and Europe, the number of those graduating from high school and college grew exponentially. Since 1890, as the number of high schools increased by 19% per year, and the number of students attending high school had been rising by an average of 30% per year. The number of college graduates was also increasing: from a mere 1% of the population in the 1870s to 8% by the 1920s. A month earlier, Gene had just become one of the 8%-ers. Since most, but not all, of the competition occurred in college meets, most of the track and field participants, the core of the American team, hailed from the college ranks, which was less true for the other sports, such as boxing or swimming.

Colleges began adding more sports, and the high schools followed. In the early 1900s, Rockne's high school had its first football team that only lasted a year. His high school had an unsponsored track team—for which he was expelled. Even in 1924, there was controversy about the emphasis on sports in college. Rockne felt compelled to write an essay a year earlier in the 1923 Notre Dame Dome yearbook, defending athletics as an important element in the development of a well-balanced, ethical man. He stated that athletes' test scores were statistically higher than the average student's (82% versus 80%).

By the 1920s, due to the rapid productivity improvements of the industrial age, the 40-hour workweek and child labor laws applied to most of the developed nations. Now the working class and children finally had leisure time to indulge in all manner of sport.

The British ideal of an amateur, gentleman athlete still prevailed though. Its two *Chariots of Fire*, athletes Harold Abrahams and Eric Liddell, illustrate the ideal well. Eric, who studied to be a minister at Edinburgh, was born in China to missionaries. With arms and feet rotating like a windmill, head looking upwards towards heaven, the courageous runner's style looked atrocious. With skilled coaching, he would have vastly improved his technique, but this is not something that occurred to him or to the few British coaches who witnessed his inadequacies and might have improved his style. To them, performance stemmed from natural talent and drive, something Eric possessed in abundance, rather than style and training provided by persistent coaching.

Harold Abrahams hailed from a wealthy, athletic, Jewish family. He hired a coach, Sam Mussabini, to perfect his running technique, something that was controversial and frowned on at Cambridge University where he attended. Sports was a social institution that helped define the British upper classes, and they zealously guarded its amateur character, thinking that sports enhanced the cultural ideals of sportsmanship, discipline, balance, fellowship, and fair play. Training with coaches was something the lower classes might do for their sports, such as boxing.

The emblematic opening scene in the *Chariots of Fire* movie, showed the British team in white shorts and jerseys running along the ocean shore, bare feet rhythmically slapping the waves to throbbing music. In the picturesque scene, the young, handsome athletes gave the impression that they ran for the pure joy of running. These were the amateur English gentlemen who defined the Olympic ideals of sportsmanship and fair play. They looked at the American team with all their coaches as being contrary to that principle.

Gene fit the Olympic ideal well. Based primarily on his natural, God-given talent, he had only participated in his event for two full seasons. He did not swear or indulge in smoking, carousing, or drinking. He was an outstanding student who had studied the Greeks and aspired to Aristotle's and to the leading motivator's concept of success, illustrated in *Pushing to the Front*. As demonstrated by his passing on the scholarship Rockne offered, he fiercely believed in amateur athletics and thought, as the Greeks had—that athletics was an important aspect in the development of a universal or Renaissance man.

———

"The war to end all wars" was still prevalent in the minds of those who attended the Olympics, particularly to the French, where most of the brutal trench fighting occurred, who were still, to a degree, recovering from the brutality and devastation.

As Gene witnessed on his journey to Paris from Cherbourg, Europe's story differed vastly from America's, for they continued to reconstruct their ruins after that horrendously destructive war. The U.S. fought in the war, but their country was not ravaged by it. Instead, its industries boomed to supply the war effort, and afterwards, to supply resources to rebuild Europe. From 1916 until 1920, the U.S. economy expanded 250%, producing half of the planet's oil, copper, cotton, and wheat and a third of its gold and coal. Thanks to Henry Ford and his assembly line, a working man could now afford a car, something reserved for the well-to-do in Europe. As Gene witnessed, the French still transported most of their goods by horse-driven carts. The Americans sadly lost 50,000 men during the war, but Europe tragically lost 9 million combatants and another 7 million civilians. In effect, although the term has not been coined, these countries likely suffered from systemic, national PTSD. The wounds of war needed time to heal, and the Olympics provided a tonic to soothe the pain.

As exemplified by Prohibition, a large segment of America was still somewhat puritanical, and many looked upon Europe as being decadent. The Allies loved their American saviors, but they were also a little jealous and thought these brash, naive athletes to be uncultured or even uncouth, particularly in Paris, the cultural capital of Europe and, indeed, the world.

The Paris Olympics would be Baron De Coubertin's last, set in his hometown. The French built Colombe stadium in a rundown portion northwest of Paris, where most of the events would transpire, but like future Olympiads, there would be other venues spread throughout the city. The pool was the first to be built in what would become the standard 50-meter Olympic size. In the previous Antwerp Olympics, swimmers were chilled in the canals where the swimming and diving events took place. Here there were defined lanes and gratefully, heated water!

———

Gene decided not to attend the opening ceremony at Colombe on July 5th because the athletes were required to wear their standard-issue, low-cut shoes, which would not fit over his enlarged feet, ankles and braces. Although he wanted to see the opening, he also did not want to jeopardize his performance by walking and standing on his club-like feet for hours the day before he competed.

The ceremony started with the parade of nations to loud cheers for the American and British teams, the French people's victorious allies. For only the second time, they raised the Olympic flag. The Baron had copied the design for the flag from an altar stone unearthed in Delphi, Greece. The five rings symbolize the five continents represented by six colors (blue, black, red, green, and yellow on white). Each participating nation's flag had at least one of the six.

The Baron and the French Premier briefly addressed the audience, doves were released, and a French participant, Géo André, read the Olympic Oath. André had competed in four Olympics in seven events. The oath was first taken in Belgium in 1920 and administered by the Baron as follows,

> "We swear. We will take part in the Olympic Games in a spirit of chivalry, for the honour of our country and for the glory of sport."

These proceedings were not elaborate, but the ceremony contained all of the vital Olympic elements, except the lighting of the Olympic torch, which would not occur until the next Olympiad.

Gene rested that afternoon and evening, preparing for the big event the following day. Since this would be only the Americans' second showing in the javelin, they could not expect to fare well against the intimidating Finns and Swedes who dominated the event. He had faced tests before in track and on the football fields against mighty foes like Army and Princeton, the national champion, but this constituted the most important day of his life—a defining moment. Still, as the fourth man on the team, he did not pressure himself; rather, he would do his best.

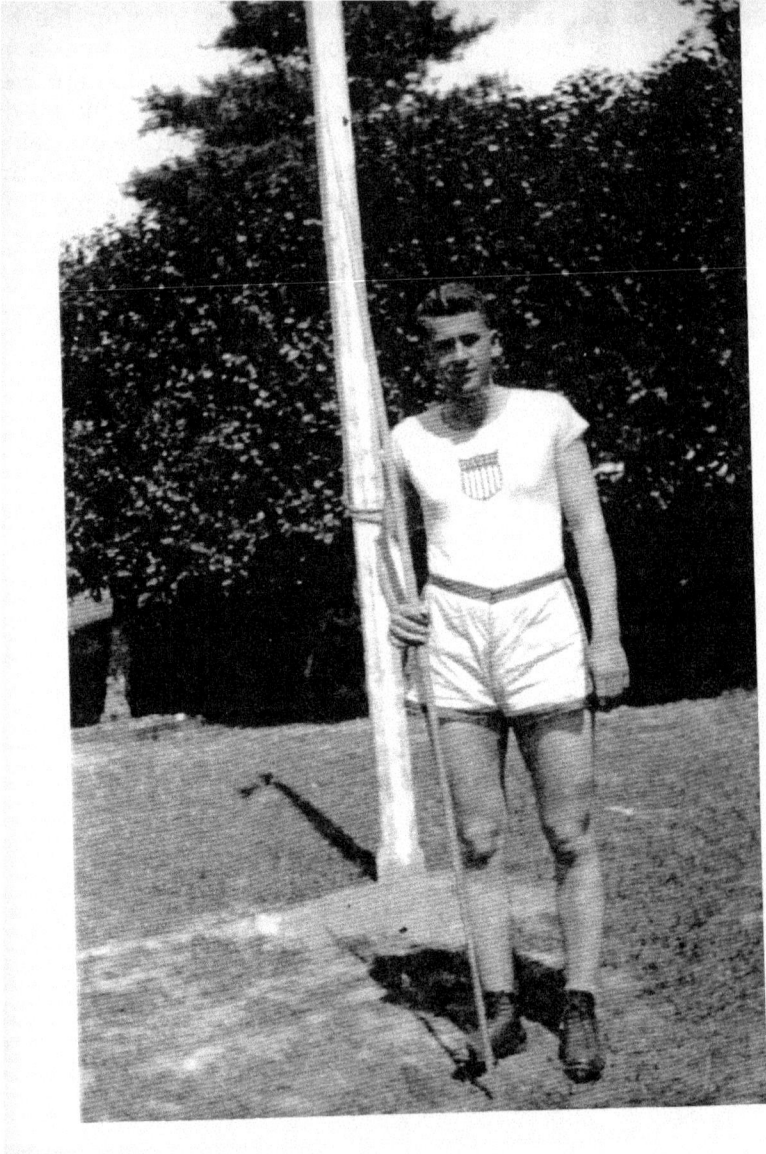

Gene in his Olympic uniform with wooden javelin

He rode the bus to Colombe with Tom, who was uncharacteristically silent. As they entered the venue, Gene felt encouraged when he saw the iconic poster for the VIIIth Olympiad, an artistic impression of a muscular man throwing the javelin with the globe and Paris filling the background, which also appeared on the front page of the program In a sense, the javelin was the featured event of the VIIIth Olympiad. They had lunch at noon, and after resting, Gene with butterflies bouncing around his stomach, nervously walked through the cool, moist, cement hall and entered the hot, noisy stadium around 3:00 P.M. Coach Tom shook his hand, patted him on the shoulder and wished him well, encouraging him to make Notre Dame and the USA proud.

Forty thousand people filled the stadium, but in the numerous major stadiums where Gene competed, he had never paid much attention to the crowds. Following his normal routine, which tended to relax him, while stretching and warming up, he noticed the broad variety of participants spanning the world. Some were tall, while others were short or heavy. The athletes that caught his attention most were those from Africa, "Looking as if they were direct from the jungles of Africa. They were long lanky beings but not skinny. One had gold rings in his ears, and all of them had tufts of wool projecting upward from the head." He thought they ought to be some of the best javelin throwers in the world, but found that to be a mistaken impression. (Then, most of Africa was still under various European countries' rule. With pictures of newly discovered African tribes practicing their centuries-old traditions appearing regularly in National Geographics, much of the continent was yet to be explored.)

As the competition got underway, Gene approached the runway for the first time with a lump in his throat, for his dream was coming true. He had been in some big events like the football game against Rebel yelling, Georgia Tech, or the crowded Army game in New York or the prestigious Penn Relays, but this was his first challenge on the world stage in front of all those people from around the globe, who did not even speak English. Because the field was wet, his friend Harry Frieda gave him a pair of his track shoes—the first he had ever worn. Gene thought the thinner spikes might gain more traction and speed in the sod.

His first mighty toss, unfortunately, hit the reddish-black cinder track encircling the field, resulting in a disqualification. This initial showing on the world stage had been embarrassing, but fortunately, no one was hurt. His second effort was gratefully in bounds measuring 53 meters (173 feet). Gene could see that five or six of the contestants had further marks, and unless he could get a better result on his last attempt, he knew he would not qualify for the finals; his Olympic dream would vanish, and he would experience the agony of defeat. This was extremely disappointing compared to his marks throughout the year, which were as much as 30 feet farther. At least his roommate, Lee Priester, had a good result and might qualify if he did not.

As with the broad jump or any of the other Men of Steel's events, the shot put, discus or hammer, if you foul or fail to obtain a good result on your first two attempts, regardless of your superior historical results, that last chance is nerve-raking and a true test of courage. Gene had set the records at prestigious meets throughout the nation, but none of that mattered now. He had one last chance for glory. This was it!

After the fourteen others had taken their turns standing at the line it was Gene's turn. He had been in similar situations before—pitching on the mound with bases loaded and one out or waiting for the ball to be hiked when he was the key down-field blocker for the speediest man ever on the field, Elmer Laden, who, with seconds remaining could score the winning touchdown. He walked off his prescribed number of steps, stopped, turned, and warmed up his arm by lifting the javelin over his shoulder and swinging it back and forth several times. Then Gene took a deep breath, jumped up, and ran as fast as he could, bent back, and with a mighty effort fired the muscles from his toes through his legs, back, shoulder, arms, hands, and twisting fingers, launching the projectile upwards. This throw felt effortless and sailed far out into the cloud-shrouded sky. Seeing the shaft's flight pattern, Gene worried that it might be out of bounds again, but after cresting, it sliced through the heavy air back to earth and stuck into the wet sod with a twang. He could see that it was thankfully in bounds.

The faraway flags marking each participant's distances had been spread throughout the field, so Gene was not sure how well he had done, for several marks appeared to be close to his. He was also not sure how well the other group, Bill and Homer's group, would fare, so he could finish high in this group and still be knocked out. When the results were announced, Gunnar Lindström of Sweden placed first with a distance of 60.81 meters (199.1 feet), with Jonni Myyra, the Finn, second at 59.3 meters (194.5 feet). Gene thankfully placed third with 57.97 meters (190.2 feet). As long as no more than three made it from the second group, he would be in the final six. Rooting for Bill and Homer, he settled in and watched the second group, hoping they would qualify if he did not.

Gene was overjoyed to witness Bill Neufeld's victory in his bracket with a throw of 56.98 meters (186.95 feet), securing his spot in the final. The final six would, as usual, include two Finns and two Swedes. However, for the first time, two Americans, including Bill, would be among them. This was a historic moment, a first in the competition's history. Out of the 29 participants, Gene had finished third. He was a bit disappointed as he had thrown over 12 feet further at the Indiana meet. Nevertheless, he had made it to the finals and had three more chances to deliver a superior throw.

Jonni Myyra had won the gold medal in the 1920 Olympics, but two of his first three throws were poor too. In the past, the Finns used their own javelins, as did the Americans, but in Paris, the Olympic Committee provided standard Spalding javelins. Myyra struggled with the new javelins, as did Gene and Bill, who said that because the javelins were made of hickory and bendable, they were all warped and wobbled in the air, thereby losing distance. When, after each round, the officials gathered the mud-tipped javelins sticking in the field and deposited them in a pile, the competitors rushed to grab the better ones, which was the luck of the draw, with medals possibly going to those who happened to grab the least wobbly ones.

Smiling broadly, shaking hands vigorously, and patting each other on the back repeatedly, Gene and Bill were thrilled to see each other in the final round. "Not bad for us, Yanks, hey Gene?" Bill might have said as they congratulated each other. They talked about the inferior javelins. Both were used to sculpting their own, and the balance points on the provided ones were off, especially for Bill. Not having his own javelin altered Gene's routine, but this was the Olympics, and he could not let that disturb him. As he had learned from other football and track competitions, he had to forget it and press on—to put it out of his mind, to be in the present as *Pushing to the Front* prescribed.

Before the finals began, it rained harder, and the field became a slippery mess. In their three distinctive uniforms, the competition had boiled down to a triangular meet between the presumptive favorite Finns, the Swedes, and the upstart USA men. With the focus now on the remaining six contestants, Gene approached the line, breathed deeply, ran his short distance, leaned back and let the javelin fly, but dirty from the mud and in the thick rain-soaked air, the projectile did not travel as far as his earlier tosses. Other than Yrjö Ekqvist, the other Finn, none of the six could improve their marks by more than a few inches. Gene noticed that the Finns had a different style, though. Instead of running, leaning back, and throwing, they took a cross step to set up for the toss. The cross step allows the runner to preserve more of their speed before the toss.

On his next attempt, Gene gave it all he had, hoping at least to beat the Swede's throw, but he slipped in the mud and went beyond the line, resulting in a foul, thereby disqualifying the attempt. He thought it might have been better to wear the old football shoes that gave more traction in mud rather than the unaccustomed track shoes, but he would not have time to retrieve them. The track shoes did not have the support of his high boot-like football spikes that granted him more speed and more solid footing. He had an advantage, though. Since he could not run as fast, he did not rely on a lengthy, sloggy approach to build speed; rather he relied on his upper body. Due to the slippery conditions, none of the other participants could get off vastly better throws either until Myyra strode to the line.

Jonni Myyra, the handsome, short-haired, blond Finn with strong, thick thighs, was next up. He quickly ran up to the line, executed the cross-step, bent far back, launched a magnificent spear, and mightily hopped forward, heading for the line. His right foot's spikes dug in, and just as his left foot was about to step over the disqualifying line, he rotated it parallel to the line, missing it by an inch or less. Even in the damp air, Gene could see that this spear was flying long and far, landing with a reverberating stab into the muddy soil. The toss registered a remarkable 62.96 meters (206 ½ feet). Myyra's speed, fluid form, and force imparted to the javelin amazed Gene. Lindstrom, the Sweed, could only better his qualifying mark by a few inches, something that was well within Gene's range, that is, if he happened to grab a solid javelin.

Due to repeated use, the approach became even sloppier, and on the last mighty attempt, Gene gave it all he had. Despite slipping at the very end, he got off a mighty throw. It flew high and far, and he thought this was surely the one. Because he slipped, he could see it was heading towards the cinder track, and he feared it might spear someone. The javelin flew over the track surrounding the field, thankfully not hitting anyone—another disqualification. Gene was heartbroken, for his Olympics were over, and he had not done well. He had not lived up to his lofty expectations, and it was all over.

With his remarkable performance, Myyra ended up winning the javelin competition by a substantial margin of 7.5 feet, with Lindstrom garnering second place. Even though he had done so poorly in the finals, Gene was pleasantly surprised to see that his first-round result was good enough to gain a third place and a glorious bronze medal. Like Gene, Bill too was frustrated that he could not improve his previous mark, and the other Finn, Yrjö Ekqvist, took fourth, but Bill still finished 5th—not bad for the Americans competing in the event for only the second time. Against the world's best, out of the 29 participants, their cabin mates Priester and Whelchel finished 11th and 12th, and the USA captured four of the top twelve positions overall, a great showing for American javelin men—the first of the Men of Steel to compete. Despite the less-than-ideal conditions, their friendly competition, companionship, and throwing javelins tied to the back of the ship had paid off.

If Gene's furthest throw was measured on the arc, as would be done soon for future Olympics for all the throwing events, it would have measured over 204 feet, enough to beat Lindstrom but not quite enough to beat Myyra's toss of 206 1/2 feet. If measured on the arc, his furthest toss at the Indiana meet a little over a month ago, the farthest in America that year, would have resulted in up to 215 feet. The wet conditions and unfamiliar javelins affected all the participants, with few being able to record their best distances. Under better conditions using his own javelin, Myyra had thrown nearly 10 feet further in the '20 Olympics when he set the world record, which was not beaten on this inclement day. Gene would have admired Myyra's remarkable form and liked to adopt the crossover to qualify for the next Olympics. The complex foot movements and explosion at the end was something Rockne would appreciate and perhaps coach him on.

Back of Gene Oberst's 1924 bronze Olympic Medal
Showing one athlete helping another up & Olympic rings

After the event, the three athletes received their medals from their coaches, with Walter Christie handing Gene his bronze medal, shaking his hand, and congratulating him with a smile and a pat on the back. Myyra received the gold and Lindstrom the silver. Since the Olympic customs that now seem entrenched were still evolving, there was no formal award ceremony or victory stand, and the Finnish anthem was not played, as it would be later. However, this was the first Olympics in which the three flags were raised. Having endured the rain, mud, and slippery conditions; after not registering a better throw in the finals, Gene was elated to receive his medal, thinking that would be all the recognition he would receive. After all, this is something he had dreamed of his whole life, and as the last to qualify for the American javelin team, it was not something he expected.

For the first time, officials attached three flags to tall flagpoles and pulled the flags upward to the sky with Finland's blue cross on a white background on top, Sweden's yellow cross slightly below, and on the other side, the USA's seven red and six white stripes along with six horizontal rows of eight white stars on a blue background. Surprised to see the flags rising up the poles, struggling not to let the tears gathering in his eyes flow down his cheeks, shivers went down Gene's spine as he saw the American flag rise in his honor and heard his name over the PA system, "Troisième, Gene Oberst, Les États-Unis d'Amérique, Third, Gene Oberst the United States of America." His was the first medal for America and, consequently, the first time the Stars and Stripes flew over the Paris Columbes stadium or any Olympic stadium for that matter, and the first time the Stars and Stripes ever flew to honor an American. It was also the nation's first medal in the javelin and it would be the only USA javelin medal in the first 50 years of the Modern Olympics.

Later, Gene received a large certificate with a Greek figure recording his place and distance, signed by the Baron—the last he would sign. The top six places garnered this honor, so Bill won one, too.

Front of Gene Oberst's bronze Olympic medal
Showing date and various summer and winter games implements

Gene later looked closely at the medal, seeing that the back contained a variety of sporting implements such as a javelin, discus, and shot put. Some of the figures looked unfamiliar, though, such as skates, skis, and poles for the same medal that had been awarded at the first Winter Olympics earlier that year in Chamonix, France.

Olympic Certificate
Presented to the top six places
Signed by Baron De Coubertin
With place and distance

Afterward, Tom likely met Gene with a broad smile, shook his hand vigorously, and gave him a big bear hug. The usually reserved Kentuck could not avoid an immense, toothsome grin. Tom said, "Rock will be so immensely pleased, Kentuck." Gene said, "It's your turn now, Tom. Let's make it two medals for the U S A and good old Notre Dame." In addition to being his teammate and friend, Tom was also his coach, which added another degree of pride.

Following the first day's events, the score stood at Finland - 30 points, Sweden - 21, USA – 6: the points Gene and Bill earned. The scoring for each event consisted of 10 points for first place, 5 for second, 4 for third, 3 for fourth, 2 for fifth, and 1 for sixth place. Therefore, Gene scored 4 points and Bill 2 for good, old USA. On that day, July 7th, the New York Telegram's coverage of the event read, "Yanks broke up the former Russian subject's complete mastery four years ago. Earnst (Eugene) Oberst of Notre Dame University got third place and Bill Neufeld of the University of California fifth scoring the six points that the Americans were not counting on."

After the event, while still charged with excitement from the competition, Lee and Bill decided they wanted one of the Olympic flags flying on all the flagpoles around the stadium as a souvenir to commemorate the event. They talked a French boy into climbing up the pole to get an Olympic flag for them. The boy climbed up and then looked down to see two gendarmes standing behind Lee and Bill. Struggling to formulate an excuse, they told the policemen they were applauding the flag, and the gendarmes let them go.

Gene and Bill registered the first, but many more spectacular performances had yet to transpire for the Americans and the world's competitors.

19: Joy of Victory

The next day Gene looked forward to attending the much-publicized 100-meter dash, deciding who would be the fastest man in the world. Eric Liddell, the fastest British runner, might pose an obstacle for the two American phenoms, Jackson Schulz and Charlie Paddock, who had been christened "the fastest man alive."

When the schedule came out, Liddell, a ministry student, noticed that the preliminaries would be held on Sunday, which his religion forbade participating in. The British Olympic Committee, including the Prince of Wales (soon to be King), tried to persuade him to compete, but Eric struggled with his conscience. The British saw that their best chance to win gold in the esteemed race would vanish if Liddell did not race. Despite the intense pressure from the British Olympic Committee, the Royals and the press, Eric decided he could not compete. The controversy appeared in papers throughout Britain, the U.S. and Paris, so Gene had read about it. Instead of the 100m, they decided he would run the 400m.

However, the Americans would not be guaranteed a pass to sweep the medals because the Brits had another outstanding sprinter in Harold Abrahams, the gentleman from Cambridge. Abrahams had not fared well at the Penn Relays a couple of months earlier when Liddell soundly defeated him. After breaking the Relays record by 12 feet, Gene had witnessed the event. Under Sam Mussabini's tutelage, he had made rapid progress, though. Abrahams had already broken the British long jump record at 24 feet 2½ inches, a feat not bettered until 32 years later in 1956, but now he concentrated on his running.

Since shorter faster piston-like steps produce more speed, Sam worked with Harold to quicken his start and increase the number of steps by placing pieces of paper at a measured interval on the track for him to spike as he ran. Abraham's major flaw was that he tended to look at other contenders as he ran, which Mussabini constantly tried to correct, instructing him to concentrate on his race and nothing else. In a preliminary, Scholz grinned at Abrahams, which disturbed his concentration and resulted in a poor start, after which he finished second. Sam scolded him severely for doing that and warned him not to do it again—concentrate, concentrate, concentrate.

Abrahams, a nouveau riche Jew, and Mussabini, an Arab/Italian immigrant, felt they had something to prove to the British elites. As a non-credentialed coach, Sam would not be allowed to enter the stadium to watch the race, but his hopes would be with Abrahams. Prior to the race, Sam sent Harold a note that he read in the tense, subdued locker room. "Only think of two things—the report of the pistol and the tape. When you hear the one, just run like hell until you break the other." The note helped Harold focus.

The four favored, speedy Americans all made it through the numerous preliminaries to the finals. Before the race, the Prince of Wales shook the hand of each of the participants telling "the fastest man alive," Charlie Paddock, "Dinner for your whole team at my club when we get back to London. You win, I pay. Abrahams wins; you pay. He went over to Abrahams and said, "Do your best. That's all we can expect."

The tension before a sprint is comparable to that of a taught wire about to snap and, for most, is unbearable. There you are in the footholds, ready to explode. Once the gun goes off, you must use every muscle in your body, not just those in your legs, to explode off the line, charge as fast as you possibly can, and, in fewer than ten seconds, it's all over. Unlike other sports, after the start, there is no second serve, no second down, no second strike, no second chance, one mistake, one imperfection, and you're out. Any sprint at any level is like this, but imagine the tension, competing against the world's best for fewer than ten seconds in front of the world with only one such opportunity every four years.

The gun went off, and Harold had a lightning-fast start. At the 25-meter mark, the runners bunched together. At the 50, he took the lead with Scholz and another American, Bowman, in hot pursuit. Then he gained a foot, then two, and hit the tape. He was the fastest man in the world. Scholz came in second. Gene saw Liddell run through the crowd to be one of the first to congratulate Abrahams. The Prince of Wales smiled broadly to the French Premier and then went down to congratulate Abrahams. Harold and Sam felt a mix of elation and vindication.

––––––

That Wednesday featured the 200-meter dash, in which Gene's teammates fared better. Scholz won the gold medal and Paddock the silver. Liddell finished third to garner a bronze, with Abrahams sixth.

The 400-meter would be the next major race. Gene followed the controversy surrounding Liddell, discussing it with The Men of Steel. As a religious man, he could understand Liddell's perspective. He was grateful he did not have to compete on Sunday but did not think it would have been against his conscience to do so. He later met Eric and found him to be an impressive, character-laden, spiritual man, someone you could look into his eyes and instantly admire.

Sixty runners competed from 27 nations in the preliminary, quarterfinal, semifinal, and final heats. In the successive races, Liddell finished first, second, and first again. He had been a sprinter, the best in Britain and, indeed, Europe, but the 400 was relatively new to him.

The 400-meter is a challenging race combining elements of the sprints and longer-distance races. In the sprints, you go all out the entire distance, whereas in the longer races, you must pace yourself until the end, saving up for that final, all-important sprint to the finish line. With your core in constant, perfect alignment, you take longer, more efficient strides that feel like you are gliding powered by rhythmic footfalls off the cinders. Running at 85% of full speed, the 400 is a controlled sprint. It's like running with a full tank of energy reserves. As you run one full lap around the circular track, your energy gauge gradually falls, and you want to reserve enough in your tank to go all out at the end. If you do not, you will stall out. So, you want to get up to speed quickly, then maintain that speed as you run in your lane in 5th gear, and downshift at the end for a burst of speed. It's a gutsy and painful race that requires extreme courage, one in which many contestants collapse or throw up at the end due to their intense exertion.

As in any race, form and precision are of utmost importance, which the superbly coached Abrahams and the Americans mastered well. It's like running on a tightrope. Liddell had absolutely no form or precision; instead, he ran on guts and spiritual reserves. He planned to dedicate his life to God and return to China as a missionary like his parents. His primary reason for racing was that he believed God had given him this gift and intended for him to use it for God's purpose.

Before the Olympics, Liddell had never broken 49 seconds, whereas two racers, Horatio Fitch of the United States and Guy Butler, one of Eric's British teammates, had. Fitch set the Olympic record in the first semi-final at 47.8, with Butler only a tenth of a second behind.

Eric received a note in the locker room as he dressed for the race. He opened it and read, "In the Old Book, it says, 'He that honors me, I will honor." All his teammates signed it. If any controversy lingered, the note vanquished it.

Eric lined up in the outside lane and, with his trowel, dug holes in the cinder track to anchor his feet, one for each foot about two feet apart, which the sprinter pushes against at the start for an explosion of speed. The outside lane is the worst because you cannot see the other competitors, and the fastest men in the world use you as a target to run you down.

When the gun went off, Eric shot out as if he was running a sprint. His 200 time of 22.2 was only .3 second behind his bronze medal-winning time in the 200—unfathomable. He ran at 99% of his sprint speed, substantially beyond the world-record pace. At this pace, his tank would surely soon be emptied, but he just kept running. Two of the five runners who tried to chase him fell to the ground because they could not match his ridiculous pace. Fitch and Butler were less than two steps behind, thinking the foolish Scott would soon exhaust his tank, stall out, and they would speed by him. He continued to run with his head looking up to the sky and his legs and arms churning like a windmill. At the end, Fitch and Butler downshifted, expecting Liddell to be out of gas and easily pass him, but instead, Eric sprinted ever faster, increasing his lead by another couple of meters. He snapped the tape in a new world record of 47.6. Winded, Finch and Butler finished nearly a second and several steps behind. Afterwards, Eric went back to John Taylor, an American, who had fallen, to help him to his feet. The crowd stood up, cheering and clapping wildly. Gene thought this was the best Olympics performance thus far and could not imagine any better, but there was more to come. Since his event was over, he could enjoy it all.

DeHart Hubbard

On the SS America, Gene remembered seeing a "Negro" onboard. At first, he thought he might be a porter, but DeHart Hubbard was instead one of the first black American Olympic team members. Gene may have had mixed feelings about having him on the team as a Southerner, but many of the people he liked most in Owensboro were black, and his dad employed over a dozen in the brickyard. Even though Kentucky was a border state and the city was on its northern border, Owensboro's Davies County had slave owners prior to the Civil War.

Harriet Beecher Stowe, who lived upriver in Cincinnati along the Underground Railroad, based her foundational, attitude-changing *Uncle Tom's Cabin* on the life of Josiah Henson. Josiah rose to the position of overseer on an Owensboro plantation before escaping with his family along the Underground Railroad. As a Catholic from Notre Dame, who had witnessed such prejudice firsthand from the KKK in Georgia, Nebraska, and their invasion of South Bend, he could sympathize with DeHart's plight.

DeHart, the son of a chauffeur, grew up in Cincinnati always running—running to school, running to deliver his newspapers. He was one of the few blacks admitted to Walnut Hills College Prep, where on the football team, he scored four touchdowns in one game, after which the prejudicial school board insisted he be cut from the team.   This sounds unbelievable, but it was the 1920s, during the time of the Jim Crow laws, during the KKK's resurgence, when the KKK dominated much of the Midwestern landscape, including most of the political offices in nearby Indiana.   In a show of solidarity, his supportive white teammates refused to play another game unless DeHart would be allowed to join them. Thanks to the students' principled stand, the school board wisely relented.

When the Cincinnati Enquirer sponsored a contest, Lon Barringer persuaded fellow Michigan University alumni throughout the country to buy subscriptions so DeHart could win a college scholarship to Michigan University.

Michigan's coach, Fielding Yost, along with Capp, Stagg and Rockne, was one of the greatest early coaches, winning six National Football Championships up until 1923. Early In the 20th century, he had won 56 games in a row claiming four national championships. Yost grew up in the South and, due to his prejudice, did not allow blacks on his football or track teams. Lon somehow persuaded Yost, also the athletic director, to let Hubbard join the track team, a fortunate decision for Michigan, for Hubbard would set numerous Michigan, Big Ten, NCAA, AAU, and national records in the sprints, the broad jump, triple jump and hurdles, helping Michigan to win numerous meets including the conference championships. Yost might have also won a couple more football championships if he had allowed one of the fastest men alive to play.

DeHart's Michigan broad jump record of 25' 10 ½" stood for over 50 years and remarkably, nearly 100 years later, still ranks second. As if this was not enough, remarkably, he captured the world record in the broad jump and tied the 100-yard dash world record. Therefore, he was one of the two fastest men in the world. Demonstrating his intellectual capacity, DeHart also graduated with honors.

In the '24 Olympics, Hubbard was one of only three blacks on the team. Gene had witnessed Hubbard's spectacular performance in the 100-yard dash and long jump at the Conference Championships at Michigan in '23. Gene ate with DeHart and the other blacks onboard the S.S. America and at Rocquencourt. Dining with blacks in 1924 was not something many white athletes would do, especially Southerners, but Gene didn't care and may have caused others to be more accepting of their accomplished teammates.

Hubbard wrote back to his parents, "Tell Papa I got his letter, but have been busy traveling, etc., and have not had the time to answer. Tell him I'm going to do my best to be the FIRST COLORED OLYMPIC CHAMPION."

In the broad jump, after injuring his heal, on his last jump, DeHart soared 24' 5" inches to capture Olympic gold—the first individual gold medal for an African American in the history of the Olympics, after which he watched the American flag hoisted in his honor.

As one of the fastest men in the world, Hubbard also qualified to compete in the 100-meter dash and the high hurdles but was denied the chance because he was black. Many more would follow in DeHart, though.

Two other African Americans were among the first to join the Olympic team: Charles Brookins of Iowa in the 400-meter hurdles and E.O. "Ned" Gourdin of Harvard, who won the silver medal in the long jump. Ned would later become a Massachusetts Supreme Court judge.

Without evidence of their tours through Paris, one can wonder about their impression of Parisian life, where the highly civilized French treated blacks as equals and even celebrities. DeHart would later live near Gene. (As a coach, Gene would stand up to prejudice in the South and champion black athletes.)

Like Jackie Robinson of the National League and Larry Doby of the American League, Arthur Ash in tennis and Tiger Woods in golf, Hubbard broke down barriers so other renowned athletes could follow in his footsteps. Two other outstanding athletes who benefited from his pioneering spirit would become his best friends in Cleveland—Jesse Owens and Harrison Dillard. Jesse Owens thwarted Hitler's master race ideology by winning four gold medals in the 1936 Berlin Olympics and ranks sixth among 20th-century athletes. Harrison also won four gold medals, winning both the 100-meter dash and the 100-meter hurdles, making him the "World's Fastest Man" in 1948 and the "World's Fastest Hurdler" in 1952. In his eulogy to DeHart, Dillard remembered him as being intelligent, articulate and of the highest character. "There was a sense of the gentleman about him."

In addition to his incomparable athletic ability, it took an extremely intelligent and humble person, someone with impeccable character and resilience, to break down the massive barriers he faced. (The author nominated, somehow forgotten DeHart Hubbard to the Cleveland Sports Hall of Fame and had the heart-felt honor of sitting next to Harrison Dillard, who at 95 gave DeHart's induction speech.)

Johnny Weissmuller

One of America's most promising athletes, Johnny Weissmuller, grew up on the mean, gang-infested streets of Chicago's North Side. He lived in an abusive household where his Austrian father beat his wife and two sons regularly. The father left the family when Johnny was in sixth grade, leaving his mother to raise the boys herself by taking a job as a cook.

Johnny had polio, and according to the story, his mother worried about her spindly child's health; she sought the advice of a doctor who recommended he try swimming. She took sickly Johnny down to the sandy beach on Lake Michigan. There, young Johnny took to the water like a dolphin, transforming his underdeveloped frame to that of a mighty athlete. He lied about his age, saying he was 12 when he was 11, so he could join the YMCA, where he soon won all the swimming competitions. Johnny soon left school to help support his mother and younger brother.

Bill Bachrach, a cigar-smoking, 350-pound coach and eventual Olympic swimming coach noticed the tall, long-armed swimmer and invited Johnny to join the Illinois Athletic Club's (IAC) team, the same club Rockne ran for ten years earlier and where Tom Lieb set the AAU discus record that year, the same club that Alonzo Stagg belonged to and Gene would soon join. Athletic clubs were the only real pathway for a poor athlete like Johnny to make it to the Olympics. There, Bachrach coached gangly Weissmuller until he became a successful swimmer.

In the first Olympic-sized pool, Johnny Weissmuller won three gold medals in the 100-meter freestyle, the 400-meter freestyle and the 4×200-meter relay. He also won a bronze medal in water polo, becoming the most decorated American Olympian in Paris. All but one of the water polo team members were from the IAC. Johny was the first to break the 1-minute mark in the 100; his 51.0 mark would not be broken for 17 years, which he would again break at the age of 36 with a time of 48.5 seconds. In total, he broke 67 world records.

The French went wild for Johnny. When he won, they stood and cheered for two or three minutes. In between events, Johnny and Stubby Kruger, another swimmer, entertained the crowd at the natatorium. Johnny, with his Atlas physique, would perform a classic swan dive, followed by Stubby in a striped, baggy suit who would perform a clumsy, slapstick, crash landing, duck dive. The French crowd loved this type of humor.

The U.S. men's and women's swimming teams had a glorious Olympiad winning 11 out of 13 gold medals. Johnny, Duke Kahanamoku, and his brother Samuel would sweep the 100-meter race becoming the fastest swimmers in the world, while the American women would sweep the 100-meter and 400-meter races, becoming the fastest women.

Initially, Gene was not particularly fond of Weissmuller though. To him, he seemed crude and uncouth. Earlier on the train from Cherbourg to Paris, some French children rode their bikes alongside of the train cheering for the team. To show off, Johnny jumped off the train and pushed one of the lads off his bike, then jumped back on the train. Gene thought this was despicable. Gene later saw Johnny heat some coins with a match and then throw these to some French children, who, upon picking up the coins, burnt their fingers. As Johnny began laughing, using his skill in handling boys' bad behavior, Gene touched him on the shoulder, looked him squarely in the eye, and told him to never do that again. Later, Johnny lived less than a mile away from Gene at the Alcazar Hotel in Cleveland Heights. Both were invited to the same events, where Gene got to know him better as they relived their Olympic experience when Johnny had matured.

Johnny would go on to make 37 movies, acquiring fame as Tarzan and Jungle Jim.

Paavo Nurmi

Another Finn, Paavo Nurmi, was the Olympian whose star shown the brightest in the '24 Olympiad. At a time when the population of the United States stood at over 100 million, Finland had a little over 3 million people, yet, surprisingly, next to the U.S., it was the most dominant Olympic power. Finland won their independence from Communist Russia in 1920, so this was a heady time for the Finns buoyed with self-confidence and national pride. Besides the javelin, their prowess extended into distance running too.

A reclusive runner, Nurmi had a rigorous, secretive training regime. The only other runner who could challenge him was another of the Flying Finns—Villa Ritola. After winning gold medals in the 1,500-meter and 5,000-meter races, Nurmi entered the 10,000-meter cross-country race, which would be contested over a brutal course featuring water, steep, bramble-laden cliffs, fences, and a pollution-belching electricity plant. Running one distance race at the highest level would be a daunting enough task, but running three seemed unimaginable. To check his pace, Nurmi always ran with a stopwatch in his hand

The temperature on that sweltering July day registered 86 degrees Fahrenheit in the shade and as high as 113 in baking, sun-drenched Colombe stadium. With no one in sight, Nurmi was the first to enter the stadium, winning the individual gold medal. Of the 42 well-conditioned athletes who started the course, only 18 entered the stadium and only 12 managed to cross the longed-for finish line, most staggering to do so. The rest faltered or collapsed en route with many of them being hospitalized. Because this event was so brutal, it would not be continued in future Olympics.

As with any cross-country race, points were also awarded based on a team's order at the finish line. Nearly a minute and a half later, his teammate Ritola, who was later hospitalized, captured second, with Heikki Liimatainen finishing eighth to win the team gold. The U.S. was more tightly compacted finishing third, fifth, and sixth for the silver, with France capturing the bronze—the only teams to have the three required finishers.

Ritola also won the 10,000-meter long-distance race (10k, 6.2 miles), a race Nurmi thought the Finnish Olympic committee should have allowed him to enter, but they thought he would not have enough time to recover for his fourth long-distance race.

The next day, Nurmi went on to help his team with the 10,000-meter relay, setting a World Record of 30:06.2. He had won five gold medals, the most in the Paris Olympics—a remarkable feat. Ritola would have the second most, with four golds and a silver.

———

Since Gene completed his event on the first day of the Olympics, he spent his time watching the other events and touring Paris, in a relaxed, joy-filled manner. While wandering through the verdant half-mile-long Jardin des Tuileries, he grabbed a baguette, some cheese, and a café au lait at an outdoor café on a beautiful, sunny, hot July day, then settled in near a splashing fountain and watched the life and people streaming by as he feasted on his meal.

He visited the adjacent Louvre, amazed by what he saw there, with entire halls dedicated to the famous artists he loved, such as Rubens, Murillo, Velasquez, and Van Dyke. There he saw the works of Titian, Bartolommeo, Raphael, Da Vinci, and other famous masters, some so realistic they jumped out at you. He spent hours viewing the sculptures of the Assyrians, Egyptians, Corinthians, Romans, and Greeks. He marveled at the Egyptian antiquities that dated back to 3000 BC, such as the Great Sphinx of Tanis and the Seated Scribe, which looked like it could have been sculpted in his time.

He admired the armless sensuous, 2nd century BC, white marble statue of Venus de Milo, depicting the Greek goddess Aphrodite, with a bare torso and drapery over the lower half of her body with raised leg like that of a model. He gazed at Da Vinci's enigmatic Mona Lisa and the huge 30-foot by 20-foot-high painting of the Coronation of Napoleon by Jacques-Louis David.

With his appreciation of French history, the sword of Charlemagne, who conquered nearly all of Europe, fascinated him the most. He left the Louvre stunned, unable to believe that so much beauty and expression could be contained in one place.

Gene had drawn doodles in his notebooks at school and inspired by what he saw, thought someday he might like to paint. If he took a coaching job, an advantage would be that he would have the summers off to develop his art. After all, this was something a true Renaissance man, as he aspired to be, would do. If he did so, he thought he would like to adopt the classic style that overwhelmed him at the Louvre. (Gene would eventually paint over 200 paintings in four generations of styles.)

Later that day, he rode an elevator for the first time to the top of the Eiffel Tower, at 975 feet the world's tallest structure. There he had a glass of cold beer and purchased some souvenirs for those back home. Afraid to get too close to the railing from such a height, he thought, "Paris, with its streets, gardens, parks, buildings, vehicles, and people seemed like a toy city of teeny, weenie people. A horse appeared much like an ant crawling on the ground. The Seine seemed to be a broad dirty white ribbon carelessly thrown by the hands of a giant across the toy town of Paris just below my feet."

The ride down the elevator seemed like a vast telescope focused upon the ground. The nearer he approached the earth, the better the focus grew, increasing the toy city's size more and more to what he was accustomed.

———

Anxious to hear news from home, Gene received a letter. Brother Albert wrote him on July 3, 1924, which would take a week or two to arrive, since there was no airmail yet. Gene missed home and appreciated hearing the latest news of his family from his favorite brother. In the letter, Albert told him that even though he would have competed by the time he received the letter, he knew he would have done his best and that they were all pulling for him. Gene imagined the celebration the family had once they learned he had won a medal. He thought they would all gather in the parlor and toast his victory with their best homemade wine or bourbon.

Albert enclosed pictures of Gene he had made for him to hand out to Olympic friends. These would prove a valuable remembrance when the team finally ended their monumental trip together and went their separate ways. While he was out of the country, he had asked Rockne to contact Albert regarding any potential job prospects. Albert wrote about the position Rockne had arranged for him, "Received a letter from Father Walsh of St. John's in Shreveport, Louisiana about your position, and he asked that I write the contract. So, I am going to submit a copy to him."

Last day

On the last day of the athletic events, Gene went to Colombe to see Tom compete in the discus. There, he was thrilled to see him win a bronze medal too. He could not wait to give him a well-earned bear hug. Rockne would soon read about their success. Another man of steel, Bud Houser, won the gold in the discus, setting the Olympic record of 46.155 meters (151'5"). Later that summer Tom would break this and the world record with a toss of 156'2".

Bud Houser went on to win gold in the shot put too. Along with Glenn Hartranft and Ralph Hills, the U.S. swept the event. Gene was proud of them all, men of steel, who threw the ancient weapons as he did. He especially enjoyed seeing the three American flags flying.

The men who threw the hammer and lived with them in their cabin, also performed well with a couple of big Irish cops, Fred Tootell and Matt McGrath, taking gold and silver. Overall, The Men of Steel took 8 of 12 available medals in the four throwing events—the javelin, discus, shotput and hammer.

The last event consisted of the Marathon. This, too, was an extremely hot day, so the runners tied cloth to their heads that looked like turbans as they ran through the steaming Parisian streets lined with throngs of cheering fans. When they reached the refreshment tables, they would reach into a tub of water lying on the ground with both hands and splash the liquid over their hot body, head, and turban. They might also drink a glass of water or milk or wine before running off.

Another Flying Finn, Oskar Stenroos, won the grueling contest, finishing the 26+ miles in a "fine manner" with a time of 2h.41m.22s Oskar was evidently not exhausted as he ran a victory lap after finishing as if he was just getting ready to run. Gene, along with all the spectators, rose and shouted to honor this great athlete who finished 6 minutes ahead of any of the other 55 starters. An Italian, Bertini took second with the American, De Mar third, who was from Madeira, Ohio, and a Harvard grad. With this achievement, the flag of Finland floated over the Stadium once again, being the first and last flag to be seen there. The U.S. flag also flew first and last.

During the brief closing ceremony, Baron de Coubertin urged the Olympic torch to illuminate forever "an always more ardent, braver and purer humanity."

Afterward, Colonel Thompson read the names of the fifty athletes who were invited to go to London for the London Relays. Gene was tickled to be on the team and have the opportunity to see London too, a wonderful bonus. They went to the grand Continental Hotel where they were the guests of the British Olympic Team. The Americans would soon travel with the Brits to London to compete in the London Relays, which would prove to be an unexpected, interesting experience, perhaps not as glorious as the Olympics, but more intimate and in some ways, richer.

20: London

Throughout the Olympics, the mood in the newly built clapboard village at Rocquencourt became increasingly more festive as the Americans accumulated more of the precious gold, silver, and bronze they gleefully displayed to their fellow Americans. The Men of Steel were particularly pleased with the fruits of their labor, their eight medals, a crescendo they had been building towards for their entire lives.

Between witnessing their successes, Gene pursued his passion of seeing the historical battlefields—scenes of destruction, despair, and devastation wrought by the First World War. He toured Belleau Woods, Chateau Thierry, and the Marne first all within 20 miles. At Belleau Woods, he saw the recent graves of 2,200 American soldiers then walked up the hill and entered the woods along a path where a French worker was laying fresh gravel. According to Gene:

> *The woods is a mass of vines, small trees and underbrush, through which one cannot see more than 25 feet. Hundreds of splintered tree stumps gave mute testimony of the scenes enacted there. Bullet holes, large and small, were in practically every tree."*
>
> *"There still was a large number of machine gun nests and sniper holes throughout the woods, the same as those were left by the soldiers just 6 years earlier, only that the bottoms are filled with water that cannot dry up in the thick woods. Helmets, shells, hand grenades can be seen lying around rusting rapidly.*

He secured several shells as souvenirs and brought away a vertebra of either a dead German or an American soldier.

The caretaker, who tended to the continuing grizzly work of the woods, informed him that approximately 100 American soldiers were buried somewhere in the woods that they could no longer find, a testament to the terror that still haunted the grounds even on a fine July day. Just that very morning, they had found the skeleton of a German soldier hidden in the woods. On the return to Paris, they passed a German graveyard wherein 16,000 Germans reposed.

Following the Russian surrender, the Germans transferred 50 divisions to the Western Front, hoping to defeat the Allies before U.S. forces could be deployed.   By June, the Germans had conquered Château-Thierry, less than 60 miles from Paris, an hour's drive. The allies hoped they could stop them at Belleau Woods before they rolled into Paris, only 30 miles from de Gaulle Airport.

In the afternoon of June 3rd, 1918, German infantry attacked the Marine positions through the grain fields with fixed bayonets. The Marines waited until the Germans were within 100 yards before opening fire, which mowed down waves of German infantry before they retreated into the woods. Over the next two days, the Marines repelled continuous German assaults.

Six times the Marines attacked across open wheat fields and the woods that were swept with German machine gun and artillery fire. Many Marines were cut down. They fought in hand-to-hand combat using bayonets and fists. It was not until June 26 that the Marines and a Machine Gun Battalion cleared the area of Germans, whose advance towards Paris was finally significantly stopped.

The United States suffered 9,777 casualties and 1,811 deaths. White crosses and Stars of David mark 2,289 graves in a 13-deep, semi-circular pattern at the edge of the fatal woods. An additional two-hundred-and-fifty headstones were dedicated to unknown soldiers. As Gene could attest to, many of the dead would never be recovered from the deadly tangled woods, for the names of 1,060 missing men adorn the wall of the Romanesque, marbled memorial chapel at the center of the field.

In July, the Allies went on the offensive and defeated the Germans at the Second Battle of the Marne. In this battle, they suffered over 122,000, mostly French, casualties to the Germans' 139,000. They also captured 29,000 Germans. This victory and that at Belleau Woods marked the turning point of the brutal war, which, as a result of these battles, would be over in three months.

Gene's future son, Captain Albert Knute (named after Rockne) Oberst J.D., would promote and maintain a memorial to the World War I veterans, Liberty Row, for over 50 years. After the war, school children planted White Oaks along Cleveland's Liberty Boulevard donated by John D Rockefeller, that spanned from Lake Erie through the Shaker Lakes in Cleveland Heights and Shaker Heights. Beneath each of the over 800 Oaks was a brass plaque set in concrete honoring the Clevelanders who perished in World War I. Many of these valiant service members would have died at Belleau Woods and the Second Battle of Marne. Over 100 years later, although many of the memorials have disappeared, and some of the oaks died, thanks to Al's and other's efforts, many are preserved.

Just 15 years later, Europe would plunge into another World War, and France would be invaded again. Several of Gene's nephews would fight in that war and one, Gerald Oberst, would die in a German prison camp after his plane was shot down. His niece, Mary Josephine Oberst, would be one of the Angels of Baton who was imprisoned in terrible conditions in the Philippines ministering to sick and dying soldiers. She would be one of the last Angels to die and would receive a commendation from Congress.

————

Back in Paris, the athletes who scored points (the top six) were given tickets to the opera. The performance would commence shortly, so they had to attend in the same grimy clothes, in which they had toured the battlefields. As they entered the opulent opera house, probably the most famous in the world, the actual setting for the *Phantom of the Opera*, with long magnificent golden, gilded halls that were up to five stories high, with magnificently painted colorful, scenes painted on the ceilings, lit by huge ornate chandeliers as breathtaking as Versailles, they attracted shocked looks from the well-dressed, society crowd, a stunning contrast to the grizzly scenes they had just witnessed. Hidden in their boxes, they enjoyed the performance quietly, where they saw Strauss's mesmerizingly sensuous Dance of The Seven Veils by Salomi, who danced faster as the veils fell to the floor. Bill followed the dance closely but was disappointed when he saw that "She had an eighth veil on."

After a long day of touring, Karl Anderson, a hurdler, went out to acquire sandwiches for the famished athletes. Their box seats were five feet above the audience, where the dignitaries, including the President of France, Douglas Fairbanks, and Mary Pickford sat in their beautiful gowns and fine tuxedos, looking refined and elegant. As Bill remembered, "We didn't dare eat our sandwiches openly, so we ducked behind the banister every time we took a bite."

After leaving the Opera, they passed the site where, during the French Revolution, the revolutionaries guillotined Marie Antoinette and Louis XVI. They stopped at the Arc de Triomphe, visiting the tomb of the Unknown Soldier, where a torch burned continuously, adding to its solemnity. To Gene, it seemed to be, "an ever-present reminder to the French people of the fire of hate and preparedness that must always burn in their heart against their enemy who had caused so much death and destruction."

Revelers celebrating Bastille Day halted the bus carrying the Olympians, enticing the Americans to come down and join in their celebration. According to Bill, "There were a lot of ladies, and I happened to be unfortunate enough to get a rather heavyset lady, and dancing on those cobblestones was quite an ordeal—particularly with my companion and I not knowing anything about dancing in the first place."

The next day, Gene met Pat Hurl, an Owensboro native and Notre Dame alumni, who fought in the Great War and stayed over in Paris as a journalist.   Pat offered to show Gene Paris from a local's perspective.   He brought Gene to St. Gravais Cathedral, which was destroyed by the huge German howitzer Big Bertha.   During mass, the immense, 150-ton artillery piece fired a massive 1871-pound shell that shattered the church, tragically killing 80 people and injuring 60.

Next, they visited the Medieval Sorbonne established in 1253 (part of the University of Paris), and toured the adjacent Cluny Museum, where 2000-year-old Roman baths had been unearthed. After saying farewell to Pat, Gene entered the Luxembourg Garden, where he rested beneath the shade of one of its many trees—a welcome respite from the hot July sun.   There he watched "prettily dressed little French children at play."

Following the team's return from the London Relays, continuing his much-anticipated war tour, Gene visited Verdun, Soissons, Epernay, Rheims, the Argonne, Meaux, the forests of Compiegne, and Versailles where the Treaty of Versailles was signed ending the war. Verdun was the first battle of the war, where a devastating 400,000 – 500,000 Frenchmen lost their lives in the muddy, noisy, terrifying trenches of a struggle that raged for over a year.   Tragically, France lost 1.4 million people and a quarter of her young men with another million permanently injured.

London

On the 17th of July, the relay team traveled to Calais and crossed over the English Channel to Dover, then on to London where they would compete in the London Relays at Stamford Bridge.   The British and American athletes first crossed the Atlantic in the late 1800s when Cambridge and Oxford athletes sailed over the "pond" to compete against the elite universities of the Ivy League, such as Harvard, Yale and Penn. Afterward, the Ivy League athletes sailed across the Atlantic in the opposite direction to compete against the Brits.

Renewing the spirit of competition, following "The War to end all wars," Britain instituted the first London Relays after the 1920 Olympiad.   During the inaugural event, the two teams tied.   The relays would also be held after the IXth Olympics in Amsterdam in 1928.   Since these three Olympics were close to England (Antwerp, Paris, and Amsterdam), it was an easy extension of the Americans' trip.   In a sense, the British were saying, "While you're in our neighborhood, why don't you stop by? We'd like to see you, Yanks?" The Americans did not continue the practice after the 1932 Los Angeles Olympics because it was during the depths of the worldwide Great Depression when funds for such activities were tight. Just funding the Olympics was difficult enough for the Americans to accomplish, when adding another event would be impossible to politically justify.

The competition proved to be an excellent opportunity for Yanks and Brits to compete one more time in a hearty spirit of conviviality. Stars and medal winners from both teams such as Scholz, Paddock and Houser, Abrahams and Liddell, would be there competing one more time. Athletes throughout the British Realm attended including a few each from Canada, New Zealand, Australia, Scotland, and South Africa.

The Americans stayed at several London hotels. R.G. Hills of Princeton, who placed third in the "Putting of the Weight" as the British called the shot put, roomed with Gene. They remembered playing against each other in that pivotal football game at Princeton that fall, when the Irish beat the previous year's national champions, Princeton. R.G. had been enrolled in pre-med and served as the captain of the Princeton track team.

R.G. and Gene met their fellow relay members in the hotel lobby: the other javelin men, Bill and Homer, and the two other "putters of the weight" Bud Houser and Glenn "Tiny" Hartranft, who captured the gold and silver medals thereby sweeping the medals. Together, the six men of steel set off to attend a scheduled affair. Three of them captained their respective track teams: Bill, Homer and R.G; and three hailed from sunny California: Bill, Bud and Glenn. Bill, no longer outnumbered by Southerners, enjoyed being with his fellow Californians.

With Hollywood good looks, Bud Houser from USC would later become the dentist to the stars. Glenn Hartranft of Stanford, who weighed in at a beefy 245 pounds and also competed in the discus, later broke the discus world record, a mark that would soon be set by Gene's buddy, Tom Lieb. Walking down the street, the six huge men made quite an impression on passers-by, who quickly moved aside for fear of being trampled by the big, strong Men of Steel.

According to Bill, "We had tea there with several English ladies. That was quite an affair. The trouble was that we were all pretty hungry and we took advantage of that and ate all the sandwiches and pastries that were available." Bill always seemed to be hungry. The well-dressed, well-mannered, English society ladies were likely shocked or at least entertained by these huge, young athletes' uncustomary behavior, but, after all, they were American, who, despite their cultural ignorance, appreciated the elegant ladies' hospitality.

———

Unlike the Olympics where individuals compete, relays are a team event. In races of various lengths, four runners form a team to run the prescribed distance. For example, in a mile relay or 4 x 440, each member runs a quarter of a mile handing a baton off to the successive runner. For the field events, the distances are combined for each of the three participants on a team.

The Stamford Bridge Stadium held up to 70,000 spectators and currently is the home of the championship football team Chelsea. There, the American javelin team had the furthest three results in their event—Whelchel (187'8"), Neufeld (180' 7") and Oberst (173'11"), winning by a substantial margin. Gene had not touched the javelin in a couple of weeks, and his results were atypical, but perhaps he felt little pressure.

The U.S. won 11 out of 14 events, with British teams winning the mile relay, two-mile relay and three-mile team race. Eric Liddell anchored the mile relay that they won. The Americans, Scholz, Paddock, Bowman and Lecony set a new world record in the 4x100 relay of 37.8 seconds and they didn't even field one of the fastest men in the world, DeHart Hubbard. Abrahams, now "the fastest man alive," anchored the British team but, against four finalists from the Olympics, could not make up the lost distance by the time he felt the baton slap his outstretched hand.

There was an extravagant, formal banquet after the meet at the magnificent Opera-Baroque-style Trocadero Restaurant, at which the two teams socialized in a relaxed, elegant atmosphere. Gene especially enjoyed meeting Eric Liddell and Lord Burghley, the hurdler who gave up his place to Liddell in the 400, both of whom were well-spoken and affable gentlemen featured in the *Chariots of Fire* movie. The young, handsome blond Lord Burghley (David George Brownlow Cecil, 6th Marquess of Exeter) was the decedent of the chief minister to Queen Elizabeth I, William Cecil, in the 16th century. David was the president of the Cambridge Athletic Club and would go on to win a gold medal in the 400-meter at the 1928 Olympics. Later he would become a conservative member of Parliament and president of the AAU.

On a trip to London decades later, Bill Neufeld would tour gracious Lord Burghley's spectacular, ornately decorated, 2200-foot-long 200-room castle, reminiscing about their Olympic experience. (The Burghley castle has been the site of several movies, including The *Da Vinci Code* and *Pride & Prejudice*).

There were several speeches prior to dinner highlighting the conviviality and friendship felt between the allied nations represented by the best of its youth. When they sat down at the banquet, Prince Henry made a brief speech.   The program listed several members of the royal family including King George V, Queen Mary, Queen Alexandra (the Queen mother), and the Prince of Wales, but Prince Henry was the only royal in attendance.

Henry, the Duke of Gloucester, was the king's third and favorite son who grew up sickly, until, following in his esteemed father's footsteps, he embraced sports and joined the Army. He enjoyed his whiskey and had affairs until he wed and, perhaps afterwards, like others of his class. When King George V died in 1936, his eldest son, the Prince of Wales, who attended the Olympics as a member of the British Olympic Committee, became the King. He wanted to marry the twice-divorced American, Wallis Simpson, which was not acceptable, so he renounced his throne.

As the second oldest son, Albert, feeling a sense of duty, reluctantly ascended to the throne, becoming King George the VIth. Bill noticed that Henry, unlike some of the other speakers who tended to go on and on, had a short speech. This is because Henry, like his favorite brother Albert (Berty), had a stutter, which was the subject of an Academy Award-winning film, *The King's Speech*.

Prince Henry became a close and trusted advisor to Albert and was third in line to the throne. If Albert died, he would become regent to his young niece Elizabeth until she turned 18. She would later become the longest reigning monarch of 70 plus years, surpassing her great-grandmother, Queen Victoria and namesake, Queen Elizabeth I.

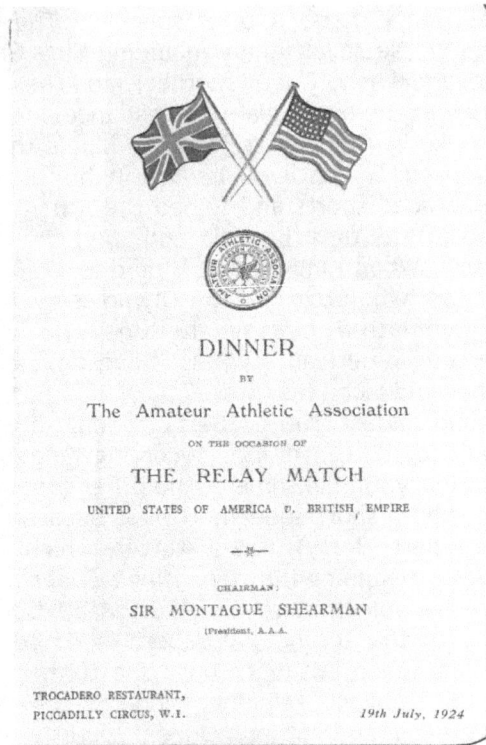

DINNER

BY

The Amateur Athletic Association

ON THE OCCASION OF

THE RELAY MATCH

UNITED STATES OF AMERICA v. BRITISH EMPIRE

CHAIRMAN:

SIR MONTAGUE SHEARMAN

(President, A.A.A.)

TROCADERO RESTAURANT,
PICCADILLY CIRCUS, W.I.   19th July, 1924

London Relay dinner program

A man dressed in a red coat with brass buttons stood behind the prince and made all the announcements. He would start out with "His Majesty the King of England, Her Majesty the Queen of England," and then "the President of the United States, and Vice-President of the United States," and then he would name some dukes, then finally, "The British and the American Olympic team may now eat," as Bill recalled, who as usual could not wait to dig in. But Bill would not go away hungry this time.

When he sat down to the opulent meal, Gene was highly impressed by the number of assembled silver utensils and crystal glasses for various wines. At least he knew to start at the outside and work his way in as the multiple courses appeared, but also watched the interspersed English nobles closely to confirm his utensil choices. Judging by the expression on many of his startled teammates' faces, he was not alone in his wonder and confusion. He noticed that the British athletes, who largely hailed from Cambridge and Oxford, seemed at ease with the confusing array. With the last of their competitions over, the athletes no longer in training, and no Prohibition in England as there was at home, there was no restriction on indulgence, and the fine wine flowed freely. This was by far the most elegant, elaborate meal Gene would ever enjoy.

The menu consisted of the following courses, each having a famous American or British Olympian assigned, many accompanied by fine wines.

MENU

1. Consome double "Abrahams", Crème a la "Scholz"
   (Thick consume with cream)

2. Salmon d' poche', Sauce "Liddell et Lowe" (Poached salmon)
   Concombres (cucumbers)

3. Selle d' Agneu poelee a la "Kinsey" (Lord Burleigh)
   (Saddle of sautéed lamb)
   Petis Pois Noveaus "Taylor" (Small new peas)
   Pomes Palace (Potatoes of the palace)

4. Sorbet "Americaine" (Sherbet)

5. Poulardines de Surrey en Cocotte "Osborne"(Chicken casserole)
   Coeurs de Laiture "Hubbard" (Romaine hearts)

6. Caprice Glacee "Tootell" (Ice cream)

7. Friandises (Candy)

8. Dessert

9. Café

Fred Tootell, the gold medal hammer thrower and fellow Man of Steel, was thrilled to see his name attached to his favorite dessert, ice cream. Not understanding French and without translation, Gene had little idea of what he ate, but it was all delicious, one dish after another.

Captain Jackson Scholz, the famous American sprinter and new world record relay holder, rose to speak. Back in Paris, nervous about delivering such a speech in the presence of royalty, he asked the team for advice, whereupon they told him to just make it short. Jackson, in accordance with protocol, started his speech very formally, thanking the majesties, presidents, and distinguished attendees, whether they attended or not, and then got stuck. He pulled out a wad of papers from his back pocket and started to read. Prince Henry, surprised at the sight of the unsightly wad, spilled his goblet of red wine all over the white tablecloth covering the table in the rich ruby-colored liquid. When the prince handed the awards to Homer, Bill and Gene, they had to reach across the "Red Sea" to receive their medals and shake his hand.

———

The sumptuous affair highlights the contrasts between American and English athletes. Since many of the English participants hailed from colleges such as Oxford, Cambridge, and Edinburgh, they possessed the impeccable manners of a British aristocrat. In British colleges, the university did not sponsor sports or hire coaches, but rather the students formed and managed the athletic clubs that competed. After University, the Achilles Club offered the former athletes of Cambridge and Oxford the opportunity to compete and train for the Olympics. To them, athletics played an essential role in a gentlemen's upbringing to be enjoyed and heralded as an expression of one's "God-given" talent and courage—a strictly amateur pursuit—certainly not something to be professionally pursued.

Most of the Americans hailed from well-respected colleges but, by the 1920s, college admission was no longer restricted to the elite, as evidenced by De Hart Hubbard and the Gipper, who grew up poor and Gene, who had worked his way through college. Colleges had just begun to award scholarships, which would allow more needy athletes to attend. Those who did not attend college could qualify for the Olympics through athletic clubs such as the Illinois Athletic Club or individually through the AAU. Some gifted, poor athletes like Johnny Weissmuller, who might not have made the Olympic team otherwise, acquired professional coaches such as Bill Bachrach. Johnny Weissmuller belonged to the highly successful IAC in Chicago along with other luminaries such as Tom Lieb, Gertrude Ederle, Alonzo Stagg, Rockne, and Gene.

Still, for the Americans, this was, for the most part, a time of innocence in sports. It was a time when an athlete such as Gene, who first picked up a javelin at the end of his sophomore year in college and had little coaching could medal at the Olympics.

The British program was more exclusive, whereas the American program was more inclusive, something that contrasted the two nations at the time and led to the Americans' overwhelming success. Over the coming years, the Olympics would evolve and the spirit of the Olympics would remain, but this was a special time when sports were purer, unspoiled, and closer to the Olympic ideal. The '20s were a unique, naïve, wonderful, transitory period in sports history when many sports came into their own, and for the first time, large numbers of fans had the leisure time and means to attend sporting events—why this was called the "Golden Decade of Sports." Many sports grew rapidly in the magic decade that are still featured today; swimming, football, boxing, hockey, basketball, tennis, golf, etc.

The path to the Olympics is much more difficult now, for which young athletes must dedicate themselves to one sport in middle school or even grade school, and join traveling teams with professional coaches, parents spending large sums of money and time to cart them around to practices, meets, competitions and games that may be out of state. In the 1960s and 1970s, such requirements did not exist. Back then, we were favored to win the league basketball championship until our best player was disqualified because he attended a camp in the Summer. Playing on a traveling team, if it existed, would also result in a disqualification.

Despite their parents' desire and support, the odds are extremely long that such superb athletes will qualify for the Olympics. For every American athlete who competes in the Olympics, there are hundreds of disappointed kids and parents. Out of 1,000 outstanding hopefuls competing in the 2024 Indianapolis swimming qualifier only 54 will make Olympic team. Once a young athlete joins the team, the odds of winning a medal are still long. Before the pandemic, in 2016 about 11,000 athletes were competing at the Rio de Janeiro games. A whopping 972 medals were awarded to those from 87 nations, but still, the odds of winning a medal were one in eleven. Back in 1924, an Olympic medal and world record holder like Tom Lieb excelled in four sports and his buddy Gene in three—something very rare these days.

Sixty years later in an interview, Gene commented on the changes over the years:

> Those who competed in 1924 and before were Olympic pioneers and that the athletes were true amateurs with a great spirit of competition. Just being there was reward enough. Those competitors were not just set on winning a gold medal or setting up lucrative deals.

> Just making the team and competing is a great achievement. It's terrific to win, but the competition and the fellowship also means so much.... We must strive to get back as close as we can to true amateurism. - back to the Olympic ideal.

Gene later enjoyed the wonders of London visiting the British Empire Exhibition, St. Paul's, Westminster Abbey, London Tower,

London Bridge, etc.　They returned to Paris on July 21-22 via the Folkestone-Boulogne.　His joyful, Olympic experience would end soon and he would sail back over the broad, blue Atlantic to America and triumphant parades.

21: Victors Arrive Home

The Olympics ended on July 28[th,] the same day the American team left Paris sailing from Cherbourg on the SS America. The main events of the VIIIth Olympiad (the Track and Field competition) transpired within a week after the opening ceremony. Most of the other sports such as swimming, fencing, wrestling, and boxing occurred either before or afterward, lasting well over a month.

The United States garnered 99 total medals—45 gold, 27 silver, and 27 bronze. Amazingly, tiny Finland finished second with 37 medals, 14 of which were gold. The host nation, France finished third with 13 gold and 38 overall medals. Great Britain, the London Relays host, claimed fourth with 34 medals.

Of course, then the scoring was not based on medals, but on points, with the top six finishers earning points for their nation, such as Bill did for the U.S. There appears to be no existing record of the points scored by nation, so it is difficult to summarize the actual order.

Finland had 14 gold and 37 overall medals, whereas France had 13 gold and 38 total medals, which resulted in the same number of points. So, depending on the number of 4th through 6th places, the host nation may have been second. Even though they had one less gold than Italy, tiny Switzerland, with nine more medals, likely captured fifth with Sweden and its 15 medals sixth.

So, including all the points, the likely order was:

		Medals
1.	U.S.A.	99
2.	France	38
3.	Finland	37
4.	Britain	34
5.	Switzerland	23
6.	Italy	15

Considering the number of superior athletes competing in the 21st-century Olympics and the current odds of winning a medal so small, it seems worthwhile to recognize the other top athletes with some reward such as a gilded certificate and possibly points scored for the nation.

During the voyage, President Coolidge sent the team a long telegram congratulating each of them on their fantastic performance. Gene cherished his telegram. While back in the States, the interest in the team and their stellar performance received constant coverage in the news and, for the few that had a receiver, on the newly popular radio, which allowed Americans to follow the action daily. The long trip provided the American Olympians plenty of time to enjoy and relive their victories in the company of their teammates—a halcyon time for all.

On board, Gene formed a close relationship with Coach Alonzo Stagg as indicated by his reference to Alonzo as his "Second Daddy" in his journal. It is not clear how this relationship formed. One of Gene's friends, Harry Frieda, the '23 javelin champion and decathlete, who gave Gene the ill-fated track shoes, starred for Stagg at nearby Chicago U. Alonzo who founded the first NCAA championship where Gene stood out, would likely have seen Gene set records at the Penn, Kansas and possibly Drake relays and certainly seen him during the Olympic trials likely playing a role in his selection to the team

In addition to track and being an innovator of American football, second only to his mentor Walter Camp, Alonzo had been an outstanding pitcher—something else he and Gene shared. When Stagg started playing baseball, there were no baseball gloves, and even when he played in college in the 1880s, the glove was little more than a work glove with the fingers cut out. As Yale's pitcher, Alonzo won five championships, striking out 20 batters during a Princeton game. Six professional teams competed to have him sign with them, offering him a fabulous salary, but he turned them all down because he did not want to associate with players of questionable morals—the image of baseball pros then.

Alonzo was a member of the Illinois Athletic Club and asked Gene to join the club. If Gene did so, he would be able to stay competitive for the 1928 Olympics in Amsterdam. Even though he had just graduated from nearby Notre Dame, he was unsure where he might end up. If Gene found a position in the Midwest, he would be able to travel to the meets, which would be no further than many of those he competed at while at Notre Dame. The IAC sponsored several Olympic champions such as Johnny Weissmuller, the top American medal winner at Paris, fulfilling a role similar to Achilles Club in London, helping college graduates and non-college athletes to stay competitive.

Gene could not believe all he had seen in France and London—all of those historic sites he had read about in his beloved history books and all of the interesting battle sites. Beautiful Versailles was his favorite, with its magnificent grounds, the Louvre and the towering Eiffel Tower close seconds.

———

While sitting on a deck chair looking out to the sea, waves crashing against the hull and the scent of fresh sea air filling his lungs, the sun tanning his skin, there was plenty of time to reflect on what he would do with the rest of his life. Until then, he had been too busy to spend much time thinking about his future. He felt with his success in football, setting records across the USA in the javelin, graduating from Notre Dame, and competing at the Olympics that he had lived up to his lofty expectations inspired by *Pushing to the Front*. He majored in foreign commerce, which after the war in the 1920s, was a booming, promising field. His experience in France and England gave him an even broader appreciation of what that might be. The foreign students at Notre Dame he spent holidays with could prove to be valuable contacts. He learned from Rockne the importance of a network of such acquaintances. Still, like many new college grads, he was not sure where to start.

On the other hand, he had gained valuable experience coaching the Minims in four sports and achieved resounding success in two. At the Olympics competing with the world's best, he acquired an even greater perspective of what coaching might be like. In addition, he thought his mentor, Rockne, to be the finest coach in the world, to which many would attest—not just as a coach but as a man. With his background in academics, science, art, athletics and business, Rockne seemed like a Renaissance man to Gene, something he aspired to do too.

Rockne was a great promoter of the team, football, and himself, as testified by his unequaled results. Attendance at games was soaring from around 50,000 a year to what would become over 500,000 under Rockne. Something the administration previously considered eliminating, the Notre Dame/Army game would draw over 125,000 fans alone. The upcoming USC game would soon draw an additional 123,000 that fall. Rockne worked well with Alumni and the Chamber of Commerce in South Bend to help the administration see the benefits of the program and those expensive road trips. Not only had football become a revenue maker, it greatly enhanced student spirit and after graduation, alumni interest and donations. Football also drew students from around the nation to Notre Dame, for those Irish and Catholics who rooted for Notre Dame wanted their sons to go there. Largely due to Rockne, the little Midwestern College with a small enrollment would become one of America's premier colleges to which only top students would be accepted, a far cry from accepting students that did not even have a high school diploma.

Rock would represent the Studebaker auto company throughout the country as a motivational speaker. He would continue to expand his coaching seminars during the summer, for which he earned over $25,000 ($400,000 today). He would also become a popular speaker and conduct coaching seminars around the nation, in which he would advance the art of coaching and the science of football while, in a collegial fashion, training many of the top coaches of the next half century who would win numerous national championships. Later, he would team up with Pop Warner, another legend, to teach these popular seminars.

Gene learned the importance of promotion and much more from his mentor. He also saw from Rockne's activities that his background in commerce might serve him well as a coach. Plus, like Tom, he would be able to continue improving his javelin skills and perhaps win gold or silver at the '28 Olympics while competing for the IAC. Mc Grath, his compatriot, the hammer thrower, who participated in four Olympics, was still going strong at 47 and Gene was barely 23. Talking to Tom and seeing Tom's enthusiasm as Rockne's assistant also inspired Gene's interest in coaching. Rockne mentioned the opportunity in Louisiana, which his brother Albert, in his letter, said he was working on. If it were not the greatest job, at least it would be a start; a chance to prove himself again, and like Rockne, he might be able to work his way into business during the summers.

––––––

As they approached America, Colonel Thompson spoke about how the Olympians' friends and neighbors would treat them royally when they returned to their hometowns—there would be parades, brass bands, and dinners in their honor. He told them of how the Greeks tore down the walls of their cities to welcome their victorious Olympians. Gene remembered reading about the Greek Olympiads and how the Greeks honored their Olympic heroes. During the original Olympics, 2,700 -3,000 years ago, there was a Sacred Truce, when Greeks could travel freely to Olympus regardless of the ever-present wars between the various city-states. Winners received a wreath and a hero's welcome back home. They might marry rich women, enjoy free meals for life, invitations to parties, and the best seats at the theatre.

Gene had not been home in a year and desperately wanted to see his family, wondering about how his mother and each of his ten siblings fared. They would certainly be pleased to see their returning hero. He also looked forward to seeing the expanding tribe of nieces and nephews. He could imagine all of Owensboro turning out to regale him—brass bands, the mayor with a proclamation, or perhaps a key to the city.

On August 6ᵗʰ, as the S.S. America steamed into New York's harbor, Gene saw the Statue of Liberty, a gift from the French he so admired nearly two months ago—what a fabulous adventure they had been on during the intervening time. A large crowd greeted them at the peer, followed by a ticker-tape parade down Broadway. Thousands of people cheered wildly for their returning heroes, ticker-tape streaming from the skyscrapers onto their heads and shoulders as the athletes waved to their adoring fans. The glorious parade, like those in Athens following an Olympiad, ended at City Hall where Mayor Richard T. Hylan presented them each with a gold medal. That evening, they were guests of honor at a fabulous dinner, not quite as elegant as in England but still sumptuous.

Gene soon realized that his Olympic buddies would each go their separate ways, back to their home cities and towns throughout the nation. Most he would never see again, but some would intersect his future life in unusual ways. They had shared much together; small rooms on the ship and at Rocquencourt, practices on the deck, trips to see the spectacular wonders of Paris, the unimageable, sumptuous beauty of Versailles, the battlefields of France, the London relays, the sights of London and that glorious Olympic stadium with the roaring crowds cheering them on to glory. He would miss The Men of Steel most, those big men like himself, with whom he spent most of his time and who performed so brilliantly. One's first impression of these big, strong men roaming the streets of Rocquencourt, Paris or London might have been that they were just big, dumb jocks, but that was far from the truth. They were highly intelligent college graduates, captains of their track teams and highly respected police officers.

Gene felt verklempt when he said farewell to Homer, Bill, and Lee, the outstanding gentlemen he had lived within the cramped stateroom and plywood room at Rocquencourt that would be lauded by their coach in his report to Congress. They had done so well in Paris, had gotten along so well, and had so much fun. He felt a special bond with Lee and would greatly miss Bill's flamboyant personality that kept them lose.

Gene said goodbye to Tom the next morning and vowed to follow the Notre Dame football team next year knowing he would see him again. As Alonzo Stagg had suggested, Tom had convinced Gene to join the Illinois Athletic Club. Gene planned to join Tom for a meet later in August.

On the train ride home, he anxiously waited for Owensboro to appear, expecting a band to be playing with the whole town showing up to welcome their conquering hero, perhaps with the mayor holding that key to the city—similar to the receptions he experienced in South Bend and New York for football and in Paris. Gene thought about what he might say. He took a trip to the small train restroom at the end of the car to comb his wavy locks and checked his pocket for his written notes regarding the speech he planned to deliver to the assembled crown, which he ran through one more time.   "The familiar scenes passed by: Crossroads, schools, corn fields, houses, factories, the distilleries, children at play. Finally, the train came to a screeching stop."

When Gene stepped off the car, he saw no brass band, no reporters, no mayor, no cheering throng, not a single person showed up to welcome him back not even his family. As he dejectedly walked down the platform and picked up his bag to head home, a porter he had known as a boy passed by and remarked, "Hi' ya Oberst, been someplace?" which could have been anywhere, South Bend, Louisville, Evansville. He wanted to say he had been to Paris, to London, to the Olympics, but dejectedly, just walked on.

At home, his family was elated to see him. Gene passed around his medal letting the nephews and nieces hold it and feel its heft. He brought many gifts back from Paris for them. One nephew, Charlie, Albert's son, later remembered the lace gloves and French perfume Gene brought for his mother that she cherished.

A few days later, he received his Olympic diploma in the mail of a grand Grecian scene with a fair maiden and olive branches signed by the founder of the modern Olympics, Baron De Coubertin, showing his place and results in meters, one of the last the august Baron would sign. He was also featured in a textbook.

According to the Owensboro Messenger, "Mr. Oberst's fine physique has been used by Bobbs Merill Company, publisher of the textbook on physiology and hygiene as an exemplification of its text as to the relation of muscles to nerves. His picture is in the act of casting his javelin, which is printed in the textbook, which is used in the public and parochial schools."

In late August, Gene joined the Illinois Athletic Club where he competed alongside Johnny Weissmuller, and Tom Lieb, got to know Gertrude Ederle, and met Alonzo Stagg better.

With the Olympics over, Gene turned his attention to the next phase of his life in faraway Louisiana. Like any graduate, no longer sheltered by school, he would now enter the real world, one of life's major passages.

La Fin

❧

Afterword

After returning from the Olympics, filled with enthusiasm, Gene set off for his first coaching assignment in Shreveport, deep in the bayous of Louisiana, where he would be St. John College's first coach, athletic director and trainer, coaching football, basketball, baseball and track. In addition, he would teach English, history and algebra. Not being familiar with Louisiana sports, he would schedule games against some of the most formidable schools in the state, including one that would soon play for the state championship. During the game, eight of his sixteen players succumbed to injury with five heading to the hospital. Having run out of subs they would have to forfeit the game and the remainder of the season. He would write to Knute Rockne about these first coaching experiences, which commenced a fascinating relationship between the two, contained in nearly 50 regular letters. Rockne would help him find his seven coaching positions as he rose in the ranks of the coaching profession.

His father had died when Gene was twenty and Rockne, whose father also passed away while he was a student at Notre Dame, became his second father, helping guide his career, teaching him the ropes, steering him through the political minefields, consoling him when the eventual loses came, and celebrating his successes. Indeed, without Rockne's assistance, he may not have been able to marry his beloved wife, Catherine. Gene and later Catherine traveled around the country to his various coaching posts, adding five children along the way, who were born in four different sections of the country. Gene had claimed that Alonzo Stagg, the second father of American football was his second father, but surely Knute was. How fortunate that Gene had two such outstanding men, two amazing and accomplished championship coaches with the highest integrity in both football and track as mentors.

Less than seven years later, when Rockne's plane crashed in a Kansas field on a flight to L.A. to star in a movie, whilst mutual friend Tom Lieb waited, Rockne tragically died. Gene was devastated. He had to endure a treacherous situation without his mentor to guide him, during the Great Depression, and then face debilitating, humiliating unemployment trying to provide for his wife and four children. He sold insurance, worked for the WPA, wrote historical novels, tried to get various businesses off the ground and started oil painting, but nothing seemed to generate enough income. Finally, relief came in the form of a telegram from Tom Connolly, his former captain, who he had sent to Rock. Tom, an All-American, captained Rockne's last national championship team. He invited Gene to be his line coach at John Carroll University in Cleveland, Ohio.

After over 30 years of coaching, discouraged with the vicissitudes of athletics and its politics, Gene obtained his master's in Political Science and started teaching at John Carroll in University Heights Ohio, where he taught for 35 years. Working with young men, helping them to learn and grow, is what Gene loved most and he finally discovered his true passion as a college professor. Just when Gene felt he was hitting his stride, in accordance with policy, the university moved to retire him at 65, but the student body initiated a petition drive to keep the popular professor. Faced with so much fervent resistance, Carroll relented and agreed to keep Gene for another five years.

The next book is about Gene's intriguing life after Notre Dame and his evolving relationship with Rockne: *Renaissance Olympian, Mentored by Rockne, Gene Oberst Becomes a Renowned Coach, Professor and Artist.*

Acknowledgments

Thanks to Angela Kindig and the Archives Department at Notre Dame, who provided a wealth of information including numerous letters between Knute Rockne and Gene Oberst. I would also like to thank Christina Clary of the Davies County Library. Both were extremely responsive and helpful. In addition, I would like to thank my brother Al and sister Pat Oberst TePas for keeping and preserving boxes of our father's documents, along with cousin Neil Mellon who formalized dad's Olympic diary, and my wife Pat for her encouragement and editing.

About the author

Rob Oberst, the author of this book, is a seasoned writer with a wealth of experience. In addition to numerous articles on various technical and non-technical topics, he has published seven other books, all of which explore the realms of history and time travel.

Time Traveler 1491 & 1492: Transported Back to 15th-Century Ireland, Rand Joins the Global Revolution. When venture capitalists steal his lucrative app, Rand seeks solace on a backpacking expedition to the bottom of the Grand Canyon, where he slips and is swept into the turbulent rapids. Nearly drowned, battered, and bruised, he seeks refuge in a hidden cave, where a mysterious galvanic force overcomes him. Barely able to move, he wakes in the bed of a beautiful maiden who nurses him back to health. While recovering, her father, Ireland's first printer, teaches him the revolutionary profession that, like the Web, is transforming the world five centuries later. Becoming embroiled in castle politics but unskilled in their weapons, Rand has one advantage—a downloaded copy of Wikipedia on his iPhone, which he must access judiciously before its battery dies.

One of Rob Oberst's most notable works is *2020 Web Vision: How the Internet Will Revolutionize Future Homes, Business, and Society*. This book, which appeared in over a dozen countries and at universities on five continents including Harvard, accurately predicted how virtual technology would transform our world. Published at the start of the millennium, it was remarkably prescient in predicting what transpired over those two and a half decades, including the rise of virtual work, online shopping, AI, and the changing migration patterns towards more desirable locations. According to its prophecies, we are in phase one of the Web's evolution with so much more to come.

The Financial Time Machine: *Predicting Our Economic Future* Based on the generations' economic behavior, generational economics forecast the Great Recession and the stagnant course of the U.S. and major world economies for over a decade, including the dangers facing us in the 2020s and 30s such as inflation, ultra-low unemployment, stagflation and a mountain of debt. This book analyzes the various generations, their economic behavior, and the cycle that has shaped our economy back to the Civil War and will continue to play a key role in the future. The book was revised in 2024, which showed how accurate its forecasts were and with the addition of four new chapters what lies ahead.

Renaissance Olympian: Mentored by Rockne, Gene Oberst becomes a Renowned Coach, Professor & Artist The narrative picks up after Gene Oberst wins the first U.S. medal at the Paris Olympics, the first time the American flag flew over an Olympics and travels to Louisiana to be St. John College's founding four-sport coach, athletic director, trainer, and janitor. As portrayed in fifty letters between Gene and his mentor, Knute Rockne (America's winningest football coach), Gene faces numerous challenges, but Rockne is always there to help. Indeed, he may not have married his wife, Catherine, if not for Rock.

Rob possesses a BS in Systems Analysis from Miami University along with an MBA in Policy and Organizational Behavior from Case Western Reserve University. In addition to being a leader in three national groups, Rob has been a guest columnist for the Cleveland Plain Dealer, Ohio's largest newspaper.

He has presented to scores of universities and management groups on various leading-edge topics. As a management consultant, he served as the regional practice manager for Towers Watson, where he co-founded its successful quarter-billion-dollar (inflation-adjusted) systems line of business. Earlier he served as a hospital CIO and project manager for TRW that launched the first satellite to leave Earth's orbit, designed the fastest chip and search engine, operated the first worldwide satellite network, and owned Atari, where Jobs first worked. As he participated in the evolution of systems technology, Rob learned over a couple dozen development languages. He designed and implemented numerous human resource, healthcare, and financial systems and has consulted on behalf of dozens of S&P 500 companies, including Kraft, Sherwin Williams, Verizon, GE, Toyota, Goodyear, BP, Bank America, JP Morgan Chase, Callaway Golf, Qualcomm, Northrop Grumman, Parker Hannifin, Eaton, Scripps Clinic and the Cleveland Clinic.

Notes

Chapter 1
- Harold Sauerbrei, "Clevelanders in Olympic Games," *Plain Dealer*, p81
- "Mr Stagg Honors," Amos Alonzo Stagg, *Liskahass.org*
- http://www.liskahaas.org/stagg/honors.htm
- Philip S. Moore, "The College of Commerce," *Notre Dame University Archives* http://archives.nd.edu/moore/moore04.htm

Chapter 2
- "Eugene W. Oberst Ancestry," *Ancestry.com*
  www.Ancestry.com
- "Joseph Anton Keifer Ancestry," *Qwest.net*
  http://www.users.qwest.net/~lawrencek/KieferText.htm
- "Köln-Düsseldorfer – Paddle Steamers," *Wikepedia*
  https://en.wikipedia.org/wiki/K%C3%B6ln-D%C3%BCsseldorfer
- "Indiana Bridges – Historic Context, 1830-1965," *In.gov*
  http://www.in.gov/indot/files/INBridgesHistoricContextStudy1830s-1965.pdf
- "Sister Cities," *Jasper German Club*
  http://www.jaspergermanclub.org/sistercities/historical_perspective.cfm
- "Jasper history," *Jasperin.org*
  http://www.jasperin.org/history.cfm
- "The Roman Catholic Diocese of Owensboro, Kentucky," p 335
  https://books.google.com/books?id=OqdNN9R9OHcC&pg=PA335&lpg=PA335&dq=St.+JOseph+Owensboro,+Oberst&source=bl&ots=J8v733zUH2&sig=EbUqv_PLgRN4AElyrjb9kkgZqFU&hl=en&sa=X&ei=NMgRVc-UK8qigwTXlITwBw&ved=0CB4Q6AEwAA#v=onepage&q=St.%20JOseph%20Owensboro%2C%20Oberst&f=false
- "Jasper Indiana--Festival," *Wikipedia*
  https://en.wikipedia.org/wiki/Jasper,_Indiana
- "Confederate Monument in Owensboro," *Wikipedia*
  https://en.wikipedia.org/wiki/Confederate_Monument_in_Owensboro

Chapter 3
"Andrew Oberst Ancestry," *Ancestry*.com
"Charles Oberst, London Ancestry," *Ancestry.com*
Tom Oberst research, *Ancestry.com*
"Oberst Family Tree," *Tennes.com*
http://www.tennes.com/family/tree/languages/en/persons/Person_862150 08.html
"Martin Luther," *Wikipedia*
https://en.wikipedia.org/wiki/Martin_Luther
"Napoleons-disastrous-invasion-of-russia-200-years-ago,"
History.com

http://www.history.com/news/napoleons-disastrous-invasion-of-russia-200-years-ago

"French Invasion of Russia," *Wikipedia*

https://en.wikipedia.org/wiki/French_invasion_of_Russia

"Franco Prussian War," *Wikipedia*

https://en.wikipedia.org/wiki/Franco-Prussian_War

"Education in Germany", *Wikipedia*

https://en.wikipedia.org/wiki/Education_in_Germany#Prussian_era

"St. Josephs and Paul," The Roman Catholic Diocese of Owensboro, Kentucky, p 146

Chapter 4

- "Life in 1914," *Macrohistory*
  http://www.fsmitha.com/h2/ch03.htm
- "american_studies/america_in_1900," *AmericanDigest.org*
  http://americandigest.org/mt-archives/american_studies/america_in_1900.php
- "richest-people-in-history," *BusinessInsider.com*
  http://www.businessinsider.com/richest-people-in-history-2010-8?op=1
- Rosanne Tomyn, "What were work conditions in American factories in 1900?," *classroom.synonym.com*
  http://classroom.synonym.com/were-work-conditions-american-factories-   1900-23383.html
- Walter Trattner, "Child labor," *History.com*
  http://www.history.com/topics/child-labor
- "About Owensboro history," *VisitOwensboro.com*
  http://visitowensboro.com/about-owensboro/history/
- "Owensboro, Kentucky," *Wikipedia*
  https://en.wikipedia.org/wiki/Owensboro,_Kentucky#Economy
- "Daviess County, Kentucky," *Wikipedia*
  http://en.wikipedia.org/wiki/Daviess_County,_Kentucky
- "Paul Tennes," *History of Daviess County*, p 655
  https://books.google.com/books?id=_xxEAQAAMAAJ&pg=PA655&dq=Paul+Tennes+Davies+county&hl=en&sa=X&ei=c84RVb7LC4jIsAT9rYHoAg&ved=0CB4Q6AEwAA#v=onepage&q=Paul%20Tennes%20Davies%20county&f=false
- "About Owensboro history," *VisitOwensboro.com*
  http://visitowensboro.com/about-owensboro/history/

Chapter 5

- "Bulletin of Holy Cross Province," bulletin number 21949
- https://archive.org/stream/passionistbullet21949unse/passionistbullet21949unse_djvu.txt

Chapter 6

- "Owensboro Public Schools," Owensboro.kyschools.us
- http://www.owensboro.kyschools.us/ohs/football/Schedules/1917%20Schedule.
- "Henderson High School," Classic High Schools.com

- http://classicschools.com/blog/ky/henderson-high-school-henderson-kentucky/

Chapter 7
- "Notre Dame Football 1920," *The Season in Review*, p 5, 19, 32
  http://www.archives.nd.edu/Football/Football-1920.pdf
- "Amos Alonzo Stagg," *Wikepedia*
  https://en.wikipedia.org/wiki/Amos_Alonzo_Stagg
- "Walter Camp History," *WalterCamp.org*
  http://waltercamp.org/history/
- "1st NCAA championships Chicago, IL June 18, 1921,"
  usctrackandfield.com
  http://www.usctrackandfield.com/1921_results.pdf
- Pete LeFleur, "Three NCAA Champions In Three Days: A Landmark Weekend in the History of Notre Dame Athletics" *und.com/sports*
  http://www.und.com/sports/c-fenc/spec-rel/041714aab.html
- *University Of Notre Dame, Track And Field, History & Records*, p2
  http://grfx.cstv.com/photos/schools/nd/sports/c-track/auto_pdf/2014-15/misc_non_event/14-15-track-media-supplement.pdf

Chapter 8
- "History of American Football", *Wikepedia*,
  https://en.wikipedia.org/wiki/History_of_American_football#Football_in_America
- Harry Stuhldreher, *Knute Rockne, Man Builder*, p 17
- Jim Lefebvre, *Coach for a Nation*, p 76
- Harry Stuhldreher, *Knute Rockne, Man Builder*, p 43
- "History of Cedar Point," *Cedar Point*, https://www.cedarpoint.com/
- Jim Lefebvre, *Coach for a Nation*, p102
- Harry Stuhldreher, *Knute Rockne, Man Builder*, p 153
- Harry Stuhldreher, *Knute Rockne, Man Builder*, 167
- "History of Neuland Labs," *Neuland Labs*
- https://www.neulandlabs.com/core-values/history-of-neuland/
- Harry Stuhldreher, *Knute Rockne, Man Builder*, 258
- Harry Stuhldreher, *Knute Rockne, Man Builder*, 271
- Jim Lefebvre, *Coach for a Nation*, p 161

Chapter 9
- "The Minim Department," *The Notre Dame Archives News & Notes*
- http://www.archives.nd.edu/about/news/index.php/2011/the-minim-department/#.VRQvw_zF-8A
- "George Gipp," *Wikipedia*
- https://en.wikipedia.org/wiki/George_Gipp
- Jack Cavanaugh, "The Elusive Gipper," *Sports Illustrated*, Dec, 30, 1991
- Harry Stuhldreher, Knute Rockne, *Man Builder*, p 220
- Jack Cavanaugh, "The Elusive Gipper," *Sports Illustrated*, Dec, 30, 1991

- John U. Bacon, "This is the real story of the Gipper," The Detroit News, *Irishlegends.com*
- http://www.irishlegends.com/pages/reflections/reflections12.html

Chapter 10
- Harry Stuhldreher, Knute Rockne, *Man Builder,*
- Ibid., p 101
- Rob Oberst, Tom Lieb Jr. Interview, 3/7/16
- Harry Stuhldreher, *Knute Rockne, Man Builder*, 192
- Ibid., p199
- Ibid., p 153
- Ibid, p92
- Jay, "The Blue Grey Sky," *Blogspot*, August 26, 2006
- http://bluegraysky.blogspot.com/2006/08/ramblin.html
- *Louisville Carrier Journal*
- Linda Wertheimer, Host, "A Clear Take On The Rebel Yell Rebel yell." *National Public Radio*, August 3, 2013, 8:00 AM ET
- Jim Lefebvre, *Coach for a Nation*, p 192
- Jerry Dorsch, "Oberst Meets Grace Kelly," *Carroll News*, 3/9/56
- Jay, "The Blue Grey Sky," *Blogspot*, August 26, 2006
- http://bluegraysky.blogspot.com/2006/08/ramblin.html
- Adam Cole, "Are NFL Football Hits Getting Harder and More Dangerous," *National Public Radio*, February 1, 201312:02 PM ET
- http://www.npr.org/sections/health-shots/2013/01/31/170764982/are-nfl-   football-hits-getting-harder-and-more-dangerous
- Amy Daughters and Chief Writer, "The Evolution of Football Equipment," *Bleacher Report*, May 16, 2013
- http://bleacherreport.com/articles/1642538-the-evolution-of-football-equipment
- Murray A. Sperber, *Shake Down the Thunder*, p 133

Chapter 11
- Jim Lefebvre, *Coach for a Nation*, p.488
- Harry Stuhldreher, *Knute Rockne, Man Builder*, p306
- "The Drake Relays", *Notre Dame Alumnus*, May 1923, p84
-
  Harold Sauerbrei, "Clevelanders in Olympic Games," *Plain Dealer*, p81
- Ibid.
- 1923 Meet History, NCAA Division I Outdoor Championships http://www.ustfccca.org/assets/record-book/ncaa-division-i-outdoor-track/rptMeetHistory-EventYearByYear.pdf

Chapter 12
- Catholic *Universe Buletin*, 1/18/46
- Harry Stuhldreher, *Knute Rockne, Man Builder,*
- Murray A. Sperber, *Shake Down the Thunder*, p134
- Harry Stuhldreher, *Knute Rockne, Man Builder*, 223
- Harry Stuhldreher, *Knute Rockne, Man Builder*, p 258-261

- Jeremy Stoltz, "The Notre Dame Box," *Chalk Talk*, 6/28/2007
  http://www.scout.com/nfl/bears/story/655115-chalk-talk-the-notre-dame-box
- Jim Lefebvre, *Coach for a Nation*, p 290-291
- Harry Stuhldreher, *Knute Rockne, Man Builder*, p236

Chapter 13

- Jim Lefebvre, *Coach for a Nation*, p 149
- *South Bend Tribune*, October 21, 1923
- Jim Lefebvre, *Coach for a Nation,* p 293
- List of the Oldest Radio Stations, *Wikipedia*
- https://en.wikipedia.org/wiki/List_of_oldest_radio_stations
- Murray A. Sperber, *Shake Down the Thunder*, p 149
- Ibid., p 77
- Harry Stuhldreher, Knute Rockne, Man Builder, p 248
- "Irish," *Racial Slur Data Base*
- http://www.rsdb.org/search?q=irish
- Harry Stuhldreher, *Knute Rockne, Man Builder,* p 243
- "Rest of the Cantos," *Notre Dame Scholastic*, p 13,
- http://archives.nd.edu/Football/Football-1922s.pdf
- "Ed Weir Profile," *Huskers.com*
- Weir http://www.huskers.com/ViewArticle.dbml?ATCLID=919693
- "Upset of the Year," *Huskermax.com,*
- http://www.huskermax.com/games/1923/05notredame23.html
- Lincoln Eleven Outplays Rockne's Men, *Associated Press*, *The Gazette Times*, 11/10/23, Third Section, P 9.
- https://news.google.com/newspapers?id=8KZRAAAAIBAJ&sjid=c2gDAAAAI BAJ   &pg=3529,4719395&hl=en
- Chuck Heaton, "A Gentle Giant at 83," *The Plain Dealer*, July 22, 1984, pp 16-19
- *South Bend News-Times*, October 27, 1923
- "A football official tells of the thrilling human games behind the lines," *The American Magazine,* October 1932
- "All-American Selections," *Notre Dame Daily*, December 18, 1923, p 8
- http://www.archives.nd.edu/daily/ND_Daily_1923-12-18_V2-050.pdf
- p8
- Tim Hyland, "National Champions," *About.com*
- http://collegefootball.about.com/od/nationalchampions/a/champions-list_5.htm

Chapter 14

- 1925 *Notre Dame Dome*, p325
- Harold Sauerbrei, "Clevelanders in Olympic Games," *Plain Dealer*, p81
- "Varsity Defeated By Stong Illini," *Notre Dame Daily*, May 4, 1924, p 1
- http://www.archives.nd.edu/daily/ND_Daily_1924-05-04_V2-111.pdf
- "Eugene Oberst," *Cleveland Sports Hall of Fame*
- http://www.clevelandsportshall.com/oberst-eugene/
- "Timeline at Penn Relays – Highlights 1924," *pennrelaysonline.com*
- "the highlight for 1924," *Penn Relay site*

- http://news.pennrelaysonline.com/about-2/timeline-at-the-penns/
- "Minims to Hold Track Meet," *Notre Dame Daily*, May 27, 1924, p1
- Gene Oberst Enters Trials at Ann Arbor, *Notre Dame Daily*, May 27, 1924, p 2
- http://www.archives.nd.edu/daily/ND_Daily_1924-05-27_V2-124.pdf
- "Notre Dame Has Javelin Star in Big Ten Games," *Chicago Tribune*, 5/27/1924, p 21
- http://archives.chicagotribune.com/1924/05/27/page/21/article/notre-dame-has-javelin-star-in-big-ten-game
- "Mens Pole Vault Records," Track and Field (http://trackandfield.about.com/od/worldrecords/fl/Menrsquos-Pole-Vault-World-Records.htm
- *Buffalo Times*, April 5, 1931

Chapter 15
- Tom Lieb Bio, *Notre Dame Sports*
  http://www.und.com/sports/c-track/mtt/lieb_tom00.html
- "ND Trackmen Bid for Olympic Games," *Notre Dame Daily*, April 19, 1924, p 4
  http://www.archives.nd.edu/daily/ND_Daily_1924-04-29_V2-108.pdf

Chapter 16
- Simon Winchester, "The Wave King," WSJ, Oct. 3 -4, 2015, C15.
- Gertrude Ederle, *Sports Reference.com*
  http://www.sports-reference.com/olympics/athletes/ed/gertrude-ederle-1.html
- "Bill Neufeld Bio," *Calbears.com*
  http://www.calbears.com/ViewArticle.dbml?DB_OEM_ID=30100&ATCLID=210 281499
- William L. Hayword, "US Olympic Committee Report for the VIII Olympiad," p 35
  http://library.la84.org/6oic/USOC_Reports/1924/USOCReport1924.pdf
- Richard Hymans, "The History of the United States Olympics Trials--Track and Field," p 56
  https://www.usatf.org/statistics/champions/OlympicTrials/HistoryOfThe Oly mpicTrials.pdf
- "Homer Whelchel History," *Whelchel.org*
  https://www.whelchel.org/history/homer--diary same as Gene's
- William Neufeld, *An Olympic Oral History*, p18
  http://library.la84.org/6oic/OralHistory/OHNeufeld.pdf
- "Jack Kelly Sr.," *Sports Reference.com*
  http://www.sports-reference.com/olympics/athletes/ke/jack-kelly-sr-1.html
- "Matt McGrath," *Olympic.org*
  http://www.olympic.org/matt-mcgrath
- "Athletes at the 1924 Summer Olympics," *Wikipedia*
  https://en.wikipedia.org/wiki/Athletics_at_the_1924_Summer_Olympics _%E 2%80%93_Men%27s_hammer_throw
- Ellen Phillips, "The VIII Olympiad," p 12

- "Caroline Smith," *International Swimming Hall of Fame*
  http://www.ishof.org/caroline-smith-(usa).html
- William Neufeld, *An Olympic Oral History*,
  http://library.la84.org/6oic/OralHistory/OHNeufeld.pdf
- Eugene G Oberst, "Eugene G. Oberst Olympic Oberst Diary," 1924

Chapter 17
- William Neufeld, *An Olympic Oral History*,
  http://library.la84.org/6oic/OralHistory/OHNeufeld.pdf
- "Quarters Chosen for Olympic Team," *The New York Times*, July 24, 1923,
  p 18
- Michael K. Bohn, *"Heroes & Ballyhoo: How the Golden Age of the 1920s
  Transformed American Sports,"* pp107-122
  https://books.google.com/books?id=pc1KD4AaCKoC&pg=PR9&lpg=PR9&d
  q=Johnny+weissmuller+act+Paris&source=bl&ots=iYPu62b6Sm&sig=65_tU
  EO5OjyJdUX2WP7M9BlU38s&hl=en&sa=X&ved=0ahUKEwiQlu70xc3LAhXJez
  4KHci4AaIQ6AEIPTAE#v=onepage&q=Johnny%20weissmuller%20act%20Pari
  s&f=false
- William Neufeld, *An Olympic Oral History*,
  http://library.la84.org/6oic/OralHistory/OHNeufeld.pdf
- W. E. Garrett Gilmore, "Single Skulls", *US Olympic Committee Report
  for the VIII Olympiad*, P 81
  http://library.la84.org/6oic/USOC_Reports/1924/USOCReport1924.pdf
- *NY-Herald*, July 4,1924
- "Hormer Whelchel History," *Whelchel.org*
  https://www.whelchel.org/history/homer
- Neil "Paris Wildly Cheers U.S. Team on Arrival," *The New York Times*,
  June 26, 1924, p 26
- Inti Landuaro, "A First-Class Way of Going Coach," *WSJ*, 5/14/16, p C12.

Chapter 18
Michael K. Bohn, *"Heroes & Ballyhoo: How the Golden Age of the
1920s Transformed American Sports,"* pp107-122
http://www.fsmitha.com/h2/ch03.htm
Ellen Phillips, *The VIII Olympiad*, p 49
Ibid., 32
William Neufeld, *An Olympic Oral History*,
(http://library.la84.org/6oic/OralHistory/OHNeufeld.pdf)

Chapter 19
- W.J. Weatherby, "Chariots of Fire," p 155
- Ellen Phillips, "The VIII Olympiad," p 48
- Ibid., p 53
- Ibid., p 53
- Michael K. Bohn, "Heroes & Ballyhoo: How the Golden Age of the 1920s
  Transformed American Sports," pp107-122
- Ellen Phillips, "The VIII Olympiad," p 62
- Ibid., p 22
- John J Lucas, "The Greatest Gathering Of Track And Field Olympians,"
  Journal Of Olympic History, September 1999, p 1-3

- http://library.la84.org/SportsLibrary/JOH/JOHv7n3/JOHv7n3l.pdf
- Ibid.
- Ellen Phillips, "The VIII Olympiad," p 103

Chapter 20
- William Neufeld, An Olympic Oral History,
- P27 http://library.la84.org/6oic/OralHistory/OHNeufeld.pdf
- Ellen Phillips, "The VIII Olympiad," p 26
- William Neufeld, An Olympic Oral History, p 26
- Ibid., p 42
- John J Lucas, "The Greatest Gathering Of Track And Field Olympians," Journal Of Olympic History, September 1999, p 1-3
- Owensboro Messenger-Inquirer Sunday, December 13 1983, quoting Plain Dearly 1984 article

Chapter 21
- Amos Alonzo Stag, *Honors.com* http://www.liskahaas.org/stagg/honors.htm
- *Chicago tribune*, November 23, 1930
- *Ancient Greeks: Olympic Games*, BBC, http://www.bbc.co.uk/schools/primaryhistory/ancient_greeks/the_olympic_games/
4. Chuck Heaton, "A Gentle Giant at 83," *The Plain Dealer*, July 22, 1984, pp 16-19
- Aloma Williams Dew, "Hometown Hero," *Messenger-Inquirer*, 12/13/1998, p 3E
- Emerson and Betts, "Physiology and Hygiene," *Boobs-Merrill*, 1924, Indianapolis, p 57

www.ingramcontent.com/pod-product-compliance
Lightning Source LLC
La Vergne TN
LVHW051502080426
835509LV00017B/1885